THE 7 HABITS OF HIGHLY EFFECTIVE FAMILIES

Also by Stephen R. Covey

The 7 Habits of Highly Effective People

Living the 7 Habits: Stories of Courage and Inspiration

The 8th Habit: From Effectiveness to Greatness

The Leader in Me: How Schools and Parents Around the World Are Inspiring Greatness, One Child at a Time

The 3rd Alternative: Solving Life's Most Difficult Problems

Primary Greatness: The 12 Levers of Success

Life in Crescendo

Principle-Centered Leadership

First Things First

THE **7** HABITS OF HIGHLY EFFECTIVE FAMILIES

Creating a Nurturing Family in a Turbulent World

Fully Revised and Updated Edition

Stephen R. Covey

With Foreword and Insights from
Sandra Merrill Covey

ST. MARTIN'S
ESSENTIALS
NEW YORK

The information in this book is not intended to replace the advice of the reader's own physician or other medical professional. You should consult a medical professional in matters relating to health, especially if you have existing medical conditions, and before starting, stopping, or changing the dose of any medication you are taking. Individual readers are solely responsible for their own health-care decisions. The author and the publisher do not accept responsibility for any adverse effects individuals may claim to experience, whether directly or indirectly, from the information contained in this book.

Published in the United States by St. Martin's Essentials,
an imprint of St. Martin's Publishing Group

THE 7 HABITS OF HIGHLY EFFECTIVE FAMILIES. Copyright © 1997 by FranklinCovey Company. Foreword copyright © 2022 by FranklinCovey Company. All rights reserved. Printed in the United States of America. For information, address St. Martin's Publishing Group, 120 Broadway, New York, NY 10271.

www.stmartins.com

Designed by Steven Seighman

The Library of Congress Cataloging-in-Publication Data
is available upon request.

ISBN 978-1-250-85777-4 (trade paperback)
ISBN 978-1-250-85848-1 (ebook)

Our books may be purchased in bulk for promotional, educational, or business use. Please contact your local bookseller or the Macmillan Corporate and Premium Sales Department at 1-800-221-7945, extension 5442, or by email at MacmillanSpecialMarkets@macmillan.com.

First St. Martin's Essentials Edition: 2022

10 9 8 7 6 5 4

For all children, our common mission

CONTENTS

WELCOME TO THE FULLY REVISED AND UPDATED EDITION

For as good as our father, Dr. Stephen R. Covey, was as a consultant, author, and public speaker, he was an even better husband, grandfather, and dad. Our mother, Sandra Merrill Covey, was every bit his equal. In fact, Dad would say she was his superior in many aspects, and most particularly in her contribution to what went on at home.

As you are about to discover, we are not the perfect family. Yet we keep trying. The same 7 Habits that we were taught as children—along with the examples of our parents—continue to guide and bless our lives as we now do our best to raise our families in this hectic digital age.

We fully recognize that our family is not your family. What worked well for our family might not work exactly the same for your family. Perhaps you will relate more to the insights from the many other families mentioned in this book. We have confidence in your ability to find ways to apply the principles found in this book to your one-of-a-kind family.

As this book now celebrates its twenty-fifth anniversary

and our parents have both passed away, we have given the book a substantial refresh. This fully updated version:

- is more concise for the busy reader.
- includes some of our father's more current insights and stories.
- contains insights from our mother, whose spunky personality and practical ways of handling difficult family issues contributed much to our family.
- has expanded global and digital-age relevance.

It is with much gratitude and respect for our parents and the many lives and families they touched that we pass on their heartfelt insights to you.

Sincerely,
The children of Stephen and Sandra Covey

FOREWORD

FROM DR. STEPHEN R. COVEY

Never in my life have I had such a passion for a project as I have had for writing this book. Why? Because family is what I care about most.

Every family is different. Your family is undoubtedly different from my family. Yet families also share similarities. What family doesn't worry about how to become more united, how to reduce contention, how to raise children who prefer not to be attached to their phones, or simply how to experience more happiness?

For Sandra and me, having the 7 Habits to rely on in difficult family times has been a blessing. The habits have enabled us to be more effective as individuals, as parents, and now as grandparents and great-grandparents. The habits have helped us work through some of our greatest challenges—every family has challenges. I believe that you too will come to see the value of the habits as you read the marvelous accounts of how people from around the world have applied the 7 Habits in their families.

On many occasions, people have asked me to share specific examples of how Sandra and I have used the 7 Habits with our family. On the one hand, I don't want to sound as if we have all the answers, nor do I want you to feel like you need to do things the way we did them. Yet on the other hand, I also don't want to hold back from sharing our family's experiences with the remarkable power of the habits. So in sharing examples from our family, please know that I have done so with humility and with the hope that a story or insight might inspire you with ideas for how you can tailor and apply the habits to circumstances in your family.

Above all, I desire for this book to provide you with feelings of courage and hope. These are unusual times to be trying to raise and sustain a family. Yet I honestly believe the principles found in this book will provide you with timely and practical guidance. The more you apply the principles to your family situations, the more they will become sources of constancy, strength, and peace within this ever-turbulent world.

I firmly believe that family is the building block of society and that the most important work you or I will ever do will be within our family relationships. If we as a society were to work with all our might to improve all other areas of life and yet neglect the family, it would be analogous to spending our time straightening the chairs on the deck of a great ship that is in the midst of sinking.

FROM SANDRA MERRILL COVEY

At the end of one of our son's basketball tournaments, a mother turned to me and said, "I'm surprised your husband has been here for almost every game Joshua has played. I know he's busy writing, consulting, and traveling, so how has he managed to come?"

The first response that flashed into my mind was to say that he has a great wife who organizes his life. But instead I simply replied, "He makes it a priority." And he does.

As Stephen built his reputation as a consultant, speaker, and author, he did travel a lot. When our children were young, this required planning ahead so that he would not miss important occasions such as their athletic events, school productions, and other performances. When he was traveling, he called nightly to talk with each child. "Somebody get the phone," I would hear. Then one of the children would holler back, "You know it's going to be Dad again. I talked to him last night. Tell him to call back when the movie is over."

When Stephen was home, he was totally there. He was so much a part of the children's lives that I'm not sure anyone remembers him being gone. He truly tries to live the principles he teaches, and he has an uncommon sense of humility that makes me want to be like him.

Raising a family takes effort—a lot of it. What strikes me as funny is that people often remark to me, "Sandra, you have nine children. How wonderful! You must be so patient!" I've never been able to follow that line of reasoning. Why would

I be patient because I have nine kids? Why wouldn't I be an exhausted, raving maniac?

But this book is not about Stephen, nor is it about me. It's about you and your family.

Since only you will ever fully understand your family and its unique qualities, I encourage you to take from this book only what feels right for you. I see it as a vast library of practical ideas that you can explore and customize to fit your needs. Please don't even think about trying to do them all. Perhaps a story or a quote will touch your heart and give perspective for how to help one of your family members, or create more family unity, or strengthen yourself. Use the ideas in the manner that you feel best.

If you—like me—ever feel overwhelmed or feel you have made past mistakes, really blown it at times, or even lost trust with a child due to poor choices, then this book is meant to give you the hope to never give up. It is an evergreen source of positive inspiration for bringing progress and happiness to you and your family. Of that I am convinced.

Please accept my every good wish for you and your family.

INTRODUCTION

Creating a Nurturing Family Culture

Whenever I write or speak on the topic of family, I feel that I am treading on sacred ground. I have a deep reverence and respect not only for my family but for all families.

Family is where people experience many of their greatest joys, their most lasting friendships, and their most penetrating sorrows. Family is where minds are enlightened, fun is had, confidences are kept, and hearts are mended. Family is where people sacrifice for others, sometimes even at the risk of their own lives, such as when a mother gives birth. In saying this, I fully recognize that some people may view their families more as battlegrounds, not sacred grounds. Maintaining a united, loving family is never easy.

So in writing this book, I do so with sincere respect for who you are as an individual and the role you play in your family. I do not know all that you and your family have been through together in the past, nor do I claim to know what you are going through now. You know your family far better than I. Therefore, my intent is to identify some principles of effective living, and then to fully trust you to decide how to best apply the principles to your specific family needs and purposes.

FAMILIES ARE "OFF TRACK" MUCH OF THE TIME

All families—even great families—are "off track" much of the time. And that's okay! The important thing is that they have a sense of purpose and destination, and that they keep trying.

Family life is somewhat like the flight of an airplane. Before a plane takes off, the pilots have a clear destination in mind for where they intend to go. They also have a flight plan and a compass system to help them navigate their way. Yet during the course of their journey they may encounter delays at the terminal, traffic on the runway, or storms and headwinds in the sky that require deviations to the plan. Nevertheless, barring anything too major, they make the needed adjustments and arrive safely at their destination.

> All families—even great families—are "off track" much of the time. And that's okay!

And so it is with families. All families encounter turbulence, adverse conditions, pilot errors, or other life delays. So occasionally they need to adjust their plans and find a way to get back on course. My wife, Sandra, and I have certainly experienced our share of chaotic moments in raising our family, as our son Sean reveals:

In general, I'd say that our family had as many fights and problems as most other families when we were growing up. But I am convinced that it was the ability to apolo-

gize and to start again that made our family relationships strong.

For example, when preparing for our family trips, Dad would always have all these plans for us to get up at five in the morning, have breakfast, and get ready to be on the road by eight. The problem was that when the day arrived we'd all be sleeping in and no one wanted to help. Dad would lose his temper. When we'd finally drive off, hours after the time we were supposed to go, no one would even want to talk to Dad because he was so mad.

But what I remember the most is that Dad always apologized. And it was a humbling thing to see him apologize for losing his temper—especially when you knew that you were one of the ones who provoked him.

As I look back, I think what made the difference in our family was that Mom and Dad would always keep trying, even when it seemed that all their plans and systems for family meetings, family goals, and family chores were never going to work.

As you can see, our family is no exception. I am no exception. We've had our share of times when we've struggled to be the family or individuals we wanted to be. But we've also had our successes and happy times. So I assure you from the beginning that whatever your family circumstance may be, even if you are currently facing painful setbacks or sensing that your family is flying in the wrong direction, there is hope in not giving up. History has proven that even battlegrounds can be turned into sacred grounds.

PURPOSES OF THIS BOOK

I'm delighted to share with you *The 7 Habits of Highly Effective Families.* If you are familiar with my earlier book, *The 7 Habits of Highly Effective People,* you will recognize that the habits are the same in both instances. What makes this book different is that its entire focus is on applying the 7 Habits to family situations.

This book has three main purposes: to emphasize the importance of the family, to help you see more clearly how you can be a leader in your family, and to show how you can use the 7 Habits to address your challenges and to create a nurturing family culture.

The importance of the family. Families come in all different shapes and sizes; no two are exactly alike. This is why I resist when people ask me to define what I mean by "family." I prefer that people define their own family.

However, if there is a definition—or description—of a family with which I do strongly relate, it is this: family is the most important organization in the world.

Family is the most important organization in the world.

The number of organizations I have worked with over my career ranges into the thousands. I have engaged with the presidents and prime ministers of several nations. I've worked with all kinds of businesses, large and small. I've consulted with schools, governments, and not-for-profit organizations—all having noble purposes. Yet not one of them has convinced me that any organization is more important than the family.

Family is not just one more relationship. It is not merely another group or association. Family is very unique in its contribution to society. In fact, the more I go through life and mature in my view of the world, the more the role of the family stands out to me as having the most vital influence within any society. The world desperately needs healthy families.

As you progress through these pages, I hope you too will come away with a greater appreciation for the irreplaceable role of the family.

Your role as a leader in your family. This is a book about leadership. More specifically, it's about your role as a leader in your family.

Like the previously mentioned airplane pilots, one of the primary responsibilities that leaders of any type of organization take on is to establish a clear destination for where they want to go as an organization and a plan for how to get there. That's why I begin my work with top executives by asking such questions as: "What is the purpose of your company?" "Where do you want it to be in five years?" "Do you have a company mission statement?" "What are your top three goals?"

More often than not, I'm impressed with the answers I receive from the executives. Yet when I speak to audiences on the topic of family and ask similar questions, I am often stunned by the dull mix of answers I receive. I hear things like, "We've never really thought about our family purposes, Stephen. We never set goals." Or, "We don't have time to pause and clarify our family values or make plans together. We're lucky if we even see each other at dinnertime."

Given the important role that families play in society and in each individual's life, I would hope that more families would have a clearer vision of their purposes, their values, their dreams, and the type of family they want to become. This is why one of my primary purposes in writing is to invite you—as a leader of your family—to consider how you can develop an even greater sense of purpose and direction for your family.

Insight from Sandra

I heard Stephen tell a group of high-powered businesspeople, "If your company was falling apart, you would do whatever you had to do to save it. You would not give up easily. Somehow you'd find a way to make the needed changes."

The same reasoning applies to a family. As our family grew and our lives became busier and more complicated, Stephen and I realized that successful families don't just happen. They take every bit of energy, talent, vision, determination, and rescue efforts a person can muster. They take prioritizing, planning, and sacrificing. They require family members to be willing to say, "I'm sorry," and to do whatever is needed to make adjustments.

Yes, in times of storm or calm, families need someone who is prepared to step up, not give up. Someone who is ready to lead.

Using the 7 Habits to address your challenges and to create a nurturing family culture. This is perhaps the most central purpose of the book. I will illustrate why by first sharing a real-life example, one to which many parents will relate.

Years ago, a friend expressed to me his concern about a deteriorating relationship with his son. The more he tried to improve the relationship, the worse it became. "Stephen," he said, "it's gotten to the point where if I come into the room to watch television with him, he walks out."

"My guess," I responded, "is that your son may not feel understood."

"Oh, I understand him," my friend said with some cynicism. "And I can see the problems he's going to have in life if he doesn't listen to me."

I told my friend about Habit 5: Seek First to Understand, Then to Be Understood. I explained how to listen to others without judging or evaluating them. Thinking he knew exactly what to do after that one brief discussion, my friend went to his son and said, "I want to listen to you. I probably don't understand you."

"You have never understood me—ever!" his son replied. And with that, the son stood up and walked out, like he had done on previous occasions.

The following day my friend returned and said to me, "Stephen, it didn't work. I can't see any hope."

"He's testing your sincerity," I replied, "and what did he find out? He found out you don't really want to understand him. You want him to understand you. You want him to shape up."

"He should!" my friend fumed. "He knows what he's doing is wrong."

I responded, "Look inside you. You're angry, frustrated, and full of judgments. In that state of mind do you really think you can use some surface-level listening technique and it will get your son to open up?"

I suggested he try again. But this time I suggested he try to listen from within his son's frame of reference, not his own. And, if necessary, to first apologize for his own past mistakes.

My friend saw that he had in fact been listening with the intent to get his son to make changes, not with the intent to genuinely understand and respect him.

Eventually my friend determined he was ready to give it another try. "He'll test your sincerity again," I cautioned.

"That's all right," he replied. "It's the right thing to do."

That night my friend sat down with his son and said, "I know you feel as though I haven't tried to understand you, but I am trying and will continue to try."

Again, the son responded coldly and stood up to leave. Taking courage, my friend said, "Before you leave, I want to say that I'm sorry for the way I embarrassed you in front of your friends the other night."

His son whipped around. "You have no idea how much that embarrassed me!" he said, as his eyes began to fill with tears.

"When I saw those tears," my friend later told me, "for the first time I *really* wanted to listen."

And he did. The two of them talked into the early morning hours with the father mostly listening. The next day, with tears in his own eyes, my friend said, "Stephen, I found my son again."

My friend did more than rediscover his son that night. He began to discover the power of the 7 Habits. He learned the value of Habit 1: Be Proactive, which involves first working on one's self and taking responsibility for one's actions and emotions instead of trying to change others. He learned the value of Habit 5: Seek First to Understand, Then to Be Understood, which encouraged him to listen through his son's frame of reference, not his own. In fact, without knowing it, my friend used several of the 7 Habits to arrive at his desired destination with his son that night.

Your challenges are likely different from my friend's. You may be worn out from trying to raise children all by yourself as a single parent. You may be struggling to balance the competing demands of work and family. You may be trying to rekindle the fire in your relationship with your partner. You may be trying to raise your grandchildren. You may be struggling to connect with a child whose only desire is to connect with the internet. Whatever your challenges, you can use the 7 Habits to diagnose the root issues and to lay out a plan for addressing the challenges. In my experience, the greater the challenges become, the more relevant the 7 Habits become.

If this is your first exposure to the habits, then you may wonder where the 7 Habits come from. Years ago as a university professor, I conducted an in-depth review of two hundred years' worth of "success literature." I researched hundreds of studies and classic books to search out the qualities that the world's experts had indicated would lead people to be most successful in life. From that research, I identified seven themes, or habits. They have a logical sequence to them.

I eventually published *The 7 Habits of Highly Effective People*.[1] Never did I imagine the notoriety it would gain. Each time I shared the 7 Habits with an audience—even in tough business settings—almost instantly I began receiving such questions as: "Stephen, how can I get my daughter to listen to me?" "What do I do with my failing marriage?" And so forth. People wanted to know how to apply the habits to their closest relationships— their family relationships. The demand for this book was born out of the frequent and sometimes intense questions I have received about how to apply the 7 Habits to family matters.

Please know that Sandra and I have never considered ourselves to be model parents. In leading our family, we have done a lot of course correcting. So we find it somewhat daunting when we are asked for advice on how to lead a family. However, where we have taken courage in sharing our insights is through our unwavering trust in the 7 Habits. Each habit is filled with very practical, doable insights that can be applied on a daily basis.[2] Each contributes to a nurturing family culture.

A NURTURING FAMILY CULTURE

So what do I mean by "a nurturing family culture"?

A family culture is the overall spirit of a family—the feelings, vibes, and atmosphere within a family. It is the way family members relate to one another and how they feel about one another. A family's culture grows out of the collective behaviors, habits, and beliefs of each family member.

Like a tender plant, a family's culture must be nurtured with consistent care and attention. Since families are made up of individuals, this means that each individual must be nurtured with consistent care and attention until they mature to a point where they can withstand the buffeting winds of today's turbulent world.

Different family cultures have different feelings and outcomes. Below are examples of two very different family cultures. Review their descriptions and imagine how you would feel living in either of them.

Family Culture #1	Family Culture #2
Be Reactive Lose temper. Blame others.	**Be Proactive** Stay calm. Apologize.
Begin With Nothing in Mind Don't plan or set goals.	**Begin With the End in Mind** Have clear purposes.
Put Low Priorities First Be too busy for family.	**Put First Things First** Make time for family.
Think Win-Lose Always compete and compare.	**Think Win-Win** Respect each other's needs.
Seek Only to Be Understood Pretend to listen. Interrupt.	**Seek First to Understand** Listen to each other.
Minimize People's Strengths Focus on weaknesses.	**Synergize** Value each other's strengths.
Live an Unbalanced Life Burn out. Stop learning.	**Sharpen the Saw** Exercise. Learn. Have fun.

What words describe the feelings you would feel if living in Family Culture 1? What words describe the feelings you would feel if living in Family Culture 2? Which family culture do you think would lead to more productive outcomes?

Just as every family is unique, no two family cultures are meant to be identical. So no, I am not going to prescribe what your family culture must be like. That's for you and your family to decide. But I do believe that as you learn about the 7 Habits of Highly Effective Families (which are the basis for Family Culture 2), you will quickly see the relevance of the habits and how they provide a foundation for creating a nurturing family culture.

A TURBULENT WORLD

Personally, I love life. I love nature and its beauties. I love the grand diversity of ethnicities, cultures, and belief systems that provide variety to life. I love the many advances that result from the innovations of creative people from all parts of the world.

Yet at the same time, what family does not feel the turbulence that comes with today's fast-changing economic, social, political, and digital environment? No family is immune to these effects. Many parents feel overwhelmed and struggle to keep up with all the changes and turmoil. At times they may even feel as though their family is under attack. My brother, Dr. John Covey, and his talented wife, Jane, have taught the 7 Habits of Highly Effective Families workshop across the world for the last two decades. On such occasions, Jane likes to share the following experience, which metaphorically captures the magnitude of the challenges that today's families face:

We have a cabin that's eighty years old. It is full of mice, but we love it. It sits on the shore of a lovely lake and is surrounded by a thick forest with lots of wildlife.

One summer, we spotted a large grizzly bear in front of our cabin. We knew it could be dangerous and we didn't dare go outside. Yet we had little children and teenagers with us so we also didn't want to stay inside the entire day. Therefore, we packed a picnic, made a dash to our cars, and drove to a spot on the other side of the lake—far, far away from the grizzly. There we enjoyed a lot of activities and fun.

As I viewed the scene through a grandmother's eyes, I couldn't help but think, "Wouldn't it be great if this was how it was in our world? If families knew exactly where the dangers were and could easily get away and be safe."

But families don't always know that today. A family might have a seventeen-year-old daughter sitting in her bedroom streaming a grizzly bear into her room via the internet. It could be a predator, a cyberbully, or a social media post implying that she is not good enough. She doesn't know it's a danger, nor do her parents know it is happening.

Or a family might have a son who has started to experiment with drugs or is delving into abusive pornography. In either case, it's a grizzly that he's entertaining and it dreadfully frightens his mother. How does she convince him that he's in danger? How does she get him to safety?

Grizzly bears come in many forms. Debt, contention, disease, societal unrest, trauma, malnutrition, and selfishness are other big ones. I truly believe that most parents are sincerely concerned about the vast variety of grizzly bears that roam freely in today's society, and they are trying diligently to shelter their family from them. In fact, I believe that most parents today are trying harder than their parents or grandparents tried, yet still they find their families under attack.

When Sandra and I attended school, the top disciplinary problems were chewing gum in class, running in the hallways, and quarreling on the playground. Today the leading problems that parents and educators deal with include drug abuse, bullying, depression, anxiety, disrespect for authority, campus violence, teen pregnancy, and suicide—more grizzlies. We live in a day when instead of going to Mom or Dad to seek guidance or love, children go to their phones to ask for advice and to social media to find their emotional hugs. Things have changed.

I'm not going to try to convince you that the 7 Habits are the solution to every family challenge. The 7 Habits are not a magical bear spray. But they are an excellent place for families to start when attempting to address their challenges and create a nurturing family culture. So as you go through each chapter—each habit—be thinking about what one or two challenges are most threatening your family's progress. Try asking, "What from this particular habit can help me and my family better address these one or two challenges?"

I am convinced that the more you learn about the 7 Habits and the more you apply them to your family challenges, the more you will see positive impacts—maybe even immediately.

Insight from Sandra

I had a happy childhood. I remember playing games with my neighbor friends. We would lie on the cool green grass and watch the clouds make pictures in the sky. We frequently slept outside on summer nights and gazed in wonder at the billions of stars in the Milky Way. I'd see my parents walk hand in hand to get ice cream at the nearby store.

So that was the picture I had in my mind whenever I thought of what an ideal family and childhood should look like. I dreamed of having the same for my children when that day came. But those days are gone. Today's world is nothing like what I imagined. Things have changed— dramatically. Turbulence is everywhere and seems to be picking up in its pace and intensity. As a result, Stephen and I have had to figure out how to adapt and lead our family in new ways.

What about for you? Have your childhood dreams of what your future family life would be like turned out how you expected? Or have they also changed? How have you adapted?

HOW TO CHANGE A FAMILY CULTURE

If you feel your current family culture is not strong enough to fend off metaphorical grizzlies, or that your family is not as nurturing as you want it to be, then how do you go about changing it? The answer is not a simple one, but I offer a few suggestions.

Start with Yourself

Highly effective families are made up of highly effective individuals. So to improve a family culture requires the individuals within the family to improve.

> Highly effective families are made up of highly effective individuals.

When thinking about how to improve your family, you may be tempted to think first about the other members of your family and what they need to do to change. "If only that son of ours would change, then things would be so much better!" "If only my spouse could be on time, then I wouldn't get so mad all the time." After all, isn't it more fun to try to "fix" someone else rather than to try to change your own behavior?

While it may be more fun to focus first on changing someone else's behavior, it is not nearly as effective. Leadership—including parenting—is an *inside-out* process. That means you first work to improve yourself before you attempt to influence others. By improving yourself, you automatically improve your family culture.

Work from a Strengths-Based Paradigm

A "paradigm" is the way you *see* the world. It's the lens through which you view life. Paradigms are important because they greatly influence what you *do* in life, which in turn influences the results you *get*.

Let me give an example. I spoke to a large audience one afternoon and my totally loyal mother was in attendance. However, she became distracted by a man and woman in the front row who kept talking during my keynote. "How could they be so inconsiderate?" she kept thinking. Afterward she commented to a friend about the rudeness of the two individuals. The friend responded by explaining, "Oh, that woman is from Korea and the gentleman is her interpreter. He was translating for her."

Mother was embarrassed. Suddenly she saw the whole thing differently. Her paradigm shifted. She was ashamed that she had allowed herself to be distracted and miss much of my presentation as a result of her incorrect paradigm.

Mother's nature was to be positive and friendly. So I'm convinced that if her paradigm (see) that day had been accurate, then she would have made extra effort (do) to befriend the two individuals, to get to know a little about them, and to perhaps introduce them to me so I could get to know them.

The woman and her interpreter would have left the event feeling entirely welcomed and happy, and Mother would have left feeling good about her contribution instead of leaving embarrassed (get).

In that example, can you see how the way we *see* things (our paradigms, our thoughts) drives what we *do* (our behaviors, our habits), which in turn influences what we *get* in life (our results, our outcomes)? This pattern is illustrated by the "See-Do-Get Cycle," or sometimes I call it the "Change Cycle." The cycle suggests that if we want to create sustainable change—such as improving our behavior or our family culture—then the most powerful way to start is by focusing on changing our paradigms. Focusing on changing behaviors will bring small results, while working on changing paradigms has the potential to bring quantum leaps in improvement.

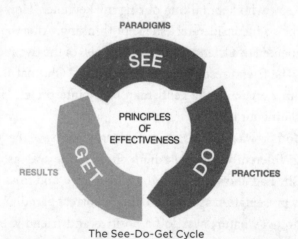

The See-Do-Get Cycle

Two of the most important paradigms are the paradigms we have of ourselves and our families. Unfortunately, many people view themselves and their family through weakness-based paradigms. No matter how well things are going in life, they focus on their weaknesses. Weakness-based paradigms have never been a reliable source for positive change in individuals or families. So if you find yourself reading this book through a paradigm of "I am a horrible parent, I never do any of these things!" or "We are a terrible family," then pause and shift to a strengths-based paradigm. Identify some strengths—what you and your family do well—then think of ways to use those strengths to better apply the principles found in this book.

Live by Principles of Human Effectiveness

You may have noticed the words "principles of effectiveness" in the center of the See-Do-Get Cycle. Principles are found in many aspects of life, particularly in nature and science. For example, pilots must adhere to principles of flight, such as gravity, thrust, lift, and drag in order to go up and down, right and left, to stay on course, and to achieve their destination. Those principles have been around for as long as birds have taken flight, and are the same no matter where in the world one flies. This makes them timeless and universal. If pilots ignore or try to go against the principles, they will experience natural consequences that may prove disastrous.

Similar principles, known as laws of the harvest, are found in farming. Farmers who sit idle and do nothing for the entire planting season and then try to cram by planting seeds and watering heavily the week before the harvest time arrives cannot expect to reap a great crop. Why? Because their outcomes are governed by the principles and natural consequences of Mother Nature.

The same concept is true for nurturing an effective family culture. There are principles of human effectiveness that are just as real as the principles of science and nature. I refer to them as True North principles because they are as constant as True North and act like a compass in pointing individuals and families in effective directions. Living in harmony with principles of human effectiveness is essential for quality family life. Going against the principles can be disastrous to a family because, once again, principles have natural consequences that ultimately govern the outcomes.

So what are the principles of human effectiveness? Each of the 7 Habits is based on a principle of effectiveness. I'll identify some of the principles as I describe each habit, but for now let's use as examples the principles of initiative, vision, discipline, courage, empathy, teamwork, and continuous improvement. Do they feel like timeless and universal principles for being effective both personally and as a family? If you doubt them, think about living life or leading a family based on their opposites: laziness, lack of vision, no discipline, cowardliness, not listening, contention, or neglecting one's basic needs. Do those sound like principles for building an effective life or family culture? I think not.

> Living in harmony with principles of human effectiveness is essential for quality family life.

Families that center their paradigms (see) and behaviors (do) around timeless and universal principles of human effectiveness achieve (get) more desirable results. I call this "principle-centered living."

Insight from Sandra

The thing I like about principles of effectiveness is that they are full of common sense. But that doesn't mean they are always easy to put into common practice.

I have been familiar with the 7 Habits and the principles they are based on for years and yet I am still finding new ways to better apply them. I keep working at them because they help me to be a better mother, grandmother, spouse, neighbor, and person. In them, I find guidance, stability, comfort, and hope.

Involve Your Family in Your Learning

One of our company's consultants was teaching the 7 Habits to a staff of teachers as part of a strategic effort to improve their school's culture. One teacher in particular kept approaching the consultant for clarifications during the breaks. She said she wanted to understand the content to its fullest because she intended to go home and teach the habits to her husband and two sons.

A year later, the consultant was back in that same school

and happened to meet that teacher in the hallway. He asked the teacher what impact the habits were having on the school's culture, and her answers were favorable. The consultant then remembered how the teacher had planned to teach the habits to her family. "What about your family?" he asked. "Have the 7 Habits impacted your family?"

That's when the floodgates opened. She explained through tears that the reason she had been so intent on teaching her family the 7 Habits was because at that time they had been in the midst of a major upheaval. Divorce was imminent. Her husband had lost his job and was depressed, angry, and clueless about what to do. She disclosed how teaching the 7 Habits to her husband and sons had saved her marriage, her family, and maybe even her husband's life.

Your family situation may not be so extreme. It may even be that your family culture is vibrant and needs only slight mending or a fresh new outlook. Whatever your situation, I encourage you to find ways to invite your family members to learn with you and to involve them in the process of creating a more nurturing family culture. As you teach, you will come to know the habits in deeper ways. The teacher always learns the most. This is called teach-to-learn.

Perhaps you can begin by sharing with your family one story from this book and mentioning how you are personally trying to apply the related principle. Or use one suggestion found in the Reflections and Applications section at the end of each chapter. But whatever you do, don't try to do it all at once.

Be Patient and Realistic

I refer often to highly effective people or highly effective families. What do I mean by effective, or effectiveness?

I like to use Aesop's fable "The Goose That Laid the Golden Eggs" to describe what I mean by effectiveness.[3] It tells of a poor farmer and his wife who discover a goose that lays one glistening golden egg per day. Life is good as they use their daily golden egg to purchase needed items. But the day comes when their patience disappears. They don't want to wait another day to get another egg. They want it now! So the farmer grabs a knife, slays the goose, and collects the next golden egg. But in getting the egg sooner, he has killed the goose. There will be no more golden eggs.

The moral of the story is that whenever you are pursuing your desired outcomes in life—whether as an individual or family—be careful not to become impatient and kill your goose. It illustrates that effectiveness has two parts: 1) getting your desired results, and 2) doing it in a way that maintains or improves the results over time. If a family tries to implement too much change or goes at it too fast, they may burn out and ultimately kill their goose. That's not effectiveness. Similarly, if parents try to force rules on their children in an attempt to get results *now*, and they don't involve their children in the process, they may get short-term compliance out of their children but not long-term commitment. That is not effectiveness either.

The general rule for creating change in a family culture is

to be patient and realistic about how much you try to change or accomplish. Recognize that anytime you try something new, you can expect to get some pushback: "Why can't we just be a normal family? I don't want to be a highly effective family!" Or, "I've got ten minutes for this and that's it." Smile and keep moving forward at a pace friendly to you and your family. Don't kill your goose.

In short, to grow your family culture, nurture your individual family members and your family culture like you would nurture a tender plant—with great patience. Do not overwater. Do not give it too much fertilizer. Do not keep pulling up the roots to see how they are growing. Do give it plenty of sun. Do your best to keep the weeds away. And do be assured that Sandra and I created our family culture over decades, not overnight.

I share additional suggestions for how to apply the 7 Habits and create change in the final chapter. One thing I think is important for me to point out is that the many families highlighted in this book come from all parts of the world and all types of circumstances. However, I have intentionally provided few details about their demographics. Why? Because when I do, people almost always say things like, "Oh, that family is not like mine. They come from a different city or a different ethnic background or a different economic status. So this doesn't apply to me and my family." I guarantee that none of the families or circumstances mentioned in this book will match exactly with your family or circumstances. But the principles will. So rather than compare and contrast your family with the families in this book, involve your family members in finding creative ways to apply the principles and habits to your unique family circumstances.

FAMILY IS NO TIME FOR GIVING UP EASILY

I'm reminded of a little girl who had a little ritual. If something upset her, she would approach her mother and say, "I'm running away, Momma." She would then go outside and sit beside a tree and wait for her mother to come get her. After some minutes, her mother would go outside, find the little girl, hug her, and invite her back.

Then one day the girl did her ritual but her mother was busy and forgot to go out and get her. After some time, the little girl wandered back inside with sagging shoulders. "Momma," she said, "you forgot to come get me. Always come after me, Momma. Always come after me." Her mother hugged her extra tight, told her she was sorry, and has never forgotten those words, "Always come after me, Momma."

The key to creating a nurturing family culture is in how you treat the one who tests you the most.

The key to creating a nurturing family culture is in how you treat the one who tests you the most. There is no real test of leadership with a child or partner who is always cooperative, pleasant, and helpful. Rather, the real test of leadership and love comes when you're dealing with someone who feels unlovable, who is rebellious and ungrateful after all you have done. That's the time for true leadership—true love.

Home is not a physical place as much as it is a feeling. It's a set of emotions that make us want to love and to be loved. However thin they may be, family heartstrings are amongst the strongest threads in the world. Try to never let those threads break.

Particularly don't give up on yourself. My fear is that a parent will read this book and come away feeling like they have failed, thinking: "I've made too many mistakes. I must not be a good parent." Personally, I find that dwelling on my past misjudgments gets me next to nowhere, whereas focusing on the possibilities of the future inches me forward—little by little—toward a more pleasing state of being.

Some parents may read this and think, "My children are all grown. I wish I had this years ago. But now it's too late." With all respect, I strongly disagree. It's never too late to start providing positive leadership in a family.

Of course, there are times when a family relationship becomes so toxic or abusive that evasive action must be taken or a family relationship severed. I'm not naïve to that. For such cases, it is important to point out that this book is meant to be a first-aid station, a source of basic emotional triage. It is a preventative treatment. If you or your family is experiencing any form of deeper emotional wounds or abuse, or cannot resolve matters alone, or are struggling with chronic mental health issues, please seek out a trusted counselor who is professionally trained to guide you through your heavier needs. Seeking assistance is a sign of strength and is what great leaders do.

And with that as introductory context, let's get started exploring the 7 Habits of Highly Effective Families.

REFLECTIONS AND APPLICATIONS

With Self

What is one challenge you or your family are facing that you would like the 7 Habits to help you resolve?

_____

_____

_____

_____

With Adults and Teens

- Review the airplane example on page 2. Ask family members: In what ways do you think family life is like an airplane flight? When do you feel our family is most "on course"? Responses might include: when we're talking together, relaxing, going to the park together, or having a special meal.
- Ask each family member: How would you define our family? Invite them to argue in favor of the principle that family is the most important organization in the world.
- Invite family members to describe a nurturing family culture. Capture their thoughts and post them in a place where they can be seen.
- Review the story "Momma, always come after me" on page 25. Talk about why it is important to always look out for one another.

With Young Children

- Plan a bonding activity such as a visit to see an extended family member, a trip to a park, playing a sport, or sharing a story that shows how much you value your family.
- Share the story of the grizzly bear on page 13. Discuss what "grizzly bears" might be harmful for your family. How can you avoid them?
- Blindfold a family member. Lead them to a place where returning to the starting point without sight will be a little difficult. Ensure the return path is safe, then turn the person around a few times and explain that it will be their task to find the way back to the starting point. Let the person try to return. After a moment, ask if they would like some help or clues. Let family members direct the person back with instructions such as "turn left, go straight, turn right." When safely back, ask the person if it was hard to find the way when they couldn't see and had no instructions. Summarize: Help the children understand that you are all going through life together, and often you will need instructions or assistance from your family at times to get to your destination. Talk about how wonderful it is to have a family to rely on.

BE PROACTIVE

Influencing Your Family from the Inside Out

Many of the questions I am asked when speaking to audiences on the topic of family can be summed up with this one question: "How do I get more control of my life?"

Sometimes the question comes from individuals who are so busy with their careers that they feel they have no control over their private family lives. Sometimes the question comes from parents who feel their children are "out of control" with their cell phone use and they want to regain control over them. Other times the question comes from parents who struggle to control their own tempers. Whomever the source and whatever the reason, getting control over one's life and family is a common quest.

Listen to this single mom describe her efforts to gain more control:

For years, I fought with my children and they fought back. I constantly criticized and scolded them. Our family was filled with contention, and I knew my constant nagging wasn't helping.

Again and again I resolved to change, but each time I would fall back into negative habit patterns. The situation caused me to hate myself, and I felt helpless to do anything about it.

I gradually identified two sources for my negative behavior. First, I came to see the impact my childhood experiences had on my attitude and actions. My childhood home was broken. I can't remember my parents ever talking through their problems. They would either argue and fight or give each other the silent treatment. So when I faced similar issues with my own spouse and children, I had no proper example to follow and found myself divorced and dealing with my children the same way that my parents had dealt with me.

Second, I saw that I was trying to win social approval for myself through my children's behavior. I constantly feared that my children's behavior would embarrass me. Because of that, I threatened and manipulated my kids into behaving the way I wanted them to behave. I was trying to control their behavior so I would appear to be in control.

I am doing much better these days, yet I still remember those horrible feelings of being out of control and unable to do anything about it.

In this mother's initial attempts to gain control over herself and her children, she was instead becoming more and more out of control. To her credit, she was self-aware enough to recognize that her behavior was an important part of the solution, and to then take steps to regain some control over her anger and manipulative threats. Without knowing it, she was applying the principles of Habit 1: Be Proactive. The habit begins with the understanding that we as humans have the freedom to choose.

THE FREEDOM TO CHOOSE

For sure, we as humans cannot control everything that happens to us in life. Some of us are born into or fall into difficult circumstances that are beyond our control. So what can we control?

Years ago, I was doing research in a college library when a particular book caught my interest. I flipped through its pages and my eyes fell upon a paragraph that has profoundly influenced the rest of my life. It read in essence, "Between what happens to us in life (a stimulus) and our reaction (our response) is a space. In that space lies our power and freedom to choose our responses. In our responses lie our growth and happiness."

That single paragraph gave me the exhilarating feeling that, even in the midst of challenging circumstances, there are things I can choose to do that will allow me to be more in control of my growth and happiness. Within that concept is the essence of what it means to be proactive.

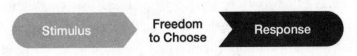

The Proactive Model

I later discovered that the paragraph I came across was based on the work of Viktor Frankl and his book *Man's Search for Meaning*.[1] Dr. Frankl was imprisoned in a Nazi camp during World War II. There, most of his freedoms were stripped away from him, and he and the other prisoners were forced to live under atrocious conditions. His captors performed horrible experiments on his body against his will. Family members were killed. While some of the prisoners gave up under those conditions, Frankl noticed that other prisoners went about doing noble acts of kindness, even offering their last morsels of food to fellow prisoners. He concluded that "Everything can be taken from a man [or woman] but one thing: the last of the human freedoms—to choose one's attitude in any given circumstances, to choose one's own way."

The concept of being free to choose one's attitudes and actions was once again brought forcibly to my mind one evening when I received a call from Sandra. "What are you doing?" she asked with fire in her tone. "You know we are having guests for dinner tonight! Where are you?"

I could tell she was upset at me but I had been involved all day in making a client video in a mountain setting. We got to the final scene and the director insisted that it be filmed with the sun setting in the background. To get this special effect forced us to delay for nearly an hour, and it put me behind in my schedule.

Out of frustration, my reply to Sandra was very blunt: "Look, Sandra, I can't help it that you scheduled the dinner or that things are running behind here. You'll have to figure out how to handle things at home. I can't leave. I'll come when I can!"

As I hung up from the call, I immediately recognized that my response to Sandra was entirely reactive. I was blaming everything on her and the director—on my circumstances. Expectations had been created and I wasn't there to help her fulfill them. It had put Sandra in a tough situation. But instead of being understanding, I was so filled with my own situation that I had chosen to respond very abruptly to her. I knew that if I had acted calmly—out of my deep love for her—instead of reacting rudely to the pressures of the moment, the results would have been completely different.

Fortunately, we completed the filming sooner than anticipated. As I drove home, my irritation was gone. Feelings of love for Sandra filled my heart as I prepared to apologize. She ended up apologizing to me as well, and the warmth of our relationship was restored. It all started the moment I began to exercise my freedom to choose.

UNIQUE HUMAN GIFTS

Not everyone's freedom to choose is the same. Some people have more freedom to choose than others, due to the effects of racism, poverty, hunger, opportunity gaps, etc. All circumstances are not equal, and numerous factors influence our ability to be proactive.

Newborn babies are fully dependent on others for the basics of survival. Someone other than the babies chooses their food, where they sleep, and the clothes they wear. So their gap between stimulus and response is quite narrow, which means their freedom to choose is limited. As they mature, however, their gap widens, their freedom to choose expands, and they gradually become more and more independent, developing what I refer to as the "four unique human gifts." Let me explain.

A favorite mountain location where Sandra and I often took our children over the years is covered with tall aspen trees. We were surprised to learn one day that that particular grove of aspens is the world's largest known living organism. Above ground, it appears to be a bunch of separate trees, but scientists have discovered through genetic testing that the trees are all connected by acres and acres of an underground root system.

As amazing and beautiful as those aspens are, however, they are the mere products of their genetics and environment. Their genes and environment "determine" their appearance, health, and longevity. The trees do not have the freedom to choose how they will respond to what happens to them on any day, or to influence what will happen to them in the future. In contrast, we humans are influenced by our genetics and our environment, but our growth and happiness is not solely determined by them. Why? Because of our freedom to choose.

A large part of what gives us our freedom to choose and separates us humans from other living organisms is what I have labeled the four unique human gifts. They are the gifts of self-awareness, conscience, imagination, and independent will.

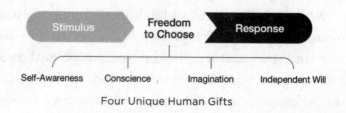

Four Unique Human Gifts

Self-awareness is our ability to stand apart from ourselves and examine our behaviors. We can step away from situations and evaluate our lives, our thoughts, and our actions. We can think about our habits and our families, and about how we might want to change ourselves. Aspen trees—impressive as they are—cannot do this.

Conscience is our ethical or moral sense, and is often referred to as our "inner voice." It houses our personal standards of right and wrong. It matures with time and helps us to make wise choices. Trees do not think, "My falling branch just harmed that other tree. I feel badly about that and won't do it again." But we humans can have such thoughts.

Imagination is our ability as humans to envision a future entirely different from our past experiences. Trees don't imagine, "This is the type of tree I am today but this is the type of tree I want to become tomorrow." Humans, on the other hand, do have the ability to imagine and reimagine the type of person or family they want to grow into. They can be resourceful and innovative, and dream of a better tomorrow.

Independent will is what enables us to respond to our genetics and environment. Trees do not have the ability to say, "I think I will choose to move to another mountain today," or "This is how I will attempt to change my environment this year." But humans not only can think such things, they can choose to do such things.

Of course, not all people take full advantage of their four human gifts. Instead, they idly allow life to act upon them. They merely respond to whatever circumstances come their way. They blame their mistakes and current happiness solely on their genetics and environment, taking no responsibility for their choices. There appears to be very little gap, if any, between what happens to them and how they respond to life. When people are this way, we refer to them as being *reactive*. Perhaps you know some people who live like this.

The Reactive Model

Meanwhile, other people do take the initiative to act on life. They don't wait for life to happen; rather they do their best to make life happen the way they want it to happen. They are self-starters. They recognize that they cannot control everything in life—including everything about their genetics or environment—but they can take responsibility for how they choose to respond to their conditions. They know that the best way to predict their future is to create it. When people are this way we refer to them as being *proactive*.

So how does a person go about becoming less reactive and more proactive, more in control of their lives and family circumstances? What follows are five proactive choices you can make on a daily basis that will enable you to gain greater control over your life and family circumstances.

FOCUS ON YOUR CIRCLE OF INFLUENCE

The first proactive choice is to focus on things you can do something about rather than focusing on things you cannot influence or control. It's what Saint Francis of Assisi was referring to when he penned his Serenity Prayer: "God grant me the serenity to accept the things I cannot change, the courage to change the things I can, and the wisdom to know the difference."[2]

Imagine your life as two circles. A larger, outer circle—your Circle of Concern—represents all the things that are of concern to you in life. Everything. In examining what's in that circle, you will recognize that many of the things that are of concern to you are beyond your influence or control. Meanwhile, inside the bigger outer circle is a smaller inner circle—your Circle of Influence. It contains the things that you do have influence or control over. (See the illustration.) Now thinking solely of your family, you will see that there are some things that concern you but that you have no control over. They are part of your outer Circle of Concern. Then there are family things over which you do have influence or control, and they fall in your inner Circle of Influence.

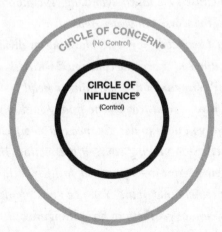

CIRCLE OF CONCERN®
(No Control)

CIRCLE OF INFLUENCE®
(Control)

The Circle of Concern / Circle of Influence

Now keep the two circles at the forefront of your mind as you read the following young man's experience with his parents:

In my teens, my mom and dad were very critical of each other. There were lots of arguments and hurtful comments.

When I was twenty-one they separated. I remember feeling at the time a great sense of duty to repair things. I would say to my dad, "Why don't you go to Mom and say, 'I'm sorry. I know I've done lots of things that hurt you, but please forgive me. Let's work at this.'" And Dad would say, "I'm not going to bare my soul like that and have her stomp on it again."

I would next go to my mom and say, "Look at everything the two of you have done together. Isn't it worth trying to save?" And she would say, "I can't do it. I simply cannot handle him."

Mom and Dad each went to unbelievable efforts to convince me that their side was right and the other's was wrong. It caused me much agonizing. The more I tried to intervene, the worse things became.

When I realized they were planning to divorce, I felt so empty and sad. I became consumed with asking: "Why me?" and "Why can't I do something to help?"

I had a very good friend who finally said to me, "You know what you need to do? You need to stop feeling sorry for yourself. Stop making yourself the victim. This is not your problem. You are connected to it, but this is your parents' problem, not yours. You need to stop focusing on what you cannot get them to do, and figure out what you can do to support and love each of your parents.

When my friend said that to me, something happened inside. My inner voice said, "Your greatest responsibility as a son is to love each of your parents and to chart your own course. You cannot choose what they do, but you can choose your response to what has happened."

That was a profound moment in my life. From then on I was choosing not to be a victim. I was choosing to focus on loving and supporting both parents and refusing to take sides. My parents did not like it at first, and even accused me of being neutral and unwilling to take a stand. But over time, and even after the divorce was made final, they came to respect my position and our relationships remain strong.

Notice how there were things in this story that the young man could not influence or control, specifically his parents' behaviors, attitudes, and decisions. In fact, the more he tried to "fix" his parents' marriage, the more his relationships with them worsened and the more his influence with them declined. It was not until the young man started focusing on what he could control—his own behaviors, attitudes, and decisions—that his relationship and his influence with his parents started to improve and his feelings of being a victim drifted away.

Much like this young man, most parents come to know that the one and only person they can control is themselves. Only as they work to control their own behaviors, attitudes, and decisions will they have greater influence with their children. Parents simply cannot "control" all their children's behaviors, thoughts, and decisions—not even with force—because those fall within the parents' outer Circle of Concern. They can only control what falls in their Circle of Influence, such as how they treat their child, the words they utter, and the opportunities and resources they offer them.

Think of your own family and its circumstances. What are the things you can control or influence? What are the things you cannot control or influence?

> The biggest difference between people who are reactive and people who are proactive is the results they get.

The biggest difference between people who are reactive and people who are proactive is the results they get. When people reactively focus on what they cannot control, when they waste time blaming circumstances for all their problems, or when they spend their efforts trying to control others—things that are in their outer Circle of Concern—the result is that they feel less in control of their lives. Their influence lessens, as illustrated below.

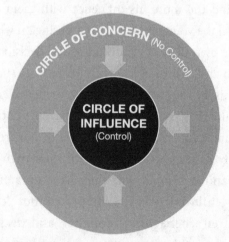

A Reactive Focus Lessens One's Influence

In contrast, when people proactively focus their energy and time on their inner Circle of Influence, and do their best to control their own behaviors, attitudes, and choices instead of trying to control the behaviors, attitudes, and choices of others, that's when their relationships start to improve. Trust increases and their influence grows, as depicted below.

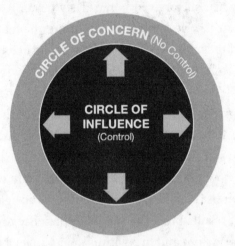

A Proactive Focus Expands One's Influence

Starting with yourself before trying to improve others is referred to as an "inside-out approach." I know a father whose daughter was destroying their family's peace. His repeated efforts to "fix" her had failed miserably. Their relationship was worsening by the day. So the father decided to inform the daughter that she needed to change certain habits or else move out of their apartment. He stayed up late that night waiting for her to return so he could inform her of his decision.

While waiting, the father began listing on a piece of paper the changes the daughter needed to make if she was to remain living with the family. Looking at the list caused him to grieve. But then he turned the paper over and began listing the changes he would agree to make if she would agree to her changes. Tears flowed when he realized his list was longer than hers.

It was in that humbled spirit that the father greeted his daughter when she arrived home. They began to talk, starting with his list. He apologized for things he had done and committed to changing some of the ways he behaved toward her. Ultimately, his choice to begin with his side of the paper made all the difference. Hearing her father apologize and ask for forgiveness brought a change of heart in the daughter. They never did get to discuss the items he had listed for her, but healing started that night.

Notice how the father's influence grew only once he focused on his list, not hers. I've seen it again and again—this is the type of results proactive people experience as they work from the inside out and live within their Circle of Influence.

USE PROACTIVE LANGUAGE

A second proactive choice is to use proactive language.

One of the best ways to tell whether you're living in your Circle of Influence or your Circle of Concern—or whether you're being proactive or reactive—is to examine your language. If you find yourself complaining, criticizing, or comparing, then there is a good chance you are living in your Circle of Concern, not your Circle of Influence. That's because when you're always focused outward—on the choices and behaviors of others—your language will be filled with words of blaming and accusing. It will sound something like:

"Those kids make me so mad!"

"If only my father was not an alcoholic, I could have . . ."

"My grandfather behaved like that, my father behaved like that, and so I behave like that."

"That's just the way I am. There's nothing I can do about it. It's not my fault."

"If only we had more money, then I could be happy."

"When that seventeen-year-old son of mine enters the room, he turns me into a witch."

Can you hear the reactive tones in those statements? Notice how in each statement the problem is always "out there," outside the person. It's someone else's fault. "I couldn't help it." "They made me do it." "If only life treated me better."

When you use reactive language, you give away control of your choices and actions to other people or to circumstances—things outside your control. You feel helpless and hopeless. You deny your fundamental power to choose. In contrast, when you live inside your Circle of Influence, your language is proactive. It focuses on things you can do something about and sounds more like:

"I chose to allow my kids to make me mad!"

"I will model the kind of loving interaction I want to see in my marriage."

"I can learn more about my father and his addiction, and work to forgive."

"I apologize. I take responsibility for my actions. It was my mistake."

"My father was that way but I choose not to be that way."

Where in those sentences is the control? It's still with you. You have not given away control of your choices or the responsibility for your behaviors. You have kept ownership for who you are and what you choose to do.

Test your tendencies toward proactive or reactive language by asking a family member to take turns with you in completing the following activity. Afterward, exchange feelings and insights.

1. Identify a specific problem or challenge in your life or family.

2. Describe the issue using only reactive language. Stay in your outer Circle of Concern and blame everything on factors outside yourself. Try to convince the other person that the problem is not your fault or responsibility.

3. Next, describe the exact same issue using proactive language. Talk only about what you can do within your Circle of Influence to resolve the issue. Try to convince the person that you can make a real difference in the situation.

4. When you are finished, examine your feelings. Discuss with the other person how you felt when using reactive language versus proactive language. Which language gave you a greater feeling of being in control? Which language most closely resembles your typical language?

If in completing the above activity you felt more natural when using reactive language, then it might be time for you to begin replacing your language with proactive words and phrases. This may take real effort and practice. You may even want to teach other family members the difference between proactive and reactive language, and invite them to hold you accountable when they catch you using reactive language.

In the end, I believe you will be surprised how much more in control of your life you feel when you make the shift from using reactive to proactive language within your family relationships.

PAUSE, THINK, AND CHOOSE

A third proactive choice is to pause, think, and then choose. See if you have ever experienced something like the following.

A parent goes off to work and behaves in perfectly calm and respectful ways. Even when their boss says something upsetting or a coworker does something annoying, the parent remains in control of their emotions. Once at home, however, the scene changes. The parent sets their emotional control aside and blows up at the smallest mistake made by a family member. They yell things in anger that they would never dare say at the workplace. They unleash words that have the potential to cause a lifetime of emotional damage.

How is that possible? Does the parent have a private persona that is different from their public persona? More likely it is because at the workplace they are accountable to someone else, whereas at home they are accountable only to themselves, and they are not very good at holding themselves accountable. In other words, at work they have learned to pause and think before acting, whereas at home they exercise no such control.

When we act reactively in anger with family members, we risk destroying the trust that exists within our most important relationships. We rupture—not nurture—our family culture.

I like to think there is a simple remedy for this, but anger is one of the things that is truly difficult for many people to control. They find it easier to blame their anger on their genetics or their upbringing than to take ownership for it. Some parents even get a momentary ego boost from yelling in anger. It's what gives a reactive parent a false sense of being in control.

When we act reactively in anger with family members, we risk destroying the trust that exists within our most important relationships.

What people need is a "pause button." Something that reminds us all to pause between what happens to us and our response to it.

When I feel upset about something, I find it helpful to imagine a pause button on my forehead. I then mentally try to push that imaginary button before I say something I will later regret. Your pause button might be something entirely different.

I have a friend who, when he feels tempers rising between him and his wife, literally steps outdoors. That's his pause button. It helps him to calm down before saying something for which he will later feel sorrow or embarrassment. He laughs when he admits that he has spent much of his marriage outdoors. Yet I might note that he has one of the best marriages I've ever witnessed.

Other people count to ten before opening their mouths. I know a family who decided that whenever an argument breaks out in their family, someone can raise their hand at any time and call out, "Can we start over?" These too are pause buttons.

A father I know has a pause button built into his daily routine. When he arrives home from his stressful job, he pauses and stays in his car for a few minutes. He imagines the feeling he wants to create when he goes inside. He says to himself, "My family is the most important and enjoyable part of my life and so I'm going to go inside and communicate my love for them." When he walks through the door, instead of finding fault with something that's wrong in the home or going off by himself to take care of his own needs, he might use a dramatic voice to call out something like, "I'm home! Please try to restrain yourselves from hugging me!" He then goes around and interacts in positive ways with family members—kissing his wife, playing with the kids, or doing whatever it takes to create pleasantness. In this way, he makes the proactive choice to mentally rise above the fatigue he feels from his challenges at work or the toils of driving in bad traffic, and to avoid any tendencies to take out his frustrations on his family. He literally pauses and chooses to become a positive force in his family culture before entering his home.

I recognize this is not as easy as I make it sound, especially in the heat of the moment when tempers are flaring. So I suggest three proactive steps to consider taking when you sense a reactive response coming on during an emotional family situation.

What Happens → 1. Pause 2. Think 3. Choose → Your Proactive Response

Pause

Decide in advance what your personalized pause button will be. Then, when the need arises—push it. If you consistently struggle with remembering to push it, tell a family member what your pause button is and ask them to help push it for you until you calm down.

Think

Think about what some possible proactive responses might be. This is a very important step because choices do have natural consequences. A person cannot ignore the principle of gravity, step off a cliff, and expect not to experience the natural consequences. The same is true with principles of human effectiveness. A person cannot constantly ignore the principle of honesty, lie all the time, and then expect others to trust them. The natural consequence of a child lying is that people will not fully trust them and they will not feel good about themselves. Being sent to their room for lying would be a secondary consequence or a punishment, not a natural consequence. Yelling at a child is a secondary consequence. Sending a mean-spirited text message to scold a sibling is a secondary consequence, not a natural consequence. Far too many parents focus on applying secondary consequences and never identify the natural consequences.

Forcing yourself to think of more than one proactive response and the natural consequences of each will often eliminate your first knee-jerk responses, which are frequently reactive responses that you may regret.

Choose

Identify the proactive response with the best natural consequences and go with it. If nothing else, by the time you have taken these three steps, you will be in a calmer, more principle-centered state of mind.

Insight from Sandra

When our oldest daughter, Cynthia, was three years old, we moved into our first house. I loved decorating and worked hard to make it into a charming, attractive place.

One night, a group of my friends was going to visit. I spent hours preparing so that every room looked perfect. I was eager to impress. I put Cynthia down for the night and thought she would be sleeping when my friends peeked in to see her, noticing, of course, the bright yellow quilt, matching curtains, and the colorful play animals, all of which I had made. But when I opened the door to show off my sleeping daughter and her darling room, to my dismay Cynthia had hopped out of bed and scattered her toys, crayons, and clothes all over the floor. And she was still going at it!

Her bedroom was a disaster. Yet she looked up at me with a big smile on her face and said ever so sweetly, "Hi, Mommy."

I was furious! In that mess, no one could see how hard I had worked to decorate the room. After shutting the door and smiling at my friends, I peeked back into the room and spoke sharply to Cynthia in an angry whisper. She sensed my fury and her lower lip started to quiver. Her eyes filled with tears, not understanding what she had done wrong.

I closed the door and immediately felt terrible for overreacting. I was ashamed I had ever opened my mouth. I knew it was my pride—not Cynthia's actions—that had set me off. At that point I was angry at myself.

Faced with the same situation today, I honestly think I would pause, think, and then laugh. What once seemed so important to me has now changed as I've matured. I've learned to back off on many of my rules, to take things less seriously, and to relax and enjoy life more. We all go through stages.

BECOME A TRANSITION PERSON

A fourth proactive choice is to become a "transition person."

I greatly admire people who have been raised in family environments that are far worse than anything I have ever imagined, and yet turn out to be the polar opposites of their upbringing. They become stronger persons as a result of overcoming the conditions in which they were raised. I call them transition people.

Transition people stop the negative transmission of dysfunctional habits from one generation to the next. They choose not to be controlled by their past, and instead to become the proactive creators of their present and future.

What stands out about these individuals is their paradigms. The paradigms of a transition person are what enable them to step away from a situation and say, "I may have had a bad past, but I can choose a different path for myself and my future. I can raise and influence my family in such a way that the paradigms of my past will no longer be part of my present family life."

I'm thinking of a man who came from racist parents. When people learn this they can hardly believe it. He and his wife have chosen to raise their family in a far different way. Looking at their circle of friends and hearing their conversations makes it clear that they genuinely value and enjoy diversity. It's not fake or for show. They have put the past behind them and transitioned themselves and their family to a new way of thinking—a new paradigm.

This topic always reminds me of the time Cousin Homer was hiking and was bitten by a poisonous snake. He had a choice. Either he could stop, pursue the snake, and seek revenge, or he could seek medical treatment. Chasing the snake had the potential to drive the poison to his heart, so he chose instead to find a hospital and obtain an antidote that would preserve his leg. Similarly, when a family member offends, treats us wrongly, or bites us in our ego, we have the choice to continue the negative behaviors by pursuing revenge—which will drive poison to the heart of the relationship—or to become a transition person by proactively stopping the negative pattern of treatment.

Some people become transition people simply by choosing the weather of their minds. Most people agree that it is natural to feel happier when the weather outside is great, and to feel more gray and melancholy when the weather outside is gloomy. Similarly, most people feel more confident or happy when family members treat them well, and more anxious or sad when family members treat them poorly. Both are cases of being reactive to the social weather. Such people turn control of their moods and behaviors over to the outside weather or to the behaviors of others. Are you ever that way?

If yes, how do you think your life would be different if instead you were to choose to carry your own weather? In other words, to proactively choose the weather of your mind. That's what transition people do. By stopping the transmission of the negative climate that surrounds them and choosing instead to carry the positive weather of their minds, transition people become more consistent in their moods and behaviors, regardless of what the weather outside is like or how other people treat them.

The intent is that you not allow your past or the actions of others to hold your present progress or future joys hostage. By choosing to become a transition person in your home, you are choosing not to allow the turbulent climates of the outer world to keep you and your family from becoming your inner sunny bests.

DEVELOP THE GIFT OF HUMOR

A fifth and final proactive choice that I will mention is the choice to develop what Sandra and I have decided is a fifth unique human gift. It's the gift of humor. Unlike those aspen trees, humans can choose to laugh, smile, and have fun in all kinds of circumstances.

Healthy humor and laughter have preserved the sanity and unity of our family culture over the years. We've learned to see the funny sides of life and to have fun together, even in turbulent times. Laughter is a great tension releaser. It produces endorphins and other mood-altering chemicals in the brain that give us pleasure and relief from stress and grief.

Humor reminds us that it is okay to be human. It helps us not to sweat the small stuff. It keeps us from taking ourselves too seriously and from being constantly uptight or battling perfectionism. People who can laugh at their mistakes and clumsiness get back on track in their journeys through life much faster than those who choose to go on guilt trips.

Sandra has been a grand source of humor in our family. She has developed the inner strength not to take things too seriously. One time she and our daughter Maria decided to attend a week-long fitness spa in a distant city. It was their way of having fun while also doing something productive together.

People who can laugh at their mistakes and clumsiness get back on track in their journeys through life much faster than those who choose to go on guilt trips.

On the first day, they walked and walked for what seemed like a hundred miles, and lifted all kinds of weights. Halfway through the evening's meal of grains and some very odd food, Sandra turned to Maria and said, "This food is for the birds—literally." Sandra and Maria had a good laugh about it, even though they could see the potential for the week turning into a grueling endurance test instead of a fun mother-daughter getaway. They recognized they had a choice. Either they could be reactively miserable all week—the victims of their own choice to attend the spa—or they could choose their own weather and find a proactive way to enjoy the time together. They chose to be happy.

When the meal was over, Sandra slyly grinned and Maria

winked back and said, "Let's go." The two of them quietly snuck out a back way and went out for Italian food, followed by a movie with soda and popcorn—extra butter. The next night it was Chinese food followed by another movie, more popcorn, and lots of humor. Each night it was a different restaurant and movie. When the week ended and their shenanigans were over, they'd had the time of their lives together, and each had somehow managed to lose six pounds. Perhaps it was from laughing so much.

People who are proactive do not take life so seriously that they forget to insert a little laughter and fun into their routines and relationships. Now, of course, like anything else in life, humor can take a family "off course" if it is not tactful. Humor that is unhealthy and mocks family members or is cruel or crude can result in a family culture of sarcasm where nothing is taken seriously and egotistical "put-downs" are common. But that's not humor, that's rudeness. When feelings get hurt and the family culture goes sour, that is not the type of humor I am referring to as the fifth gift.

Insight from Sandra

When our son Stephen was about six years old, we stopped at a small store to get some ice cream. A woman came rushing into the store and dashed past us in a big hurry. She hastily grabbed two large containers of milk and hustled toward the cashier. In the rush, the two milk containers banged together, crashed to the floor, and appeared to explode. Milk shot out in all directions.

All eyes turned toward the woman in her wet and embarrassed state. The store went quiet. No one knew what to say.

Suddenly, little Stephen piped up: "Have a laugh, lady! Have a laugh!"

At that, the woman and everyone else instantly broke out laughing, putting the incident into perspective.

Now when anyone in our family gets upset or overreacts to a minor situation, someone will eventually call out, "Have a laugh, lady! Have a laugh!"

INSPIRE PROACTIVITY IN OTHERS

To this point, the focus has been on growing your own proactivity—expanding your own freedom to choose. But how do you help others in your family become more proactive?

This is the moment when a lot of readers will get excited because they think I am finally going to focus on how to "fix" other members of their family. If you are one of those persons, don't get too excited because my foremost suggestion for helping others be more proactive is to first focus on yourself. There is no better way to inspire proactivity in others than to be a model of proactivity. It's what Gandhi referred to as being the change you want to see in others.[3]

When you choose to be proactive, other family members are more likely to make proactive choices. When you choose to stay within your Circle of Influence, others are more likely to mind their own business and focus on themselves. When you choose to pause, think, and choose your responses, others will be less reactive. When you choose to use proactive language, others will take more responsibility for their words and actions. When you choose to be a transition person, other family members are more likely to leave the past alone. Proactivity, including humor, is a contagious choice.

> When you choose to be proactive, other family members are more likely to make proactive choices.

Beyond modeling proactive behaviors, another approach Sandra and I have used when trying to inspire proactivity in our children is to create opportunities for them to make choices on their own and thereby to grow their unique human gifts. Many parents—with very good intentions—get in the way of their children learning how to expand their freedom to choose. They try to make all the right choices for their children rather than empowering their children to make their own choices. They think they are doing something *for* their children when in reality they are doing something *to* them.

By trying to "control" their children, parents often end up

losing what little control they ever thought they had. That's one reason why it is just as important to study what effective parents *don't do* for their children.

Sandra and I have found that a better way is for parents to help a child grow their self-awareness, tune their conscience, expand their imagination, and strengthen their independent will by giving them opportunities to make proactive choices. Even if it means increasing the potential and risk of the child making a measured mistake. Consider this father's experience:

My sixteen-year-old son was romantically interested in a girl named Olivia, and he knew I was not comfortable with the situation. He came to me one day and said, "Dad, what would you think if I took Olivia to the school dance?" He assumed my answer would be no.

Instead, I explained what I saw were the pros and cons and then indicated that he needed to be the one to make the choice. I wasn't going to make it for him. I did this even though I knew he might jump at the freedom I was offering and end up taking Olivia to the dance. But I also knew he needed to learn to be responsible for his choices.

To my surprise, rather than being pleased with the trust I was giving him, my son began to debate the matter with me. He wanted me to give a firm yes or no answer. I assumed he was trying to persuade me to approve so he would not feel like he was disappointing me. But I continued to put the responsibility for the choice onto him.

The debate went on for at least ten minutes until, finally, he raised his voice and said, "Dad, just say no!" This also caught me by surprise.

It turned out that my son actually wanted me to say no. Unknown to me, there was another girl he wanted to take to the dance, and he was hoping I would say no so he could tell Olivia that it was his dad's fault he couldn't take her. He wanted me to take the responsibility.

Well, I still didn't take his bait. We talked about the pros and cons of that decision, and once again I left him to make the choice on his own. Olivia may not have been pleased with his choice, but today that son is filling very responsible roles in his work and family, and I like to think that at least some of it is because of the chances we gave him when he was young to make responsible choices of his own.

Like this father, Sandra and I have found that when we work with our children and place trust in them according to their maturity, and we help them see the natural consequences of their choices—the natural pros and cons—we have been pleasantly surprised by how often they make responsible choices. At the same time, I have seen numerous parents take the opposite approach. They try to force a child to do the "right" thing, to believe a certain way, or to make a certain choice. And how often have I seen that approach work? Rarely. Teens in particular want to exercise their freedom to choose, even if it means making a reasonable mistake and then learning from the natural consequences.

Parents who succeed in "controlling" their children when they are young tend to be the same parents who see their children depart the nest early to get away from their parents' control. Either that or they are never quite successful at seeing their children become fully independent of them. This is why the goal of highly effective parents has never been to control their children. Rather, their goal is to teach children principles of effectiveness and how to control themselves, to make decisions on their own, and to become responsibly independent.

And may I add that I have never liked the word "fix" when it comes to working with people. We fix things; we inspire people. We manage things; we lead people. Not enough parents understand this and it is why many families are over-managed and underled, which reduces a child's capacity to be proactive.

HABIT 1: THE KEY TO ALL THE OTHER HABITS

Habit 1: Be Proactive is the key to the remaining six habits. The remaining six habits would be powerless without Habit 1.

In looking back over the choices associated with Habit 1, I fully recognize that for some individuals and families the idea of having the freedom to choose may be difficult to even imagine, let alone apply. They may have been born into or placed under such disadvantaged or inequitable circumstances that it may be hard for them to see or trust that their choices will bring them the outcomes they desire.

Indeed, not everyone enjoys conditions that fully nurture proactivity. Genetics and biology do play a role in all of our lives and our mental health, and I do not minimize those facts. However, by focusing our energies, talents, and resources on those things over which we do have control—

most notably ourselves—we can little by little expand our influence, growth, and happiness. We can gain more control of our lives, and feel more at peace with ourselves. We can learn to laugh a little more. And by first modeling proactive choices, we can inspire our families to become more proactive. The end result will be a tremendous lift in our family culture, even in turbulent times.

This is why the decision to be the proactive force of our life is the most fundamental choice we make every day and the key to all other habits. It is the starting place for becoming an agent for positive change in our families.

To summarize Habit 1, being proactive is the opposite of being reactive. Reactive individuals and families operate from paradigms such as: "I am merely a product of my environment and genetics." "I can't help myself." "My fate is determined by outside factors." "There's nothing I can do." In contrast, proactive individuals and families operate from paradigms such as: "My genes and environment do impact my life, but I still have the freedom to choose my responses. I can act on life rather than just letting life act on me."

Proactive paradigms are centered around the principles of choice, responsibility, initiative, and resourcefulness. As proactive people make the daily proactive choices to focus on their Circle of Influence; to use proactive language; to pause, think, and choose their responses to life; to become transition people; and to enjoy the gift of humor, they feel more in control of their lives and at peace with themselves.

Making those choices puts us in a place where we can proactively choose our life's destinations—our ends in mind. Which brings us to exploring Habit 2.

REFLECTIONS AND APPLICATIONS

With Self

Looking back over Habit 1: Be Proactive, what is the one idea or learning that if you were to apply it better would have the greatest impact on the well-being of your family?

_____

_____

_____

_____

With Adults and Teens

- Ask family members: When do you feel you are most reactive? When are you most proactive? What are the consequences of each?
- Discuss the Circle of Influence model. Have family members identify what they *do* have direct influence over and what they *do not* have direct influence over in your family. Help everyone understand that although there are things we cannot influence, there is much that we can influence. Discuss why it is more effective to concentrate efforts on what you can influence.
- Discuss the concept of the pause button. Invite family members to choose something to represent a pause button for the entire family. It might be a body movement, such as signaling with a hand, or saying a specific word, or turning lights on and off. Each time the signal is given, ev-

eryone will know the family pause button is being pushed. This signal serves as a reminder for all to stop, think, and consider the natural consequences of continuing.

- Discuss what it means to be a transition person. What are some behaviors or traditions you would not want to pass on to future generations?

With Young Children

- Develop a Conscience Treasure Hunt. Choose a "treasure" that everyone will enjoy and all can share, such as a treat. Choose a safe spot to hide the treasure, making sure that it is accessible to even the youngest child. Develop clues that lead to the treasure. To obtain all the clues, participants must answer questions that require them to exercise their conscience, such as: "Is it nice to blame others for your mistakes?" If they answer correctly, provide the first clue ("Go to the kitchen table."), and then repeat the activity until they have all the clues and find the treasure. Discuss what a conscience is and why it is important to follow it.

BEGIN WITH THE END IN MIND

Bringing Purpose and Vision to Your Family

Suppose you are about to board a plane and you ask the pilot, "Where will we be flying to today?" The pilot replies, "I don't know. We'll just load the passengers and take off. Once we get in the air and find a jet stream, we'll go wherever the winds take us."

How would you feel about getting on that plane?

Or imagine you are at a construction site and you ask the workers, "What are you building?" "We have no idea," they reply. "What does your blueprint show?" you ask. "We have no blueprint," responds the crew supervisor. "We are figuring things out as we go." "Well, what's the purpose of the building?" you persist. "We're not sure of that either," responds the crew.

What would you think about the quality of that crew?

As absurd as those two scenarios might appear, recall how I am often stunned by the number of families who have no "flight plan," no "blueprint," or no sense of purpose or destination for their family. And yet family is the most important organization in the world.

YOUR FAMILY'S MENTAL CREATION

Habit 2: Begin With the End in Mind is based on the concept that all meaningful things are created twice. First there's the *mental* creation—the plan or vision. Second there is the *physical* creation—the actual doing of the work, the carrying out of the plan. Habit 2 is the mental creation.

A family's mental creation answers the question of *why*: Why is our family important? Why do we do what we do? It also answers the question of *what*: What do we want our family to stand for? What are our goals? What do we want our family culture to feel like, sound like, and look like?

The opposite of Habit 2 is for a family to have no meaningful purposes to pursue and no proactive thinking about its values or future. It is for the family to be swept along by the flow of society's trends, going wherever the world takes them. It is a reactive approach, and many families take it. Yet by having no proactive destinations, purposes, or plans, a family significantly reduces its opportunities for growth and happiness.

There are many ways to apply Habit 2 to a family. For example, your family can plan an entire year, month, week, day, or hour by beginning with the end in mind. You can organize a special family dinner, find an apartment to live in, search for a new job, look for a family pet, join a sports team, or start a project all while asking up front, "What end do we have in mind?"

You can apply Habit 2 to a family vacation by asking in advance: What will be our vacation's main purpose? Will it be educational? Is it meant to enjoy some physical exercise or relaxation? Is it intended to be a chance to give service, or is it a time to reconnect with distant relatives? Or is it all of the above? The more a family proactively chooses clear ends in mind for a vacation, the higher the probabilities are for that vacation to be successful and fun.

The reason many families give for not doing more to Begin With the End in Mind is that they are too busy. They say they don't have time to stop and plan ahead or to set meaningful goals. And indeed most families are busy. Yet I'm reminded of Henry David Thoreau's thought-provoking statement and question: "It's not enough to be industrious; so are the ants. What are you industrious about?"[1]

GETTING AT THE ROOTS

This chapter begins the process of enabling you and your family to identify the ends in mind that matter most to your family, including your main purposes and values. But first I will emphasize why I feel Habit 2 is so vital for families in today's turbulent times.

All families face challenges. Some challenges are greater than others. When the human body faces a challenge like being out of energy, a doctor looks for root causes by asking, "Why is the body out of energy?" Often the root causes are traced to one or more deficiencies, such as a lack of nutrients, a lack of exercise, or a lack of sleep. Similarly, when families face a challenge, such as being out of love, the root causes can typically also be traced to one or more deficiencies.

In recent years, I have observed three deficiencies that

are damaging to a family's culture and reduce the love that is felt within it. What makes these deficiencies dangerous is that they are not easy to detect. They are like tiny emotional termites eating away at the very foundation of a family without the family members noticing. If left unattended, they can erode the entire stability of a family.

What are the deficiencies? They are a lack of identity, a lack of connectedness, and a lack of hope.

A Lack of Identity

We hear much these days about identity theft, where one person steals another person's financial information and uses it for personal gain. As tragic as that is, I believe the more harmful form of identity theft in today's society is not what is happening in our economy but rather what is happening amongst our youth.

Many young people truly struggle to develop their identity and to hold on to it once they've established it. Much of their early identity comes from their family where they are introduced to the basic lessons of life and a general sense of what is right and wrong. But eventually outside forces such as peer pressures, social media, or other influences start to take aim at their identity. To be "cool," they are told they need to wear a certain brand of clothing, talk a certain kind of talk, or listen to a certain type of music. To be "popular," they feel pressured to post particular content, hang out with a particular group, exhibit particular behaviors, or take particular risks. In the process, they get thrust into a frenzy of constantly comparing themselves to others in an attempt to identify how they fit in amongst their peers or how they can differentiate themselves. It's all part of their ongoing search for identity.

When young people's identities are not secure, are not supported by a strong family identity, or are not founded on principles of effectiveness, they become prime targets to have their homegrown identities stolen away from them. They are at risk for having their moral pockets emptied of the values they have been taught by their parents or other positive role models.

Crises of identity frequently manifest themselves in the form of anxiety, a loss of self-worth, rages of anger, or heavy sadness. This is why establishing strong principle-based identities and strong family values is so important—for young people and for adults.

A Lack of Connectedness

A landmark report published by the Commission on Children at Risk argues that young people's brains are literally "hardwired" to be connected in two important ways: 1) a connectedness to other people, and 2) a connectedness to moral meaning. The report asserts that both forms of connectedness are essential to good health and human flourishing.[2]

The report was sponsored by the Dartmouth Medical School, the YMCA, and the Institute for American Values, and was generated by a team of thirty-three children's doctors, research scientists, mental health specialists, and youth service professionals. These researchers were deeply concerned about the high rates of depression, anxiety, attention deficits, and conduct disorders that exist among today's young people, and their associated outcomes, such as violence, school dropout, self-harm, substance abuse, and teen pregnancy. In the end, the researchers concluded that the adverse behaviors and "disorders" all have root causes in young people feeling disconnected from other people or unattached to some form of moral meaning. When young people do not feel connected to others—lacking feelings of belonging—or do not feel connected to a moral compass, they struggle to move forward in life.

A Lack of Hope

Like connectedness, hope also comes in at least two forms. One is the hope for a brighter future—a vision of something to look forward to in days ahead. The second is the hope to be able to contribute something of worth to that better future—to feel needed and appreciated, to feel meaning in one's life. I believe these are the same types of hope that Jesse Jackson refers to when he challenges young people "to put hope in their brains, not dope in their veins."[3]

Hope is a form of vision. As the proverb recorded thousands of years ago suggests: "Where there is no vision, the people perish."[4] Yet read any news site and what do you get? Not a lot of hope. Look around many communities and what do you see? Not a lot of hope. Listen in on many family mealtime conversations and what do you hear? Not a lot of hope or

Hope is a form of vision.

of vision. A lack of hope and vision will often end in a young person perishing emotionally, if not physically.

WHO'S RAISING OUR CHILDREN?

I truly believe that all three of these deficiencies are at the root of many family challenges. So who's in charge of nurturing these roots and removing the deficiencies?

Another way of asking that question is: Who's raising our children? Where do young people go to find identity, connectedness, and hope? Where do they find a positive vision of the future? That answer is simple. They either find it in their family or they go elsewhere. And if they can't find it elsewhere, they feel desperate and may do desperate things.

Some parents resist helping their children establish their sense of identity or moral values. They argue that they want their children to have the freedom to establish their identities and don't want to force their values onto their children. Other parents claim they simply don't know how to connect with their children around such topics. By default, these parents end up leaving it to society, social media, peers, luck, or some other source to guide their child toward establishing their identity and moral foundation.

While I recognize the logic behind allowing children to have their freedoms to establish their own identities, I personally find it a highly risky approach for a parent to remain silent or to trust the trends of society or social media to be the primary teachers of moral meaning for their children, especially when compared to the more proactive approach which teaches timeless, universal principles of effectiveness to children within the security of their home. Parents who stand for nothing raise children who fall for anything.

The life lessons and values taught in the family are the lessons that last the longest and should not be left to happenchance. If parents want their family to experience identity, connectedness, and hope, then they must take whatever proactive steps they can to make it happen. If they don't, society will—for better or worse.

So how does a family go about creating a culture that is filled with identity, connectedness, and hope? I suggest three practical approaches that Sandra and I have implemented in our family. They include creating a family mission statement, sharing family values through storytelling, and communicating family members' worth and potential.

CREATING A FAMILY MISSION STATEMENT

One of the most powerful things you can pass on to your children is a sense of building a life based on a mission.

If you were to ask Sandra and me, "What has been the most transforming event in the history of your family?" both of us would not hesitate in responding that it was the creation of our family mission statement. A family mission statement is a unified expression of what your family is about and the principles you choose to live by. Writing a family mission statement is one of the most proactive ways I know to take ownership of your family's purposes and destinations. I hope you do not mind me sharing our family's mission statement and what it has meant to us.

Soon after we were married, Sandra and I went to a park called Memory Grove. We talked about the families we had each come from, what things we wanted to continue in our newly formed family, and what things we wanted to do differently. We talked about how we wanted to live our lives. We reaffirmed that our marriage was more than a contractual relationship; it was a covenant relationship with each other and with God.

A family mission statement is a unified expression from all family members of what your family is about and the principles you choose to live by.

We discussed the principles we wanted to emphasize in raising our children. When our children did begin to come along, we asked ourselves, "What kinds of strengths and abilities will our children need to be successful when they are grown?" We identified ten abilities we felt our children would need to become independent of us and to start families of their own. These included the ability to work, to learn, to communicate, to solve problems, to repent, to forgive, to serve, to worship, to survive in the wilderness, and to have fun.

As the years passed, we recognized that successful organizations have mission statements. We knew from research that mission statements are a critical ingredient in high-performing organizations and that they are fundamentally important to the productivity and happiness of the people who work in those organizations.[5] This led us to the idea of creating a mission statement for our family.

At the time, the thought of having a family mission statement was rarely, if ever, talked about. Nevertheless, we wanted to create a vision for our children of what we wanted our family to be like, what principles we would live by, and what we would stand for. It would be a mission statement created and shared by all our family members, not just the two of us.

When we began the process of creating a family mission statement, we weren't too formal about it, but we did meet as a family once a week to talk about it. We had fun activities for the children that helped to inspire and collect their ideas. We sometimes discussed related topics during a dinner meal. At one meal we asked the children, "How do you think we could be better parents?" After twenty minutes of being bombarded by their ideas that flowed ever so freely, we said, "Okay, we think we get the idea!"

Gradually, we asked about a range of deeper questions:

What kind of family do we want to be?
What kind of home do we want to invite our friends into?
What makes us feel comfortable or uncomfortable in our home?
What do we as a family most want to be remembered by?

On one occasion, we asked the children to make a list of the character traits that were most important to them. We had open discussions about why they felt the traits were so desirable. Eventually, we invited the children to write down their individual versions of a family mission statement. We read and discussed each one together. We had to smile when we read our son Sean's version. Coming from the teenage football frame of mind he held at the time, it read: "We're one heck of a family, and we kick butt!" It was not too refined, but to the point.

Everyone participated. Even my mother gave input. To-day, we have grandchildren who have become a part of it. So there are now four generations involved in our family mission statement. It hangs on a wall in our home and has been a guide to our family for many years. It has created a sense of *we*: "This is what *we* together have decided that *we* are going to be and do as a family."

Our family is not perfect in living our mission statement. Yet over the years our family has felt in general that: "Our home is a place of faith, order, truth, love, happiness, and relaxation. We try to act in ways that are responsibly independent and effectively interdependent. We attempt to serve worthy purposes in society." Those words come from our family mission statement, and now our children have their own families and their own family mission statements.

THE POWER OF A FAMILY MISSION STATEMENT

That was our family's experience with creating and trying to live by a family mission statement. But what about other families' experiences and approaches?

Occasionally, workshop participants from around the world let me know their experiences with creating a family mission statement. As I share a few of their examples, notice how their stories bring feelings of shared identity, connectedness, and hope to their families.

First, a father shares this touching story of creating a family mission statement that was originally intended solely for their family vacation:

Some time ago I was thinking about my role as a father and envisioning how I wanted to be remembered by my kids. When it came time to plan our vacation that summer, I decided to apply the principle of vision to the family. We came up with a family mission statement for the event. It described the perspective we wanted to take when we went off together on our trip. We titled it "The Smith Team."

Next, we each chose a role that would contribute to keeping the mission statement alive. My six-year-old daughter chose the role of family cheerleader. Her goal was to dispel any contention in the family, particularly while we were traveling together in the car. She made up a few cheers, and whenever there was a problem, she would break into one of them: "Smiths! Smiths! When we stick together, we can't be beat!" Whether or not we felt like it, we'd all have to join in. It was helpful in dispelling any bad feelings or quarrels that arose along the way.

We had made matching T-shirts to wear, and at one point, we all went into a store. When the cashier saw us all wearing our matching shirts, he did a double take and said, "Hey, you guys look like a team!" We got back in the car and took off with the windows down and the radio cranked up. We were a happy team!

About three months after our vacation, our three-year-old son was diagnosed with leukemia. This threw our family into months of challenge. The interesting thing is that whenever we took our son to the hospital for his chemother-

apy treatments, he would always ask if he could wear his family shirt. It was his way of connecting with "The Smith Team" and feeling the support he'd felt on that family vacation.

After his sixth treatment, he caught a serious infection that put him in intensive care for two weeks. We came close to losing him. He wore that T-shirt almost nonstop through those days, and it became covered with stains of vomit, blood, and tears. When he finally did pull through and we brought him home, we all wore our family T-shirts in his honor. We all wanted to connect to that family mission feeling we had created on our vacation.

Next, the mother of a recently blended family shares what a mission statement did to establish a sense of identity for her new family:

The difference in having a family mission statement is that you have a set of principles that commit you, and don't make it easy for you to cop out. Had I had this kind of grounding in my first marriage, I probably would have dealt with it differently. In that marriage, there wasn't a sense of shared vision or commitment for me to give answer to: "Why should I stay in this marriage? What can I do to make it work?" Instead it was, "I've had it. I'm done. I'm out of here." And it was over.

I'm now remarried and things are different. We are one. We have equal say in this family. We have a common vision and a family mission statement. With our personalities and work styles, I think it would be very easy for a blended family like ours to disintegrate or become dysfunctional. But this feeling of shared vision has given us the strength and commitment to stay together and to act like a family.

Finally, once again feel the power of a family mission statement as you hear this dad's experience with his five-year-old daughter:

As part of a bedtime game, we asked our five-year-old to identify her favorite thing that was on her bedroom wall. Of all the things on her wall—movie posters, mirrors, photos, and assorted crafts and drawings she had made herself—she chose her copy of the family mission statement. I was deeply touched. I became firmly aware of the influence for good we can have with our children, and the good that's already in each family member as we talk about what is most important to each of us.

Within each of these examples, I imagine you caught a glimpse of how a family mission statement can bring feelings of bonding, unity of purpose, and identity to a family. Through a family mission statement, you let family members know you are totally committed to them, and that the family threads will never be broken.

As Benjamin Franklin said so beautifully: "We choose the thoughts we allow ourselves to think, the passions we allow ourselves to feel, and the actions we allow ourselves to perform. Each choice is made in the context of whatever value system we've selected to govern our lives. In selecting that value system, we are, in a very real way, making the most important choice we will ever make."[6]

STEPS TO CREATING A FAMILY MISSION STATEMENT

So how does a family go about creating a family mission statement? Our family's experience—plus my experience working with other families—has led to a three-step process.

Step One: Brainstorm What Your Family Stands For—Your Purposes, Values, and Dreams

The goal for this step is to gather everyone's feelings and ideas. It requires staying in brainstorming mode, which means not criticizing or evaluating people's ideas so that everyone feels comfortable sharing. It's important that everyone has the chance to feel heard.

Family mission statements focus on possibilities, not on limitations. They are meant to be expressions of happiness and guidance, not a list of rules that constrain. They point toward a vision of a brighter future. Each word is intended to inspire.

Start your family's mission statement by setting the right tone and timing for talking freely. Big words like "family mission statement," "family culture," or "connectedness," might scare off some family members, causing them to run to their rooms screaming, "Mom [or Dad] has lost her [or his] mind—again!" In some cases, you may initially want to entirely avoid bringing up the idea of a family mission statement. You might

> Family mission statements focus on possibilities, not on limitations.

instead begin by simply expressing your love for your family and your personal interest in finding ways to strengthen your relationships.

Finding a proper time and location to discuss your family mission statement is important. If possible, go off to a quiet place where you can be uninterrupted for a couple of hours or a day. If everyone in your family is leading busy lives, you may need to schedule much smaller slices of time and spread them over a reasonable period of weeks. Sandra and I found that the more we made the discussions short and fun, the better the discussions went and the more engagement we felt from our children.

As you collect input, consider inviting a family member to record everyone's responses so that the responses don't get forgotten. Below are a few questions that you can use to ignite your thinking and creativity about the types of things you want to have in your mission statement. It's not intended that you respond to them all; they're a way to start the brainstorming.

What are the three main purposes of our family?
What do we value most?
What are our family's highest priority goals?
How do we want other people to feel when they are with us?
What are the unique talents, gifts, and abilities of our family members?
What other families inspire us, and why do we admire them?
How will we handle conflicts?
How will we lift each other when we are down?
How will we contribute to our extended family? Our community?

No involvement, no commitment.

Beyond asking questions, feel free to get creative. I've seen families begin their mission statement process by assembling inspirational lyrics from favorite songs or by gathering favorite motivational quotes. I've seen families with young children hand out crayons and paper and have each child draw a picture of their family doing their favorite things. Each child is given a chance to explain what their illustration represents, and their ideas are then incorporated into the family mission statement.

The important thing to emphasize is that everyone in the family is involved. No involvement, no commitment.

Some parents may think young children do not have much to add when creating the family mission statement. Not so. A father shared this experience:

About four years ago my wife and I, our two children, and my mother-in-law who lives with us created a family mission statement. Just recently we were reviewing that statement to see what we felt we needed to change. In the course of the discussion, Sarah, our eleven-year-old, was talking about how one person can bring stress into the family, and it affects everyone else. I think she was particularly feeling this from Grandma, because Grandma was going through some things at the time and tended to speak crossly to the kids when we weren't around. But when Sarah said it, she didn't say it about Grandma; she said it about the family.

Nevertheless, Grandma caught on to it right away. She said, "You know, I really do that, and I want to improve."

My wife and I quickly said, "You know, Grandma, we all do that. We all need to improve." And so one of the lines in our mission statement now reads, "We will recognize when we are experiencing stress in our lives and not pass it on to others."

Our daughter Catherine states:

While our family's mission statement has remained fundamentally the same over the years, it has changed a little with each child. When our oldest was only six, she said she wanted to make sure we tell lots of jokes in our family, so we added that little statement for her.

Every New Year we work on our mission statement and write out our goals for the coming year. We find that our children are excited about the whole process and add much value.

Children love being a part of creating something meaningful, even when their contribution is small. As children see their ideas valued and validated, their feelings of identity, connectedness, and hope for the future grow. In fact, the time being together and listening to one another's opinions can by itself be a priceless bonding process. That's because the process is as important as the end product. Unless people feel they have had some say in the formation of the mission statement, they will not be committed to it or feel ownership when the time comes to live it.

Insight from Sandra

Our teenaged children were not at first interested in the process of creating a family mission statement. They wanted to hurry and get it over with. But as Stephen and I found ways to make it fun, and as we kept coming back to it, their interest grew.

If you too feel initial resistance from family members, you might begin by talking with them individually and asking questions in a one-on-one setting. Perhaps you do it while working on a project or doing something enjoyable together. But don't try to do it when you feel emotionally exhausted, or angry, or are rushed, or are in the middle of a family crisis.

If the resistance is extensive, back off. Wait for a better time.

Step Two: Write Your Family Mission Statement

Once everyone's ideas are captured, you are ready to evaluate and combine the ideas into a single, simple expression that reflects the collective hearts and minds of all who have contributed. The important thing is to eventually get it into a written format—even if it is an early draft.

You may be fortunate enough to have a family member with a talent for writing and who can take all the ideas and create a first draft. If not, don't let that stop you. Because this is the point where many family mission statements come to a halt. People think, "I'm not a good writer," or "I'm not creative," and the process stops. The mission statement does not need to be long, fancy, or perfectly written. Remember that the process is as important as the mission statement itself.

What gets written is meant to prioritize all the ideas that have been brainstormed to make them simple and understandable to every person and age level within the family. Prioritizing forces families to think deeply about what truly matters most and what will bring the most bonding.

Whatever written version you come up with initially will likely be the first of multiple drafts. Family members will need to look at it, think about it, tweak it, live it, revisit it, and make changes until everyone comes to the agreement that: "This is what our family is about. We are ready to fully commit to living by it."

The following are samples of family mission statements that have gone through this process. They are not intended to be exact models for your family mission statement. Yours will reflect your family's own hopes, values, beliefs, and creativity, which means it will be one of a kind.

Our family mission is to:
Value honesty with ourselves and others.
Honor the cultures and creeds of all.

Respect and accept each person's unique talents.
Promote a kind and happy atmosphere.
Resolve conflicts with each other rather than harbor anger.
Always be loyal to each other.

Our family mission:
To love each other
To help each other
To believe in each other
To use our time and talents to bless others
Forever.

Our home will be a place where family, friends, and guests find joy, comfort, peace, and happiness. We will seek to create a clean and orderly environment that is livable and comfortable. We will exercise wisdom in what we choose to eat, read, see, and do. We will teach each other to love, to learn, to laugh, and to work and develop their unique talents.

Our family is happy and has fun together.
We all feel secure and a sense of belonging.
We strive to continually grow in mental, physical,
    social/emotional, and spiritual ways.
We respect all life-forms and protect the environment.
We serve each other and the community.
We are a family of cleanliness and order.
We believe that diversity of race and culture is a gift.
We treasure the grace of God.

Again, a mission statement does not need to be long, formal, poetic, or perfect. Especially when young children are involved. You are writing it for your family, not for worldwide review. It can even be a single phrase or something creative such as an image, illustration, or symbol. The easier it is to remember or memorize the better.

My brother, John, and his wife, Jane, were grandparents when they developed their first family mission statement. Some of their children were at home and others were married and living far away. They communicated over a series of months. Ultimately, they came up with a three-word mission statement: "No empty chairs." Those three words have profound meaning to their family. They are code words. Behind them are many deep discussions and thoughts about having unconditional love and unwavering commitment to each other: "We will include everyone." "We're not going to hold grudges." "We're going to forgive each other." Today it continues to work wonderfully for their family.

I know a family who has written a family song that they use as a mission statement. Others have created poetry and art to depict their mission statement. Still others have built theirs in the form of a collage using several photos and words cut out of magazines to represent their family values and dreams. Some families create their mission statement by building phrases that begin with each letter of their surname. All sorts of creative options exist. The format is less important than the process and the fact that the mission statement is meaningful to your family.

Step Three: Use the Mission Statement
to Stay on Track

Of course, putting a mission statement on paper or into a digital format is not as powerful as putting it into the hearts, minds, and daily behaviors of each family member.

A family mission statement is more than a piece of art to hang on a wall to impress your friends. It's meant to be the literal constitution of your family life. Just as the constitution of a country is intended to last a long time, your family mission statement can be the foundational document that will unify and hold your family together for decades—even generations. It can help you make important decisions. It can help you know what to say "no" to. You can come back to it for guidance, time and time again, especially when you get off track and need to course correct.

I recommend placing your family mission statement in a location where family members will see it and discuss it regularly. That way, in all your family's daily comings and goings, they will see it and be reminded of the kind of family they are striving to become.

Naturally, you may want to update your family mission statement from time to time. The drafting and living of a family mission statement is an ongoing habit of effective families, not a onetime event. How well you live the mission statement will set a precedent for years to come. For when you raise

When you raise your children, you're also raising your grandchildren. Patterns tend to persist to the next generation.

your children, you're also raising your grandchildren. Patterns tend to persist to the next generation.

SHARING FAMILY VALUES THROUGH STORYTELLING

Aside from creating and living by a family mission statement, a second approach Sandra and I have used to instill a sense of identity, connectedness, and hope in our children, and now grandchildren, is storytelling. Stories are excellent for communicating and reinforcing family values and vision.

My Grandpa Covey was a sheepherder. He was out on the plains in a very desolate part of Wyoming one day when he got caught in a freak, out-of-season snow blizzard. His life was literally in peril. He was a religious man and so he promised God that if He would preserve his life, then he would build a place of shelter near that very spot for others who might get stranded or were otherwise in need of shelter. Grandpa's life was preserved.

Grandpa was a man good to his word—a person of integrity—so it was no surprise that he was determined to honor his promise to God. He built a small motel next to the highway that was nearest to where he had been stranded. Nothing was within miles in any direction. Nothing! He built it anyways.

My father inherited Grandpa Covey's integrity. Occasionally he took us on a pheasant hunt and one year we decided to go out on the first day of the hunting season. We got up very early and staked out our spot by 6:30 a.m. The season wasn't set to begin until 8:00 a.m., yet at about 7:45 a.m. we started hearing shots being fired all around us by other hunters. Birds began to fly.

As boys we were eager to have our turn and didn't want to miss out on any of the birds. But Dad kept looking at his watch and holding us off. He was not about to start one second early. He didn't care that there was no authority around to catch or fine us for breaking the rules. Nor did he care what the other hunters were doing. He was going to be true to the rules and the permit he signed—no matter what. He would rather go home empty-handed than to shoot a hole in his integrity.

Sure enough, we did not get any birds that day. But I did catch a vision of my father's integrity, and to this day it causes me to recommit to my own integrity.

To everyone's surprise, people actually stopped and spent the night at my grandfather's middle-of-nowhere motel. And it grew. He eventually built a larger hotel in downtown Salt Lake City, and my father took on much of the responsibility for its management. When it came time for me to further my university studies, I was sent off to get an MBA with the intent that I would return and help run Grandpa's hotel. It would be a guaranteed living for my family. The problem was that deep inside I knew I had a passion for a different career. I wanted to be a teacher. It paid far less, but in my heart of hearts it was what I wanted to do.

If integrity is when what you do matches what you believe, then to some extent my own integrity was being put on trial. Do I go for the money or go for what my heart was telling me to do? When I returned home with my MBA degree in hand, I got up my courage and went to my father. "Dad," I said,

"I don't want to help run the hotel. I want to be a teacher." He looked me square in the eyes, paused for what seemed an eternity, and said, "Well then, you need to be a teacher." And so I went on to teach at the university for twenty-five years and have never regretted that decision.

All three of those stories occurred decades ago. Yet all three have now been told and retold many times to our children and our children's children. We use them to teach the principle of integrity, which is one of our family's core values. In all three stories, perhaps you could feel the sense of identity, connectedness, and hope that family stories can bring to family members. Young people forget lectures; they remember stories. Stories have stickiness, especially when they have a meaningful life lesson attached to them—a moral meaning.

Inspiring stories passed down from ancestors can have great impact on family members.

In cultures around the world where there are no written histories, families and tribes have used oral histories for many generations as a way to pass their values on to coming generations. In this way, entire family tribes—including children, grandchildren, great-grandchildren, and so on—all come to know in a unified, connected way: "This is who *we* are. This is what *we* value. This is who we are committed to becoming."

Inspiring stories passed down from ancestors can have great impact on family members. I recall a television program where two prison inmates shared how they had become "unfeeling" as a result of their years of being in prison. They had reached a point where they were no longer sensitive to any pains they might cause for others, and they saw little hope or vision for themselves. Then these men somehow became involved in a prison course on family history and they started to learn about their ancestors and how their grandparents and great-grandparents had lived their lives. They read about their struggles, failures, and triumphs. Both prisoners revealed how enormously meaningful their ancestors' stories became to them. Each began to think, "Even though I have made terrible mistakes, my life is not over. Like my ancestors, I want to leave a legacy that my descendants will value." Each of these men had found a sense of hope from the stories of their families' past.

What values do your family's stories promote?

Insight from Sandra

I love telling family stories. Yet I also know that children may eventually grow weary of hearing the same family stories over and over. Thankfully, there are many other forms of storytelling and many other sources from which I can borrow stories that build values.

Music, for example, is a marvelous form of storytelling. I have gathered an array of songs that our children and grandchildren love to sing. Several teach a value or spread positive thoughts. If you don't feel comfortable singing or don't know of any good songs, take comfort in knowing that there are hundreds of inspiring songs with uplifting lyrics that can be accessed at no cost online.

Reading is another grand form of storytelling. I like to find and read stories that support our family's values. I also like to tell stories about friends I know or people from history that reinforce our family values and teach timeless principles of effective living.

COMMUNICATING WORTH AND POTENTIAL

Family mission statements and family stories provide a vision for what a family is all about and what it can become. It is also important to give each individual family member a vision of who they are as unique individuals and who they have the potential to become.

So the third approach that Sandra and I have used to nurture identity, connectedness, and hope in our family is to communicate each family member's worth and potential. Recall that one of the main purposes of this book is to enable you to be an even better leader within your family. So what does it mean to be a leader? There are many ways I have defined leadership over the years, but the definition I use most is this one:

Leadership is communicating people's worth and potential so clearly that they are inspired to see it in themselves.

Leadership is communicating people's worth and potential so clearly that they are inspired to see it in themselves.

When you communicate a family member's worth—including the strengths you see in them and the value you place in them today—aren't you strengthening their sense of identity and connecting with them? And when you communicate their potential—your confidence in their ability to do well in the days ahead—aren't you giving them a vision of who they can become? Aren't you building their confidence and hope?

Communicating worth says, "I accept and unconditionally love you for who you are today." Communicating potential says, "I believe that you will make meaningful contributions in the future." These types of affirming words can impact a family member for a lifetime.

Your words of encouragement and affirmation can have a powerful impact on family members. I love the following memory of this father:

I was fifteen and had just accomplished a rather small feat. Nonetheless, I was proud of it and thought I would share it with my mother. I found her lying on our couch. She was in the final stages of cancer and the couch was where she spent her last days.

I told her about my small accomplishment and she smiled, called me by name, and said in a soft voice, "You're a good boy." That's all she said.

Those were some of the last words she ever spoke. I am now sixty-two and remember that moment like it was yesterday. I can still hear her voice. "You're a good boy."

I now have children of my own and I often think after leaving them, "What if the words I just spoke turn out to be the final words I ever speak to my children? What did those words communicate to them about their worth and potential?"

The mother's dying words were simple. Yet they put a label on that young man that he continues to try to live up to decades later as a father, husband, and grandfather. Notice how she did not say, "You're a good boy now, but when you finally mature and quit acting like a teenager then you'll really be even more special." She affirmed and accepted him as he was.

Another father shared a similar story about how his wife was able to proactively pause, think, and choose words that put a positive label on their young son. He recalled:

I came home from work and my three-year-old, Brenton, met me at the door. He was beaming. He said, "Dad, I am a hardworking man!"

I discovered that while my wife was in another room, Brenton had emptied a two-gallon jug of water on the floor. My wife's initial impulse was to yell at him. But instead she stopped herself and asked patiently, "Brenton, what were you trying to do?"

"I washed the dishes," he replied ever so proudly.

Sure enough, there on the kitchen table were the dishes he had washed with water from the jug. "Oh!" she said.

"What do you think you can do next time that would make less of a mess?"

Brenton thought for a minute, then his face lit up. "I could do it in the bathroom!"

"The dishes might break in the bathroom," my wife replied. "But how about this? What if you come and get me, and then I will help you move a chair in front of the kitchen sink so you can do the work there?"

"Good idea!" he exclaimed happily.

"Now, what shall we do with this mess that you've made, you hardworking man?" she asked.

As my wife was telling me what had happened, I realized how important it was that she had been able to pause and catch her temper, and how good it was that she had an end in mind for our son that went beyond having a dry floor.

If she had been reactive and had no end in mind, chances are that Brenton would have met me at the door and instead said, "Daddy, I am a bad boy!"

Instead of feeling embarrassed, ashamed, or even mad at his mother, Brenton felt affirmed, appreciated, and encouraged. His sense of worth and potential was strengthened. Not only did it give him a new vision of how to wash dishes, it gave him a new vision of who he was—his identity. There's a big difference between having a paradigm of "I'm a bad boy!" versus a paradigm of "I'm a hardworking man!" And I guarantee that if Brenton continues to *see* himself as a hard worker, it will positively influence what he will *do* in life and the results he will *get*.

Negative labels placed on a child have the power to thwart

all positive ambition. Positive labels nurture a budding legacy. Words and labels have the potential to become self-fulfilling prophecies. As the German philosopher Johann von Goethe said, "If you treat an individual as he is, he will remain as he is. If you treat him as he ought to be and could be, he will become what he can and should be."[7] Or slightly varied, "Speak to family members as they are and they will remain as they are. Speak to them as they can and ought to become and they will be inspired to achieve their potential."

A simple—yet often grossly underused—way of communicating worth and potential in families is to express gratitude. Saying, "Thank you for what you did for me yesterday," is a way of saying to a person, "You are of worth to me. I value you. You have made a contribution in my life." Expressing gratitude can also be a way of expressing future worth and potential by letting people know, "I'm so grateful you will be nearby when I retire," or "You have an amazing voice. I hope you come sing for my birthday every year." Words of gratitude are filled with identity, connectedness, and hope.

Another important way to communicate a family member's worth and potential is through compliments. In fact, one of the best parts of being a family is that you can affirm and encourage one another. When you see a child living one of your family's values, for example, it's a great time to compliment them: "I love your integrity. Your one hundred percent honesty." Affirmations weave a safety net throughout a family's culture that makes people feel secure and connected.

There is great value in putting your compliments and affirmations into writing so that people can hold on to them for a long time. A short while before my angel mother died,

I opened a letter from her while on a plane. She wrote such "love letters" to me frequently, even though we talked almost daily on the phone and visited in person nearly every week. Private letters were her special form of expressing appreciation and love. As I read her letter that day, I felt the tears roll off my cheeks. I felt so affirmed and treasured. I keep many of those letters.

Insight from Sandra

Children need much encouragement and many genuine affirmations. We cannot assume they will receive them from outside the family.

And something we have taught our children is that adults need a lot of encouragement too. "Compliment them," we tell our children. "They are working so hard to make a living and hold a family together. Point out the wonderful things they have done for you. Especially compliment your teachers."

Stephen and I try to model this ourselves. When we introduce a child to one of our friends, we try to point out something we like about that child and something we like about our friend. It gives our children a positive introduction to the person and teaches them good people skills.

Children don't always appreciate a parent's hard work. They just want to run off and play after a nice meal, and don't say anything. So I appreciate it when in the middle of a meal Stephen will say something like, "Kids, let's give Mom a standing ovation for tonight's dinner," and the kids all stand and give me a cheer. It may be a silly little thing, but it means something larger to me.

Children—and adults—have enough people on social media, at school, or on the job telling them what's wrong about them or placing discouraging labels on them. They do not need negative messages coming at them from within the walls of their own home. That's why, nearly every morning my brother, John, and his wife, Jane, send out text messages to their children and grandchildren—praising them, thanking them, encouraging them, inspiring them, and building them up. It reinforces their values and mission statement, and lets their family members know of their worth and potential.

And so I ask: When was the last time you communicated a family member's worth and potential so clearly that they were inspired to see it in themselves?

AND THEN LIFE HAPPENS!

Habit 1 says, "We as a family are responsible for our choices and happiness." We may be influenced by our genetics and environment, but we are going to do all we can within our Circle of Influence to influence our lives in a way that allows us to go in the directions we choose to go.

Habit 2 then says, "These are the directions we want to go as a family." It is the mental creation for your family. It's the family blueprint, the family flight plan. It's your expression of who you genuinely want to become as a family. It's your vision of your family when you are at your best. Every family benefits from having such a vision.

And then life happens! Reality strikes. Turbulence hits. And it's not easy to stay on course.

Not everything in life happens as planned. Not all dreams come true. Despite a parent's best efforts to establish clear family values, a child may choose to go in other directions. Family members get busy and become distracted from what's most important. Tragedies outside the family's control occur and throw them off course for a period. Mental illness strikes. Relationships fall apart. Contention stirs up bad feelings. Children's lives get swallowed up by their digital devices.

As the saying goes, "Life is what happens when you are busy making other plans." The family you imagined as a teen may not have turned out to be the family you have now. What worked for your parents yesterday may not work for you and your family today. You may even wonder if it's really worth the effort to create a family mission statement or to clarify your values if life is going to keep changing at such a rapid pace. Life is never easy. I know.

That all said, I still maintain that what I have observed over and over is that families who do have a clear sense of vision, values, and direction accomplish significantly more than families who do not. Life isn't always easy for these families, but it is easier for them than it would be if they were to drift aimlessly with no solid goals or values to anchor them. Why? Because there are timeless principles of effectiveness associated with Habit 2, such as vision, purpose, commitment, and meaning. When these principles are violated, there are natural consequences. In today's turbulent world, those natural consequences are manifesting themselves in the forms of anxiety, depression, or discouragement, especially among young people who lack identity, connectedness, and hope.

Vision is what helps a family over the hurdles of the past and provides them with a view of a brighter future. It's why I say that vision is more powerful than the baggage of the past. Vision inspires your family with the power and purposes to rise above past mistakes, past contentions, past hurtful comments, or past lapses in judgment. Vision enables a family to act on what matters most and this is why Habit 2 is so vital to a family.

Creating vision does not happen overnight. So be patient. Involve family members in the process. Again, no involvement, no commitment. Adjustments will be needed from time to time, but so what? The important thing is to keep trying, beginning with yourself. Work from the inside out. Create a personal mission statement and live by it. Become a living model of identity, connectedness, and hope. Then invite your family to follow. And be prepared to be forgiving and nurturing when someone slips up.

For sure, bringing your family mission and values to life on a daily basis is not always easy. Things will not always go perfectly. And for such occasions, Habit 3: Put First Things First provides some very practical guidance.

Insight from Sandra

Stephen likes to say that "vision is more power-ful than baggage." It reminds me of the time when he had a series of presentations throughout Europe, and he decided to take me and some of the children along.

We were excited to explore the beauties, cultures, and histories of that part of the world. Since we would be gone for some length of time, we packed our bags for all sorts of occasions and weather. Once we arrived, however, we realized what a mistake we had made. We had way too much baggage!

As a result, a major chunk of each day was spent figuring out what to do with all of our baggage as we shifted from city to city, meeting to meeting, and sight to sight. It became a huge burden. Ultimately, we decided to send half of our baggage home. Once we did, we were free to move around and enjoy many more sights.

Similarly, I've seen some families become so weighed down by the emotional baggage of their past that they can't seem to move a step forward. They focus so much on harmful things that were once said, past tragedies that have occurred, or sorrows they have faced, that they simply cannot see any positive future ahead. In so doing, they miss out on the present joys that could have been theirs.

Until such families set themselves free by creating a unified vision of a better future, they will always be weighed down and held back by the woeful baggage of their past. And that's why vision truly is greater than baggage.

REFLECTIONS AND APPLICATIONS

With Self

Looking back over Habit 2: Begin with the End in Mind, what is the one idea or learning that if you were to apply it better would have the greatest impact on the well-being of your family?

_____

_____

_____

With Adults and Teens

- Brainstorm examples of a mental creation, such as making blueprint plans before constructing a building or creating flight plans before making a flight. Discuss: In everyday life, what mental creations are required at school? At home? In sports? Gardening? Cooking?
- Read the statement: "If you don't take charge of your mental creation, someone or something else will." Ask: In what ways do we take charge of our mental creations as a family?
- Discuss the importance and benefits of having a family mission statement, such as having a deeper sense of identity and meaning, or a sense of hope.
- Apply the three-step process for creating a family mission statement.
- Share examples of times when people have communicated your worth and potential. How did it make you feel?
- Gather and share two or three family stories that reinforce your family values.
- Text a message that communicates worth and potential to a teen or extended family member.

With Young Children

- Ask: If we were taking a trip tomorrow, what would you pack? Don't tell family members where you are going or how long you will be gone. When they are finished making a list of what they would pack, ask what difference it would have made if you had told them the destination was the North Pole and the plan was to live for a month in an igloo. Discuss why it is important to know your life destinations.

- Ask: Does it make sense to sew a dress or shirt without a pattern in mind? To cook a meal without a recipe or an idea of what you want to make? To build a house without a blueprint? Help your family understand that a family also needs a plan to succeed.

- Take turns sharing a story of a time when a family member exhibited a family value, such as honesty, courage, or kindness.

- Distribute a piece of paper or an index card to each family member and ask them to draw things in their family life that make them happy, such as activities they love to do as a family, or good things they see other families doing that they would like to be doing. Discuss the drawings and refer to them as you develop your family mission statement.

- Make a family flag that represents your family values, select a family motto, or write a family song.

PUT FIRST THINGS FIRST

Making Time for Family Time

If Habit 2 represents a family's *mental* creation, then Habit 3 and the remaining habits represent the principles and skills for building the *physical* creation—a nurturing family culture. Habit 3, in particular, is where families find the discipline to focus their time and energy on what matters most.

Years ago, our daughter Maria had recently given birth to her third child. She was talking with me about life and confided, "I'm so frustrated, Dad! You know how much I love this baby, but she is literally taking all of my time. I'm not getting anything else done, including the many things that only I can do."

Maria is bright, capable, and well organized. She has always been involved in worthwhile efforts. And there she was feeling tormented and pulled in all directions by projects and things around the house that were not getting done.

Maria understood that her life with a new baby was going to be temporarily imbalanced. She knew that as the baby grew and entered different phases of life she would eventually be able to get back to her other goals and projects. She knew all those things. Yet still it was hard for her to not be accomplishing all she wanted.

"Enjoy the moment," I recommended. "Let this infant feel your joy. No one else can love and nurture her the way you can. All other projects or interests pale in importance for now. Forget your calendar. Stop using your planning tools if they only induce guilt. You've said that this baby is the 'first thing' in your life right now. So be governed by your internal compass, not by some calendar or clock on the wall, or by all the frivolous distractions and sideshows that life presents."

Again, Maria knew all those things. I was just there to support and remind her.

KEEPING YOUR MAIN THINGS YOUR MAIN THINGS

Feelings like Maria's are natural and are not limited to sleep-deprived new parents. In fact, as I was reminding Maria of those things, deep inside I knew I was also reminding myself. It is not easy for any purpose-driven person to relax and let some things go, even when it's clear that no one can do it all.

When presenting Habit 2 in a workshop setting, I like to invite participants to make a short list of what matters most to them. I've examined many of those lists and the vast majority of them start out with *relationships*—family, friends, God, pets, work colleagues, etc. Next comes their *values*—freedom, trust, contribution, fun, integrity, creativity, loyalty, exercise, etc. Those are then followed by their tangible *objects*—car, money, cell phone, career, projects, body, house, clothing, etc. There are exceptions, of course, but this is the general pattern.

When we then get to Habit 3 in the workshop, I next invite participants to examine their previous week. Where did they spend their time? With few exceptions, people realize that they spent insufficient time building and maintaining their most important *relationships*, and spent even less time trying to pursue and reinforce their *values*. What they ultimately confess is that their *objects* have taken over their lives. In other words, what they *say* is most important to them and what they actually *do* with their time are not in alignment.

We have surveyed over a quarter of a million people, asking them to rate how well they personally live the 7 Habits. Of all the habits, Habit 3 is the one where people consistently give themselves the lowest marks—by far.[1] With so many people rating themselves this way, it's no wonder why they also report that they feel out of balance in life or lack a sense of meaning.

The main thing is to keep the main things the main things.

What I learn from this is that even when we as individuals have done our best to identify our Habit 2 values, mission statements, and plans, unless we turn our mental creations into physical creations, we will not progress at the pace we desire or feel the internal peace we seek. This is why I summarize Habit 3 this way: the main thing is to keep the main things the main things.

OUTSIDE FORCES THAT DETOUR FAMILIES

So what prevents individuals and families from keeping their main things their main things?

In our turbulent world, families battle numerous forces that have the potential to deter them from spending more of their precious time on what matters most. I'll first identify a few "outside forces" that commonly deter families, and then identify a few "inside forces" that families can use to counter-attack the outside forces.

Media

The first outside force I will identify is media. I am not a media basher, and even see much good in it. However, it concerns me when I hear researchers argue that certain media content—such as graphic violence, degrading attacks on women and their bodies, or demeaning portrayals of racial minorities—has no influence on viewers' paradigms or behaviors, and no negative impact on a family. Then, only seconds later, I read about advertisers spending millions upon millions of dollars on media advertising. Why? Because researchers have convinced them that twenty seconds of viewership will vastly influence the thinking and behavior of potential buyers, including young people. Which researchers do you believe? It's obvious who the advertisers believe.

Sources estimate that teens spend an average of nine hours a day locked on to media screens, whether it be television screens, computer screens, or phone screens. In stark contrast, they spend only an average of twenty minutes a day with Mom and five minutes with Dad.[2] Even if the correct numbers are only half of those estimated minutes, they are a telling indicator of the influence that media can have on a child and family. Time that could be spent building family relationships or expanding each other's skills is replaced by time spent texting, filtering photos, or playing games online—often with total strangers. Many tablets, smartphones, and game consoles are uncensored and contain messages that dishearten children's feelings of identity, connectedness, and hope, and can distract a family or child from keeping their main things their main things.

Insight from Sandra

When Stephen and I were raising our children, a person needed to go to an adult bookstore or catch a late-night movie to be exposed to materials that were offensive to family-friendly standards. Nowadays, such content has not only become more graphic, explicit, and violent, it penetrates nearly every bedroom and hidden corner of a household. All a family member of any age needs is the right digital device and there it is.

Is it realistic to think that children will not be affected by the repetitious murders, cruelties, and vulgarities they watch for hours in a day? Is it reasonable to think that teens who are exposed to daily doses of cynical language or consistent screen diets of misleading sexual or drug-centered pleasuring will grow up with a wholesome view of what enduring intimate relationships or traditional family values can offer? I think not.

Employment

This outside opposing force may come as a surprise, partly because it may not be true for your family. However, in former days, a typical employee viewed their work life as being filled with stress and high-pressure deadlines, and viewed their family life as their place of refuge, joy, and relaxation. Well, for many people, those two views have traded places.

In her book *The Time Bind*, sociologist Arlie Hochschild points out how nowadays for many working people their family life has become a frantic, frenzied exercise in "beating the clock," with family members having only fifteen minutes to eat before rushing off to a soccer game, or ten minutes to try to squeeze in some bonding time before bedtime. Meanwhile, their workplaces have become their refuge of sociability, meaning, competence, freedom, and satisfaction. In describing this reversed view, Hochschild writes, "In this new model of family-and-work life, a tired parent flees a world of unresolved quarrels and unwashed laundry for the reliable orderliness, harmony, and managed cheer of work."[3]

I have observed this changing of the views in my work with a handful of top executives. On a daily basis they guide impressive organizations and lead thousands of employees with great comfort, pride, and ease. They feel in control. They then go home and find everything "out of control" and have no idea what to do about it. For them, the extrinsic rewards they receive at their workplace create a very seductive vision that draws them away from spending time with their out-of-sorts family. This happens at all levels of the workforce, not just the top.

Economy

As the quality of living has gone up in many parts of the world, so too have the costs of living. Computers, cell phones, and other advances in science, technology, engineering, entertainment, and medicine have contributed to better ways of living. Many were meant to give us more free time. Yet they all cost money. So much so that keeping up with just the basic expenses of daily life is putting tremendous financial pressures on the heads of households. Many parents have little choice but to take on multiple jobs to pay for basic expenses. The time required to obtain the additional spending money can easily draw family members away from spending time with each other. It's no wonder why finances remain a persistent source of contention and are at the root of many family breakups.

Education

Obtaining an education has by itself become a source of growing stress on families. In former days, as their child cheerfully ran off to school, parents would casually call out, "Remember who you are!" or "Be sure to tell your teacher 'thank you'!" Nowadays, parents unlatch the bolted locks on their doors to say things like, "You'd better get an 'A' or you'll never get into college!" or "Be careful and stay away from the school bullies."

Desires for their children's safety and pressures to compete for entrance into the best universities has put enormous financial and emotional stresses on families and children. Time previously spent having fun, being creative, or relaxing as a family is now spent working on endless homework assignments and dealing with the anxiety that comes with trying to get the best education possible.

Laws and Mores

In general, progressive countries and communities have laws that favor families by offering affordable housing, education, meaningful employment, food, and healthcare, and providing places where families can recreate, enjoy nature, and so forth. They are family friendly. In contrast, some countries and communities are less family centered and may even have laws that limit families' freedoms and opportunities for growth and happiness, especially when those laws favor one group of people over another on the basis of race, religion, gender, sexuality, nationality, etc.

In other cases, it is not the laws of the land but the mores of a culture or community that limit families' opportunities. Mores are the shared values of a community, nation, or people. They too can either promote or weaken the opportunities of a family, especially in areas where violence, poverty, and safety issues wreak havoc on individuals' emotional well-being. While the laws and mores of the most progressive countries are aimed at strengthening the progress and stability of all families, sadly it is not equally the case in every country, community, or culture.

So there are a few examples of outside forces that can deter or inhibit families from keeping their main things their main things. I am not suggesting that all media, employment, economies, forms of education, or laws and mores are inherently good or bad, right or wrong. I'm simply pointing out that, if left unchecked, they can place unprecedented stresses and limitations on families.

INSIDE FORCES THAT EMPOWER FAMILIES

While the outside forces concern me, I firmly believe that the forces that most deter a family from keeping their main things their main things come not from the outside but from the inside—from within the family itself. This is why I find Habit 3 so empowering. It takes an inside-out approach. It searches the Circle of Influence to find the forces which individuals and families can use to keep their main things their main things.

The most powerful inside forces are found in our paradigms—the ways we see the world. Remember, the best way to change a habit and to improve a family culture is to change our paradigms. So I will now contrast three *common* paradigms that have the potential to hinder families from putting first things first with three *effective* paradigms that empower a family to keep its main things its main things. They are summarized in the following table and then briefly described below.

Common Paradigms	Effective Paradigms
Schedules before relationships.	Relationships before schedules.
Efficiency before effectiveness.	Effectiveness before efficiency.
Urgency before importance.	Importance before urgency.

Relationships Before Schedules

Many people view Habit 3 as the habit of *managing time*. But really it's not. Rather, it's the habit of *managing important relationships*.

Sandra and I are big believers in making schedules and keeping tight calendars. But it's our relationships that drive our schedules, not our schedules that drive our relationships. It's an important distinction.

Sometimes clients or friends are slightly offended when I turn down what to them is a "big opportunity" so I can attend what in their minds is a "little family event." Often, the little family event will be a scooter ride with Sandra. It's our proactively scheduled time to be alone on a regular basis. It's our chance to get away, to talk, and to plan. It refreshes our friendship and our commitment to each other. I've never heard Sandra refer to it as a little event.

Many people attempt to live by the opposite paradigm, which is to put your schedule ahead of your relationships. You know, "Sorry, family. I've just looked at my schedule and it shows no time for you this week—again."

Some years ago, our company led a seminar that was filled with junior executives from one of the most successful big-brand multinational companies in the world. The topic was focused on putting first things first. Joining that day was one of the company's top leaders. He was a legend. He had accomplished every goal this group of younger executives could ever dream of achieving.

The top executive sat in the back and listened as the junior executives discussed "first things first" through the lenses of their careers and work objectives. He remained quiet until there came a point when he felt he could no longer sit silent. He stood up and began pleading with the up-and-coming leaders: "In your quest to accomplish your goals and meet deadlines for the company, I beg every one of you to not follow the route I have taken." The room went silent as he went on to describe with great emotion how during his climb up the corporate ladder he had not only neglected his family, he had lost them. "They no longer want anything to do with me," he said. Through his very humble expressions, he continued to urge the participants to "put relationships first and you will be happy no matter what rung on the corporate ladder you achieve."

I'm certain the junior executives never forgot the passion with which he shared his feelings. If your "ladder" is leaning against the wrong wall, every step you take only gets you to the wrong place faster. Think relationships first, then schedules.

Effectiveness Before Efficiency

Both effectiveness and efficiency are of great value, but one comes first. There's no need to do something efficiently that is not effective in the long run.

Perhaps you have heard a parent try to be efficient with a child during an emotional moment. They say things like: "So what! You just broke up with your boyfriend. Don't stress. You're tough. Now get out there and find another one." All the while, the parent has a look on their face that says, "See. That speech took only six seconds. I'm an efficient parent. Now I can get back to my television program."

> If your ladder is leaning against the wrong wall, every step you take only gets you to the wrong place faster.

Imagine a son or daughter coming to you in tears and saying, "I'm struggling to choose a major to study in college and I don't know what to do. Can you help me?" And you reply, "I'll tell you what you should do. It will take me thirty seconds. Get a pen and paper because I don't want to have to repeat myself later." How do you think that approach would go over with your son or daughter? Have you ever tried to be efficient with your partner or your child or a sibling when they are very upset with you? How did that go?

When dealing with family relationships, first ask, "What is the most effective thing to do here?" and then consider how to address it efficiently. Think effectiveness first, efficiency second.

Importance Before Urgency

We live in a busy world. Many urgent things demand our immediate attention. The phone rings and it expects to be answered—now! A child needs to go to soccer practice—can't be one second late! Your elderly parent needs to refill their medications—today! The sporting event you have been looking forward to is starting on television—right now! Everything feels urgent! Immediate! And all of it seems to end with exclamation points!

Some people operate from the paradigm that urgent means important, and so they respond to anything that feels urgent. But just because something feels urgent does not mean it is important.

In fact, some of the most important things in life are not urgent at all. For many years, I have challenged audiences to write down their answer to this question: "If you were to do one thing that you *know* would make a tremendous difference for good in your personal or professional life, what would that one thing be?" People generally come up with their answers rather quickly.

I then ask them to examine their answers and determine whether what they wrote down was urgent, important, or both. Almost without exception, people respond that the one thing that would make a tremendous positive difference in their life is important but it is not urgent.

As we talk further, people realize that the reason they don't get around to doing the "important" thing that they identified is because it is not "urgent." Because it's not urgent, they set it aside—they procrastinate about it—while they attend to other urgent but less important or not important matters. Charles Hummel suggests that these people are bound by what he calls the "tyranny of the urgent."[4]

If you think about it, there are very few true emergencies in a person's life. So don't allow every little thing that appears urgent to fool you into thinking it is important, or that it needs to be handled immediately. Especially don't let those urgent but not important things derail you from doing what you consider to be most important.

And who determines what is most important for you and your family? You do! What is most important for your family is determined by what you came up with in Habit 2— your family values and family mission statement. Families who have not proactively paid the price to create a mission statement, or are not clear about their values or goals, end up responding reactively to anything in life that seems urgent.

Think importance first, then urgency.

"BIG ROCK" FAMILY SYSTEMS

All successful organizations—including families—put systems in place to achieve and sustain effective results.

Early on in our family, Sandra and I did our best to keep our family values and mission statement alive. We talked about them occasionally with the children and built them into activities, vacations, and so forth. But for as much as we did our best to revisit our mission statement and goals on a regular basis, we knew we were doing it in a very random, unorganized way. We also knew that if we truly wanted to be both effective and efficient, then we needed to establish a few family systems—or routines.

Think about it. When a person's life is a mess, what do they say? "I need to get organized." When a family is in a mess, what do you hear? "We need to get things in order." Effective systems that are kept simple provide order and help a family keep their priorities their main things.

Now some parents and children will say, "We don't want to be so structured. We want to be free to do whatever we want to do and when we want to do it. We don't like systems."

Systems are not meant to deny freedoms, they are meant to enhance freedoms and provide order. The great British statesman Winston Churchill declared: "For the first twenty-five years of my life I wanted freedom. For the next twenty-five years I wanted order. For the next twenty-five years I realized that order is freedom."[5]

Systems do not need to be rigid to be effective. They can be very flexible and friendly while providing order. Sandra and I have found four systems to be particularly helpful in enabling our family to keep our main things our main things. We call them our "Big Rock" family systems. They are:

- Regular family mealtimes
- Weekly family time
- Family traditions
- One-on-one bonding times

Big Rock 1: Regular Family Mealtimes

I'm sensitive to families in which regular meals are not guaranteed. I'm also sensitive to homes that feel like an airport, where people come and go so rapidly to meet varying schedules that they rarely see each other except when crossing paths. But even in those instances, eating is one of the most consistent events that brings a family together.

So the first system—or Big Rock—I suggest for you to consider is to have regular family mealtimes. There are well-researched benefits to holding regular family meals that include:

- Healthier meals
- Better family communication
- Less risky behavior in teens (e.g., drugs, alcohol, sex, etc.)
- Better mental health
- Better grades in school
- More chances for parents to be role models[6]

If doing nothing more than sitting down and eating together provides those benefits, then imagine what additional benefits might result if you take proactive efforts to make your mealtimes a little more purposeful.

I love the approach my brother, John, takes when sitting down with family for a meal. As he sits down to the table he asks himself, "What is my purpose at this meal?" It's a very simple question with profound outcomes. He thinks of ways he can lift family members, listen to them, teach them something new, listen some more, lighten someone's heavy load, listen some more, express a kind word, listen some more, or share a story or quote that reinforces a family value. His mealtimes are very purposeful, and so is his bias toward listening.

If your family mealtimes are like many of our family mealtimes were when Sandra and I were raising our children, then you may need to work fast to make your meals purposeful. Our boys could eat an entire plate of food in one bite and be back outside playing with friends in a flash. Or perhaps your family experiences some of the same mealtime conversations that our family experienced at times. You ask, "What happened at school today?" and all you get in response is:

"Nothing."
"Well, what did you learn in your history class?"
"Nothing."
"Who did you hang out with at lunch?"
"No one."

Yes, those types of conversations do happen.

Children do like to talk, but they like to talk about what they want to talk about, and that may not be what you want to talk about. The key is to find out what's in their hearts and minds. What is it that they do want to talk about?

The spirit of the mealtimes I am referring to is found in this young man's recollection:

My mother was a single parent and sometimes we didn't have enough food. We never sat around a table to eat be-

cause we never had a table. Yet we were grateful for what we did have. We'd sit on chairs and talk and just catch up. We'd cook together. I'd share what was important to me because my mom was a good listener and could understand where I was coming from.

Though we couldn't afford much, the times and the things we did have were priceless.

I'm impressed by so many parents who do have meaningful discussions during their family mealtimes. They have a variety of good conversation starters at their access. They ask such research-based questions as, "What went well today?" or "Why did it go well?" or "What is one thing that you are grateful for today?" Some parents start out by sharing a success that they had that day, and then emphasize the principle that made their success a success. Then they ask their children if they have ever experienced something like that or can think of someone with a similar experience. It gets the minds spinning and conversations going.

What I find is that what effective parents do best is to listen. They listen for opportunities to communicate a child's worth and potential. As my friend Ken Blanchard says, "Catch people doing things right," and then let them know you appreciate and admire them for those things.[7]

Mealtime is best used as a time to nourish children with an occasional bite of wisdom and a steady diet of hope. Parents are wise not to use mealtimes as opportunities to criticize, to issue commands, or to scold. Nothing kills a child's appetite for sharing personal feelings more than being subjected to faultfinding or interrogations. Sandra and I have found that when we do our best to make mealtimes pleasant and devoid of judgment, our family looks forward to being together. They are far more inclined to stick around the table rather than gulping something down and running off.

I understand that many families turn their mealtimes over to their cell phones or other digital devices, rather than using the time for building relationships or growing unity. It reminds me of a brother and sister whose mother died following a long-term illness. It left their elderly father alone and with no one to talk to besides the silent walls of his home.

The two siblings decided that each Wednesday they would leave their own families and join their father for dinner. After the meal, they would watch their father's favorite television program. This went on for a few weeks until one night the father said, "Can we turn the television off?" This surprised the brother and sister who said: "We thought you liked the TV show, Dad." What they quickly realized was that their father could watch television any day of the week. What he couldn't do every day was be with them. And so they chose to extend their mealtimes and to just visit and share memories—keeping the digital devices silent.

It may not be possible for your family to gather every day for a meal, but I encourage you to do your best. The more consistent the mealtimes the better. And when you are together for a meal, try asking yourself, "What is my purpose at this meal?" At one of your next mealtimes you may even involve your family members in discussing, "If we can do just one thing to improve our family mealtimes, what would that one thing be?"

Insight from Sandra

Food is a grand gatherer of families. The better the food the more people want to gather.

Whenever I called our children to come and gather because I had a very important matter I wanted to discuss with them, they always arrived slowly and wanted to depart fast. When I called our children to come because dinner was ready, they came much quicker and were willing to stay a little longer.

And so I learned to take advantage of my captive mealtime audience by putting the time we spent eating together to more meaningful use.

Big Rock 2: Weekly Family Time

A second system to consider when trying to keep your family's main things your main things is weekly family time. I strongly suggest at least one hour per week, and preferably at a consistent day and time.

My friend and acclaimed television host Oprah Winfrey told her audience on the day she interviewed me about this book, "If you don't have the time for one night or at least one hour during the week where everybody can come together as a family, then family is not the priority."[8]

Outstanding corporate, government, and educational teams hold consistent weekly meetings to get oriented, to make plans, and to build relationships. Why would a family not do the same?

Perhaps no single system will help you build and sustain your family relationships more than setting aside a specific time each week that is dedicated entirely to the family.

Perhaps no single system will help you build and sustain your family relationships more than setting aside a specific time each week that is dedicated entirely to the family. Call it "family time," "family hour," "family council," or whatever you want. The intent is to have a designated time each week that is solely focused on strengthening the family.

A woman from Sweden shared her experience:

> When I was five years old, we started having regular family time in our home. The first time, my dad shared with us a principle of life. It was very powerful to me because I had never seen him in the role of formal teacher, and I was impressed.
>
> My dad was a busy and successful businessman and didn't ever seem to have very much time for us children. I remember how special it made me feel that he valued us enough to take time out of his busy schedule to sit down and explain how he felt about life.

I also recall an evening when my parents invited a surgeon from the United States to join us for our family time. He shared his experiences of practicing medicine and how he had been able to help people all over the world. He told us how decisions he had made in life eventually led him to reaching his goals and becoming more than he had imagined.

The surgeon's visit inspired me and left me with the feeling that it was really cool that my parents wanted to invite visitors to share their experiences with us. Today I have three children and almost monthly we bring some "outsider" into our home to get acquainted with and to learn from.

A friend of mine did his doctoral dissertation on the positive effects of establishing a regular family time. One of his more interesting findings was the positive effect that regular family times have on fathers. As one example, he shared the following account from a father:

Growing up, my family didn't talk much except to argue or put each other down. I was the youngest and it seemed as if everyone in the family told me that I couldn't do anything right. I believed them. I didn't do well in school and it got so that I didn't even have enough confidence to try anything that took brains.

So at first I didn't want to have these family times because I didn't feel I could do it. But after my wife led a discussion one week and my daughter another week, I decided to try leading one myself.

It took a lot of courage for me to do it, but once I got started it was like something turned loose in me that had been tied up in a painful knot ever since I was a little boy. Words flowed out of my heart. I told my children why I was so glad to be their dad and why I knew they could do good things with their lives. Then I did something I had never done before. I told them all, one by one, how much I loved them. For the first time I felt like a real father, the kind of father I wished my father had been.

I have since felt much closer to my wife and kids. Things at home seem different now.

When our children were very young, Sandra and I used our family time for just the two of us to communicate and plan. As the children grew older, we used the time to teach them, to play with them, and to involve them in meaningful decisions. There were times when one of us could not be there or times when we had to postpone it, but for the most part we set aside at least one hour a week as family time.

On a typical night, we would review our family calendar so everyone would know what was going on that week. We'd discuss family problems and the children would give suggestions for how to solve them. We'd sometimes have a talent portion where one or more of our children would show us how they were advancing with their music lessons. Or we would have a short lesson taught by one of the children. Many times it was nothing more than enjoying a short family activity followed by a dessert.

We viewed family time as a time to plan, a time to teach, a time to solve problems, and a time to have fun. Consider the following examples of what other families have done in these four areas, as shared by the following parents:

Planning: *A big part of our family time each week is planning. We go over each person's goals and activities, and put them on a magnetic chart that hangs on a door. This enables us to know what others in the family are doing during the week so that we can support them. It gives us the information we need to arrange transportation and babysitting, and to prevent scheduling conflicts. We also used the time to plan an upcoming activity or vacation.*

Teaching: *One of the family times our children remember most was when we played a game to teach them some principles of financial management.*

We set up signs in different places in the room that said such things as "Bank," "Store," "Credit Card Company," and "Charity." We then gave each child an object to represent work they could do to earn money. Our eight-year-old, for example, had some hand towels to fold. Our ten-year-old had a broom to sweep the floor. Everyone had work to do so that they could earn some money.

When the game began, everyone went right to work. After a few minutes we rang a bell, and everyone got "paid." We gave them each ten dimes for their labor. They then had to decide what to do with their money. They could put it in the bank. They could donate some to charity. They could buy something at the "store" where we had bright-colored balloons with the names of different toys

*written on them along with a price. If they really wanted
something from the store but didn't have enough money
to buy it, they could go to the credit card company and
borrow enough to get it.*

*We went through the sequence several times: work,
earn, spend; work, earn, spend. And then we blew a whis-
tle. "Interest time!" we said. Those who had put money in
the bank got money added. Those who had "borrowed"
from the credit card company had to pay interest. After
several rounds they quickly became convinced that it was
much smarter to earn interest than to pay it.*

*When we've asked our children to tell us about family
times they remember, this one was at the top of the list.*

Solving problems: *One time my husband lost his job, so we
used our family time to explain to the kids what had happened. We showed them the money we had in the bank, and
we explained that it usually took six months to find a new
job. We explained how we needed to divide the money into
six groups—one for each month. We divided each month's
money into what would be needed for food, house payment,
gas, electricity, and so on. In this way they could clearly see
where the money was going and how little would be left over.*

*We discussed how stressful this was for their dad and
what we could do as a family to support him. We discussed
things we could do to remove potential irritation spots,
such as keeping the house clean, turning off lights, and
saving water. We all agreed and felt very united in facing
the difficult days ahead of us.*

During the six months that followed we didn't purchase things other than bare necessities, though we did bake a lot of cakes to cheer us up. The kids continually tried to encourage their dad, telling him they knew he would get a job soon. They went out of their way to show their confidence in him because we all knew from experience that this would be an area he would struggle with.

When he finally got a new job, the children's joy was almost greater than ours, and the celebration was one we won't soon forget.

Having fun: *Family time gives us the opportunity to do something that often gets neglected in the chaos of life—to just spend time together having fun. It seems there's always so much to do at the office, at home, getting kids ready for bed, etc. that you don't take the time to just relax and enjoy being together.*

We've found that wrestling with the kids, telling jokes, and laughing together is very therapeutic. It creates an environment where it's safe for our children to tease their mom and dad. Everyone feels liked.

When things are too serious all the time, I think children wonder, "Do Mom and Dad really like me? Do they enjoy being together?"

On one occasion, Sandra and I were having a real challenge with getting the children to help out with chores, so we chose a family time to teach our children about sharing responsibilities and how we as a family are a team. As Maria recalls:

One family night, Dad went through a list of all the responsibilities that needed to be taken care of in the home. And then he went down the list and asked who wanted to do each one.

He said, "Okay, who wants to earn the money?" No one volunteered, so he said, "Well, I guess I'll do that one. Okay, who wants to pay the taxes?" Again, nobody volunteered, so he said he'd do that too. "Okay, who wants to nurse the new baby?" Well, Mom was the only one qualified for that job. "So who wants to take care of the lawn?"

Dad went on and on with all the things that needed to be done, and it became very clear that he and Mom were doing the vast majority of the work for the family. It was a great way to put our smaller list of jobs that we had as kids into a bigger perspective. It helped us realize that everyone needed to take part.

You can see that a weekly family time is much more than just sitting in the same room and watching television together. It does not need to be overly planned or lengthy. And no money needs to be spent. In fact, some of the best family times are spontaneous. If your children are mature enough, let them plan the family time or lead the activities.

So give it some careful thought. What activities would your family enjoy doing during a family time? What consistent time of the week would work best for your family?

Insight from Sandra

I think everyone's favorite family times in our family were when we would go on spontaneous adventures. Stephen would make them up as we went along, and none of us knew what to expect. It might turn out to be swimming at a local pool followed by some pizza, or having a neighbor teach us how to play a new game followed by ice cream. We might share ghost stories after it got dark and then sleep out in the backyard. Sometimes we'd watch a movie and eat popcorn. We never knew what the adventures would be, and that—along with the dessert—was half the fun.

Big Rock 3: Family Traditions

Family traditions are another great system for creating and sustaining a nurturing family culture. Traditions are always times to have fun, but they are also great opportunities to renew commitments to values, revisit the family mission statement, tell value-based stories, communicate people's worth and potential, or do other things that nurture and grow relationships.

Small children in particular love traditions. As one father shared:

Occasionally we do something new for a holiday, such as prepare a cultural meal from a distant country. The next time that same holiday comes around our kids will say, "We've got to do that meal again. It's tradition!"

My wife and I respond, "What do you mean it's a tradition? We only did it once." And the kids then respond, "No, it's tradition. We have to do it."

One year, we included our children in our wedding anniversary. We wanted to celebrate with them the birth of our family, and we made homemade ice cream using Grandma's special recipe. Now our kids expect it every year. "Mom and Dad, it's tradition!"

And that is how another new tradition is begun.

Traditions also do not need to be large, expensive, or complicated to be effective. They may be as simple as getting the family together to enjoy a sporting event, to attend an annual concert together, or to share a holiday treat. They might involve gathering for an extended family meal. But be careful. Unless meaningful purposes are proactively built into the traditions—the system—the original intent of gathering and building family bonds might instead get entirely lost in the massive busyness of preparing food and washing dishes.

One of our favorite traditions is to gather as an extended family for the Thanksgiving holiday to feast and to express thanks to each other and to God. We do it at Grandpa's hotel, even though it was sold long ago. In the summertime, we block out time to meet in a favorite vacation spot in Montana where we gather with our children and their families to mostly have fun and build relationships. Sandra is always sure to find small ways to build in connections to our family mission statement and to reinforce our family values.

What are some of your favorite family traditions? What is one family tradition you would like to start in the future?

Big Rock 4: One-on-One Bonding Times

Everyone is ultimately a "one."

A former university colleague of mine was in a lobby at the university with his ten-year-old grandson one weekend. He didn't know anyone was around to overhear their conversation. He was telling his grandson why he liked being a professor and sharing some favorite experiences. Each of them had an ice cream cone in their hand.

In a paused moment of their conversation, my friend turned to his grandson and said, "Do you know that I love you?"

"Yeah, Grandpa," the grandson nodded in reply, "I love you too, Grandpa."

Imagine that scene in your mind. The grandson is having one-on-one time with Grandpa and learning what a big university is all about. Ice cream is dripping all over his face. And then at the right moment his grandpa tells him he loves him. Bonding time doesn't get much better than that.

One-on-one time is when most of the deepest nurturing

of the heart and soul occurs in family relationships. It's when the most profound teaching and bonding take place.

I am talking about being completely present with the person. I'm referring to transcending your personal interests, concerns, and ego, and pausing to be emotionally present with them. This is particularly important in divorced families where children need to be reaffirmed that, even if their parents are no longer together, they are still loved by both parents.

One-on-one time is when most of the deepest nurturing of the heart and soul occurs in family relationships.

Sandra and I preferred to keep our one-on-ones with our children just that—one-on-ones. As soon as a third person is introduced, the dynamics change. We also tried to let the child choose the agenda. Our daughter Catherine shares the following memory of a one-on-one time she and I enjoyed:

When I was ten years old, I loved Star Wars. *So when my turn came for a one-on-one date with my dad, I wanted to go see* Star Wars, *even though I'd already seen it.*

The thought crossed my mind that my dad might prefer getting his teeth pulled rather than to watch a science fiction movie. But when he asked me what I wanted to do with him that night, it was my agenda he had in mind, not his. "We'll do anything you want to do, Catherine," he said. "It's your night."

To a ten-year-old, this sounded like a dream, so I told him my plan. I could sense a slight hesitation before he said with a smile, "Star Wars! Sounds great! You can explain it to me."

As we settled into our theater seats, popcorn in hand, I remember feeling so important to my father. When the lights dimmed and the music started, I began my soft explanation. I explained the planets, the creatures, the droids, the spaceships—anything that seemed foreign or strange to my dad. He sat listening and nodding his head.

After the show, I continued my explanations of the movie with all the emotion of my heart, while answering the many questions my father threw at me.

At the end of the evening, Dad thanked me for going on a date with him and for opening up his mind to the world of science fiction. As I was falling asleep that night, I openly thanked God for giving me a father who cared, who listened, and who made me feel important to him.

One of the ground rules Sandra and I had for our one-on-ones with our children was that we let them talk about whatever they wanted to talk about. They could complain to their heart's content, and we wouldn't give any advice unless they asked for it. As parents, we simply tried to use the time to seek to understand our children. More than once this either solved or prevented a major issue, including one described by our daughter Cynthia:

When I was five years old, our family moved to Belfast, Ireland, for three years. When we returned to the US, I had a strong Irish accent. The kids in my third-grade class thought I was different because they couldn't understand me and I didn't know how to play the games they played.

My teacher tried to help me catch up academically because I wasn't yet used to the American curriculum. I was having trouble, especially in math, but was afraid to admit it. I longed to be accepted and have friends. But instead of asking for help, I discovered that all the answers to our math worksheets were on cards in the back of the room. I began copying the answers without being caught.

It seemed for a time that all my problems were solved, as I began getting attention from the teacher and other students for doing so well in math. It felt wonderful for a while but my conscience kept after me because I knew I had betrayed what my parents had always taught me about honesty. I wanted to stop. But at that point I was in a trap and didn't know how to get out of it without humiliating myself. The problem seemed insurmountable to an eight-year-old.

My parents had the practice of having "private interviews" with each child once a month. This was a time when we could talk or complain about anything that interested us. During one of these interviews, my dad let me go off about some injustice I felt he and Mom had dealt me. He listened without defending himself or getting angry. He could sense that wasn't the real problem, but just let me talk.

Finally, when I felt accepted and not condemned, I cautiously started to open up a little to sense his reaction. When he asked if things were going well in school and if I was happy there, I said, "If you only knew, you'd think I was terrible!"

For a few minutes he affirmed his unconditional love and acceptance of me. I felt his sincerity, so I felt I could *trust him with the awful truth. And suddenly, it just blurted out from me. I found myself crying and yelling, "I'M CHEATING IN MATH!" It was such a relief to get it out, even though I still feared the consequences.*

I remember Dad saying, "Oh, how awful for you to have had this inside you for so long!" He asked if he could call my mother into the room, and then I told them both the whole story. Amazingly they helped me work out a solution that would not totally humiliate me.

To this day I can still feel the relief and the love of that moment.

I think back on that experience and wonder what would have happened if I had been so busy, so rushed, or so anxious to get on to something else that I didn't take the time to really listen. Or if I'd done all the talking myself and talked only about what I wanted to talk about.

Insight from Sandra

A dear friend and a marvelous mother whom I deeply respect shared the following memory of growing up on a farm.

Her father and brother spent many, many hours working alongside each other. Each morning and afternoon, before and after school, they milked cows, pitched hay, did daily feedings, and performed many other tasks together. But they never really talked.

Oh, they talked about the chores and what needed to get done, but they never talked about each other—their lives or their interests. Never once did the father ask the son about his schooling or plans for the future.

When the time came for my friend's brother to move out and leave home, he looked forward to the day. There were no feelings of perhaps missing home or time with his dad.

One-on-one time is not only about the *quantity* of time you spend with a family member, though quantity is important. It's really more about the *quality* of time that is spent listening, sharing thoughts, swapping dreams, and nurturing the person that matters. It's growing the relationship—not the crops—that is most important.

Meaningful one-on-one experiences don't happen without first building the foundation of trust in the relationship. That's why many of our one-on-ones with our children were a matter of just being there, having fun, and building the relationship so that if a son or daughter ever did want to open up or ask for advice, the trust was already established. Our daughter Jenny describes what this did for her:

My favorite memories of one-on-one time with Dad were during the summer. Dad would wake me up at 6:00 a.m. and we would go biking on an upper mountain road. We would spend a full hour riding alongside each other, talking things over, and telling stories. He would teach me so many things, and I could tell him anything. We would end the morning by watching the sun rise and drinking water from a fresh spring. I often reflect on those rides and what I learned.

Some children—particularly teens—will resist one-on-one times. I have a friend whose teen daughter would never consent to scheduling one-on-one time. "It's just too awkward, Dad!" she would say. However, it never dawned on her that she was having one-on-one time with her dad whenever he offered to do her chores with her. So Dad made sure to be around when she was doing her chores. I know a mother who drives her teen daughter to school each day to sneak in some daily one-on-one time. Similarly, I know a busy dad with a large family who found it hard to find one-on-one time with each child, so he put a system into place to ensure that one-on-one time happened with each child at least weekly. That system was to help each child with their weekly dishwashing assignment. The children never think of throwing their dad out of the kitchen when he is helping with the dishes and listening to what they want to talk about.

A busy mother with five boys learned how to cut hair. It is one of her built-in systems for ensuring one-on-one time. She is committed to saying only good things about the boys while they are in the barber's chair. So instead of giving tips to the barber, she is giving tips (and love) to her boys—tips for life.

A work-at-home dad knows that when his teens come home from school each day they are going to be hungry, so he plans his breaks to match their arrival and intentionally finds himself in the kitchen listening and talking about their day.

The point of these examples is to be proactive when it comes to scheduling opportunities for one-on-one times, and to not pass up such opportunities when they come unplanned. Meet family members at their critical crossroads. And don't forget about one-on-one times with your spouse or partner, if you have one. There is tremendous need for couples to be alone together, to take time to reconnect, and to carefully plan their weeks and discuss their future. Too many couples are so busy reacting to their "urgent" phone calls or other less important matters that they go for long periods without enjoying any meaningful one-on-one time with each other.

So pause for a moment and think: Who in your family is most in need of a one-on-one conversation with you? When and where will you have it?

Insight from Sandra

There is no way for me to describe the value of the one-on-one times Stephen and I have enjoyed over the years.

For years, we've gone for regular rides on our scooter. It gives us time away from children, away from phones, away from the office, and away from anything else that might distract us. We typically ride into the foothills near our house and just talk. We share what's going on in our lives. We discuss concerns.

This rich opportunity for one-on-one communication has steadily built our marriage, our friendship, and our respect for each other. It has also given me a chance to hold his hand, which is something I can't do with a text message.

PUT THE BIG ROCKS IN FIRST

So there you have four family systems—Family Big Rocks—to consider for putting first things first in your family. Sandra and I have found all four to be instrumental in creating our family culture and in keeping our main things our main things.

Now you may be thinking, "Stephen, with my busy schedule, I have no time for any of these things you're talking about!"

Believe me, I'm sensitive to busy schedules. But if you feel you are "too busy" to apply any of the four systems I have just described, then let me share an approach that Sandra and

I have used over the years that has helped us to implement these systems. It is simple, rings true with people, and explains why we call the four systems our Family Big Rocks.

Imagine a clear bucket sitting on a table. It is filled two-thirds of the way to the rim with little rocks. The little rocks represent the things you do in a week that are important to you. To the side of the bucket are seven or so fist-sized rocks. These "Big Rocks" represent the things that are most important to you. They are not just important, they are *most* important.

Let's say that one Big Rock represents your career, another Big Rock represents your health, another Big Rock represents your family, or a major project, or a specific child.

Now suppose I ask you to fill the remaining empty third of the bucket with as many of the Big Rocks as you possibly can. The one constraint is that no part of the Big Rocks can extend above the rim of the bucket.

You begin filling the remainder of the bucket with your Big Rocks, and very quickly you discover that there is no way to fit all the Big Rocks into the bucket. No matter how hard you try to squish them into the bucket or shift the rocks around to make more room, not all the Big Rocks will fit below the rim. So you end up leaving out a few of your Big Rocks.

As you look over the Big Rocks that you left out, you see that you left out the Family Big Rocks that represent your regular family mealtimes, your weekly family time, your one-on-one bonding times, and your family traditions. They are all very, very important to you, yet each remains outside the bucket. How would you feel about that?

What I have just metaphorically described is the typical week of many people. They get to the end of their week—the rim of their bucket—and realize they have left out some of the things that are most important to them—their Family Big Rocks. There simply was not enough time to do it all.

Have you ever had that happen to you? If yes, what's your recommended solution?

Consider this solution. Start over with a new bucket. First place your Big Rocks into the bucket. Make sure they are all in. Then pour in as many of the little rocks as you can. Shake the bucket and pat down any little rocks to get as many below the rim as possible.

In the end, you may have some little rocks left over that will not fit below the rim. In fact, several little rocks may be left out and scattered around the table. And that's okay. Why? Because you got all your Big Rocks into the bucket.

Not this...   ...but this.

Now let me translate this activity into real life.

Sandra and I have always been busy and have always known that was not going to change. So we needed a system to help us stay on track. The following system is what we came up with.

At the beginning of each new year, we figuratively start out with an empty bucket—a clean calendar. We first insert into it our Family Big Rocks. This includes our mealtimes, weekly family times, traditions, regular one-on-one times, and any other major family events, like our extended holiday meals and family summer vacation. By doing so, we are scheduling our priorities, not just prioritizing our schedules. There is a big difference. Our key relationships are driving our schedules instead of our schedules driving our relationships.

Next, I give our family calendar to my office assistant so she can see our plans. She adds in the company's Big Rocks and key client dates. Sandra does the same with her calendar. As you might expect, we typically find areas where our various individual Big Rocks conflict. In such cases, we either make a decision as to which of the conflicting events we will stay with, or we discuss how we will divide and conquer. When we are done, we have planned our Big Rocks into our upcoming year.

This way, when someone requests Sandra's time, she is able to look at our family's Big Rocks, her personal Big Rocks, and any other planned calendar items to determine if she is available. Similarly, when a client calls (often months in advance), my assistant can look at my calendar and say, "I'm sorry, he's not available for those weeks in June. Is there another possible date?" Or, knowing a grandson has a big basketball game at four, she can say, "Stephen's not available after three thirty on that day. Is there an earlier time?"

My assistant knows there are things on my calendar I will

not budge on, while other less important items are flexible. The good news for me is that by proactively scheduling my Big Rocks months in advance, my clients are generally fine to work around my schedule. It is much easier than trying to fit in a Big Rock after my client schedule has already been set.

PLAN WEEKLY, ADAPT DAILY

For Sandra and me, the year plan is vital. But the real key to keeping the main things the main things is what happens weekly.

At the beginning of the week, Sandra and I look at our week's calendar, almost as if it is again an empty bucket—an empty week. We consider the Big Rocks that are already on our year calendar, and any new Big Rocks that may have come up, and then decide if those things are still Big Rocks. If they are, we schedule them first into our week. Only then do we fill in the rest of the week with any little rocks that are planned for that week—at least those for which there are still time slots available. After all, they too are important. When we are done, we have our week's plan.

Next, with each new day, we look at our calendars to see what Big Rocks and little rocks are scheduled. We retain the proactive freedom to adapt daily, as needed. Personally, if something needs to drop off my day's schedule, I try to make sure it is a little rock, not a Big Rock.

So in short, we start out with a yearlong view, knowing that things will change and need updating as we go. Then we plan again weekly and adapt daily.

Of course, this process does not always go perfectly. We have our glitches and unexpected but important matters come up. But at the end of the year, week, or day, we can honestly look back and see how we accomplished far more than if we had filled in our week with little rocks and then tried to somehow squeeze in our Big Rocks.

Sandra and I are not alone in benefitting from this approach. As this executive noted:

> *In the last seventeen years of being a business executive, I've taken a lot of people out to lunch. But not long ago, as I planned my week, I realized that I hadn't taken my own wife out for lunch. And my relationship with her is the most important relationship in my life. So as a result of weekly organizing, we started doing that. And it's brought us much closer. Our communication has increased, which has led me to discover other ways I can be a better husband.*

So to any who say, "I don't have time to do these things," I suggest that you don't have time not to!

INTEGRITY IN THE MOMENT OF CHOICE

To put first things first and keep your main things your main things requires discipline. It's what I refer to as having "integrity in the moment of choice."

If you truly believe family is what matters most but then you spend hours upon hours scrolling through meaningless social media posts while neglecting your family, then that is not showing integrity in the moment of choice. I can pretty much guarantee that when you are trying to schedule weekly family time, other less important activities will attempt to interfere. A child's friend will schedule a party on that same night. A television show will come on at the exact same hour. A friend from out of town will call unexpectedly and want to go to dinner. A dozen other "urgent" but less important things will scream for your attention. And yes, there will be times to proactively choose to make exceptions.

But when you have a proactive calendar based on what matters most, you are empowered to say "no" to less important requests. When you do not have a proactive relationship-based calendar, the temptation will be to reactively say "yes" to anything. So decide what your highest priorities are and then have the courage and discipline to pleasantly, smilingly, and non-apologetically say "no" to less important things. It's easier to say no when there is a deeper yes burning within.

> It's easier to say no when there is a deeper yes burning within.

Don't be discouraged if your one-on-one times, weekly family times, or family mealtimes and traditions don't always go as planned. We've had weekly family times during which two of our children were sprawled out on the couch asleep. We've had family times that basically started with a prayer and ended with a big argument. We've even had family meetings in which the children were so noisy and so disrespectful that Sandra and I have said, "Okay, we've had it! You come and get us when you're ready!" and we've walked out. Other times we looked at each other, wondered why we even try, and burst out in laughter. But we kept trying to have integrity in the moment of choice.

Insight from Sandra

It wasn't until we had raised half of our children before I felt as though I finally had the confidence to say no to requests that were not truly important. Having an annual and weekly plan has truly helped.

I can clearly see how things would have been better if I had learned to say no earlier. Not because I get a thrill out of telling people no—I still don't like to do that. It's just that I realize that I missed out on some important opportunities and relationships.

I'm grateful that I have also learned to say no to dwelling on what I missed out on in the past. Instead I put my faith and energy into creating the future I want.

WHEN FAMILY COMES FIRST

I recall a commercial on television that showed a young girl approaching her father at his desk. His desk is covered with projects and to-do lists while he is busily filling in his calendar. The young daughter stands by him totally unnoticed until she finally asks, "Daddy, what are you doing?"

Without looking up, the father replies, "Oh, I'm just doing some organizing. I'm writing down the names of all the important people I need to talk with, and all the important things I have to do."

The little girl hesitates, then asks: "Am I in that book, Daddy?"

Goethe said, "Things which matter most must never be at the mercy of things which matter least."[9] And that is what Habit 3: Put First Things First is all about. Habit 1 provides the knowledge that we are in charge of our life and choices, including how we spend our time. Habit 2 helps us to use our proactivity to identify our "first things." Habit 3 then presents to us the principles of effectiveness—such as prioritization, discipline, focus, and integrity—that help us have integrity in staying true to our first things in our moments of choice.

> "Things which matter most must never be at the mercy of things which matter least."

So if you are feeling a need to put family first more in your life, start where you are. Choose one Family Big Rock and commit to working on it for a set amount of time, such as thirty days. Once you are satisfied that you have met your commitment to that Big Rock, choose and commit to working on a different Big Rock. Don't let the urgent but unimportant parts of life lure you away from keeping your main things your main things.

‖‖

REFLECTIONS AND APPLICATIONS

With Self

Looking back over Habit 3: Put First Things First, what is the one idea or learning that if you were to apply it better would have the greatest impact on the well-being of your family?

_____

_____

_____

_____

With Adults and Teens

- Ask family members: How much time did we spend last week doing family activities? Are we making family enough of a priority in our lives?
- Discuss the idea of family time. Ask: How could a weekly family time be helpful to our family? How could it promote planning, teaching, problem-solving, and having fun together? Discuss making the commitment to hold a weekly family time. Together generate a list of ideas for family time activities.

- Share feelings about past or current family traditions. Explore new family traditions that you might want to start as a family.
- Talk about one-on-one bonding times. Encourage family members to share meaningful one-on-one times they've had with other family members.
- Review the Big Rocks demonstration on pages 141–145 and then identify the Big Rocks for each individual family member and for the family as a whole.
- Identify one-on-one activities each family member would enjoy. Schedule one-on-one time with a child this week.

With Young Children

- As a family, schedule family activities for the next month. Consider things such as visits to extended family members, holiday activities, one-on-one times, fun events or performances you can attend together, or trips to the park. Make sure the children contribute their ideas. Then live that schedule as a family.
- Make a collection of family pictures. Talk about fun family times you have had.
- Conduct the Big Rocks demonstration described on pages 141–145 as a family. You can use small balls or marshmallows for Big Rocks and jelly beans for little rocks, or the children can bring real rocks they have painted and labeled. At the conclusion, ask each child to identify their Big Rocks—the most important things—they have to do during the coming week.

- Make the commitment to hold family times. Involve children in the planning of all you do.
- Teach children who can write how to keep track of their activities in a planner of some kind. Also have them schedule times to do special activities or services to strengthen relationships.

THINK WIN-WIN

Making Deposits in Your Family Relationships

Habits 1, 2, and 3 offer principles and skills that enable families to take charge of their lives, to establish clear purposes and plans, and to stay true to those purposes and plans. Habits 4, 5, and 6 will now provide principles and skills for strengthening the relationships between family members and for working together as a family team.

The renowned children's television host Mr. Fred Rogers said in testimony before the US Senate, "One of the first things a child learns in a healthy family is trust."[1]

Trust is at the heart of a nurturing family culture, and win-win thinking is a vital ingredient in building trust between family members. To begin exploring win-win thinking, see if you have experienced any situations in your family that remind you of the following two scenarios.

Scenario 1: A father told me of a time when his very competitive son lost an important basketball game. The father felt horrible. So when the son emerged from the locker room, the father immediately began expressing how sorry he felt for him. "You must be devastated!" he said. And then he began blasting the referees he felt were biased in favor of the other team.

When the father finished unloading his emotions, his son looked at him and said, "It's all right, Dad. Don't be upset. I felt like I played one of my best games of the season. I know some of the players on the other team, and they're in really tough situations. They don't have a father in their lives like I do. They played hard and deserved the win. I'm happy for them."

Scenario 2: Another father shared a story about his two sons who were very competitive with each other. Their sibling rivalry resulted in frequent contentions, including on this occasion. In the father's words:

> When the oldest was twelve and the youngest was ten, we went on a family vacation. When we should have been enjoying ourselves, conflicts between these two boys heated up to the point that it was affecting us all. None of us were having fun.
>
> I felt that the older boy was more to blame so I found a moment when we could talk. When I confronted him with criticism of the way he treated his brother, he abruptly announced, "The thing you don't understand is that I can't stand my brother."
>
> When I asked him why, he said, "He's always saying things to me that really bug me. I wish you would buy me a bus ticket and let me go home."
>
> I was shocked by the intensity of his feelings toward his younger brother. Nothing I said could encourage him to see things differently.
>
> I then invited my younger son to come on a short hike with us. We climbed to the top of a nearby ridge where

we sat down and began to talk. I addressed the older boy, "You said some things to me about your brother. Now he is here and I'd like you to tell him what you told me."

He spoke right up and said, "I hate this vacation. I want to go home just to get away from you."

The younger boy was hurt by these cutting words. He looked down and quietly asked, "Why?"

His older brother was quick to answer, "Because you're always saying things that make me mad."

The younger brother sighed. "I do that because every time we play a game you always win."

"Well, sure I always win," the older boy replied. "I'm better than you."

With that the younger brother could hardly speak. Yet from the depths of his heart he said, "Yeah, but every time you win, I lose. I just can't stand to lose all the time, so I say things to get even with you."

Those tearful words somehow reached the heart of the older brother. They each agreed to go easier on each other and to be more kind.

That little talk saved our vacation. It didn't make things perfect, but I don't think the older boy ever forgot his little brother's words: "I just can't stand to lose all the time."

These two scenarios remind us of just how much life, sports, and even families are filled with competitions—losers and winners. Perhaps you have experienced similar competitive situations in your family.

So why are so many family relationships turned into emotional competitions? Why is winning so important? Why is it that some family members can be happy for the successes of others, while others cannot stand to lose?

PARADIGMS OF HUMAN INTERACTION

The answers to those questions originate largely from how our paradigms are scripted in our early years, particularly within the family. Consider four paradigms that are common in relationships, including family relationships:

Win-Lose. "I am going to win and you are going to lose." People with this paradigm see life as a zero-sum competition: "Only one of us can win. So if you win, I lose."

Lose-Win. "I'll let you win even if it means I lose." People with this paradigm say figuratively, "Go ahead, use me as your doormat. Walk all over me and my feelings."

Lose-Lose. "If I lose, then you're going down with me." People with this paradigm often have motives of revenge: "I just lost to you and now I'm going to get even with you, even if it costs me more."

Win-Win. "I have the courage to stand up for my wins, but I am also considerate of your interests. I sincerely want you to win also." This paradigm actively seeks for mutual benefit.

The first three of these paradigms come from what I call a "scarcity mentality." Persons with scarcity mentalities see the world like a delicious pie. "If you get a piece of the pie, then that means there is less for me." Or, "If Mom gives you attention, that means I get less attention." Or, "If you win the game, then I lose the game." Family members with scarcity mentalities are always competing and comparing. They go for win-lose, lose-lose, or lose-win outcomes.

In contrast, people with an "abundance mentality" see the world as having plenty for everyone. "If Mom loves you, that's okay because she has plenty enough love for all of us. I like it when she gives you love because I know it makes you feel good, and that makes me feel good also." Persons with abundance mentalities go for win-win outcomes. They see a win for one family member as a win for the entire family. They are happy for the successes of others.

When it comes to creating a nurturing family culture, a win-win, abundance paradigm is the only option that will achieve the desired results.

Insight from Sandra

I believe that most parents try hard to teach their children how to be fair with others and to seek mutual benefit. That is why I think many parents are not even aware of how often they operate from a paradigm other than win-win.

For example, I've seen numerous parents go for win-lose with young children when they say things like, "Do it my way, or else," followed by their favorite threat of punishment. They're essentially saying, "I'm going to win and you are going to lose." Or maybe they say, "Whoever has their room cleaned first gets the piece of candy!" Which means one child wins the candy and the rest are losers.

Typically, such parents have learned those same win-lose scripts and methods from their parents. Now they're passing them on to their children, and they're not even aware of it.

I'm thinking of a man whose wife did not like his profession or his work colleagues. So when his work group planned a party, in spite of his pleas for her to come with him, she refused to attend. He went alone. One might argue that she won and he lost.

A month later, the wife's social group sponsored a large event. She was asked to be one of the hosts, and she assumed her husband would come along and help her set things up. She was upset when he told her he wouldn't and demanded to know, "Why not?" He curtly replied, "I don't want to be around your friends any more than you want to be around mine." She went alone. So one might now say that he won that time and she lost.

What do you think? Do you think either the man or his wife ever truly won?

From my viewpoint, they both lost on both occasions.

They were each thinking win-lose, or maybe even lose-lose. Anything but win-win.

When it involves family relationships, win-win is the only paradigm that results in high trust, mutually beneficial outcomes, and positive natural consequences. The other three paradigms all end with negative natural consequences.

COURAGE AND CONSIDERATION

Occasionally, I encounter people—mostly aggressive businesspeople—who come up to me after a workshop and say, "Come on, Stephen. You're not serious about this win-win talk, are you? This is a competitive world we live in, and frankly, win-win is for wimps!"

It's true. We do live in a competitive world and there are competitive situations in business and sports where winning is a priority. It's also true that friendly competition can make people stronger and more productive, and can even be the source of a lot of fun. But remember, we are talking about our closest relationships—our family relationships. And so I ask some of those businesspeople: "Who's winning in your relationship with your teenager, you or your teenager?" Or, "What about your marriage? Who's winning in your marriage, you or your spouse? How does your spouse like it when you go for win-lose?"

> Ultimately, win-win is the only paradigm that results in high trust outcomes and other positive natural consequences.

When family members are constantly engaged in win-lose ego battles; when they're thinking only about their own desires; when they're more concerned about *who* is right than *what* is right; or when they're always quarreling over who's the best or who gets the most, what impact do you think that has on the family culture?

The fact that we live in a competitive world is true; the argument that win-win is wimpy is not. Win-win takes effort. Win-win takes courage. In some cases, a lot of courage. Consider the following woman's story that illustrates just how disturbing the consequences of a marriage that is anything but win-win can be.

I was successful in school growing up and excelled at whatever I wanted to do. But as I started college, I knew I really didn't want a career. I wanted to be a wife and a mother.

After my freshman year, I married Steve. Being Mrs. Overachiever, I had three children in a short period of time. I remember feeling overwhelmed by all the tasks related to having young children. The most difficult part, however, was that I had virtually no help from Steve. His job kept him on the road much of the time, but even when he was home he felt that all the responsibility for the upkeep and care of the home and children was mine.

Steve expected me to be the perfect housekeeper, cook, and mother. I would offer him a piece of his favorite pie I had baked, and he would look at it and say, "You know, the crust is burned a little bit." I felt worthless. There was never praise—always just continual criticism.

I begged Steve to go to counseling with me, and he fi-

nally agreed. One evening the counselor turned to Steve and said, "You seem agitated tonight. Do you have something on your mind?"

Steve responded, "Yes. I am tired of having to constantly clean up after everybody."

I had put years of effort into creating the perfect home. I was always caught up with the laundry, and so forth. What had I missed?

The counselor said to Steve, "Could you help me understand exactly what it is that you are picking up after other people?" There was a long silence, and finally Steve blurted out, "This morning when I took a shower, someone had left the cap off the shampoo bottle!" That was the only example he could give for the day.

I remember feeling as though I was growing smaller and smaller as I sat there in my chair and thought, "Something doesn't feel right."

It was at that point when I realized for the first time that no matter what I did, Steve would continue to criticize and see things wrong. For the first time I began to realize that the problem was his—not mine.

I went through a lot of internal struggles during those years. I continued to spend a lot of time trying to please Steve and to fix me. At one point, I even went to the hospital emergency room to ask them to admit me. When they asked why, I told them I was thinking of taking my life and my children with me.

That experience scared the heck out of me. Luckily, I was lucid enough to go to the hospital and say, "I know it's not right. Please help me!"

In the beginning, this woman's idea of a win for herself was a genuine desire to make Steve happy. But as time went by, she found she was part of a one-sided lose-win relationship. It went on until eventually she was ready to break. But in the end it was the marriage that ended up breaking, not her. For after months of counseling, she built up enough courage to tell Steve she was no longer going to accept any form of "lose" in their relationship. When more months went by with no progress toward Steve thinking win-win, she moved her children to a new location, finished a college degree, and built a new life—without Steve.

So you can see why win-win is not wimpy. Win-win thinking says, "I'm not going to let you walk all over me. I will not be your doormat. I have the courage to stand up for my interests." At the same time, win-win thinking also says, "I sincerely want our relationship to be a win for you. I genuinely want you to be happy. This is not just about me, it's about us. I want to be considerate of your needs, not just mine."

In many cases, you teach family members how to treat you by what you allow them to do to you. And that's why in some situations, it really does take a lot of courage and independent will to stand up for yourself and refuse to go for lose-win.

Win-win thinking combines the principles of courage *and* consideration. When you are low in courage, you opt for either lose-win or lose-lose outcomes. When you are low in consideration, you opt for win-lose or lose-lose outcomes. Only people who combine high courage with high consideration go for win-win, as illustrated below.

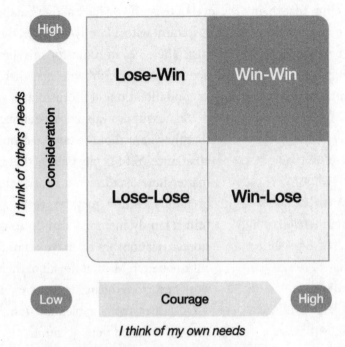

Balancing Courage and Consideration

BUILDING THE EMOTIONAL BANK ACCOUNT

So how do you build win-win relationships with family members? The fundamental answer is to start with yourself. Begin by doing your part to build mutual trust.

A metaphor I have used over the years to describe how to grow mutual trust in a relationship is the Emotional Bank Account. Sometimes I call it the Relationship Bank Account, or the Family Trust Fund. Think of it as being like a financial bank account. You make "deposits" by doing things that build trust in a relationship, and you make "withdrawals" by doing things that shrink the level of trust. If you have a high balance in your Emotional Bank Account with a family member, then there's a high level of trust. There's even room for mistakes. But if the account balance is low or overdrawn, then there's little or no trust and even good intentions are scrutinized.

Some withdrawals are large enough that they bankrupt the entire account all at once. Yet I firmly believe that no matter how overdrawn a relationship or family culture may be, there are things family members can do to restore a relationship or make a family culture better. Most, if not all of them, work best from the inside out.

> No matter how overdrawn a relationship or family culture may be, there are things family members can do to restore a relationship or make a family culture better.

A father from a blended family shared this inside-out account:

> I've always considered myself successful in my relationships with my children, with the exception of my fifteen-year-old stepdaughter, Tara. I had previously made several futile attempts to mend my broken relationship with her, but every attempt ended in a frustrating failure. She just didn't trust me. And whenever I tried to resolve our differences, I seemed to make things worse.
>
> Then I came across a question that really hit me hard: "Are the family members around you made happier or better by your presence in the home?" In my heart I had to answer, "No. My presence is making things worse for Tara."
>
> I came to the realization that if this sad truth were to change, it would only be because I changed myself. I not

only had to act differently toward Tara; I needed to commit to truly loving her. I had to quit criticizing and always blaming her. I needed to quit thinking that she was the source of our poor relationship.

I made a commitment to myself that for thirty days I would make three deposits daily into my Emotional Bank Account with Tara—and absolutely no withdrawals.

Later that day, when Tara came home from school, I greeted her with a warm smile and asked, "How are you?" Her curt reply was: "A lot you care." I swallowed hard and tried to act as if I'd not heard her.

During the next several days, I worked hard to keep my commitment to myself. I continued to dodge Tara's frequent barbs, which was not easy because my nature was to fight back. Each experience caused me to see how cynical our relationship had become. I began to realize how often in the past I had expected her to change before I would do anything myself to make things better.

I also began to see Tara in a new light. I began to appreciate her great need to be loved. I felt an increasing strength to love her without any expectations of receiving love back. I found myself doing little things for her—little favors that I knew I did not have to do. After about two weeks, she looked at me quizzically and asked, "What's going on?"

I said, "I've come to recognize some things about myself that need changing, that's all. I'm grateful that now I can express my love for you by treating you the way I know I should have treated you all along." She didn't reply, but I could tell she was thinking.

We began to spend more time talking and listening

to each other. More than two months have gone by and our relationship has been much more positive. It's not flawless, but the trust increases each day. It's due to the simple yet profound idea of making only deposits and no withdrawals—and doing it consistently and sincerely.

The quality of the father-daughter relationship improved, and so did the father's feelings about himself. That's because when you focus on your Circle of Influence and do what you can to build your Emotional Bank Account balance with others—to build relationships of trust—you dramatically increase your ability to influence others in positive ways.

What follows are five meaningful "deposits" you can make in your family relationships that have tremendous impact on the amount of trust that exists.

DOING LITTLE KINDNESSES

One-time big gifts or single grandiose deeds seldom result in high trust. More often it's the little kindnesses that are woven into the daily fabric of family life that build the most lasting trust.

I love this memory from our son Joshua:

As a nine-year-old, I spent weeks making a birthday present for my dad—a two-foot carved wooden airplane with intricate details. A couple of months later, it was almost Christmas before I remembered I had forgotten about a present for my mom. I quickly carved a small wooden car and painted it. It was one-twentieth the size and one-twentieth as impressive as the airplane I had made for my dad. Yet despite the enormous inequity in my gifts, when I gave that little car to Mom, she was overjoyed by it. She thanked me multiple times. It made me feel good.

Years went by and I was surprised one day when, as an adult, I was in my parents' bedroom and noticed something on Mom's nightstand next to the bed. It was my little car. What became clear to me at that moment was that Mom's affinity for that little car represented her remarkable capacity for love and the importance she placed on relationships.

Sandra was touched to know that young Joshua would make that thoughtful little gift for her. In turn, Sandra's warm gratitude made Joshua feel good, even decades later. Seeing how Joshua's and Sandra's little acts of kindness strengthened their relationship is a reminder that in family relationships the little things really are the big things.

One woman shared with me her thoughts about growing up in a home with a plaque on the kitchen wall that read: "To do carefully and constantly and kindly many little things is *not* a little thing," and how that saying became somewhat of a motto for her family. Of course, many of the best little kindnesses are not *things*. They cannot be wrapped in a box. They are the little compliments we give, the simple acts of service we offer, and the many small courtesies we do on a regular basis.

> "To do carefully and constantly and kindly many little things is *not* a little thing."

Another woman I met grew up under conditions of poverty and much contention. When she married and started a family of her own, the poverty and contention continued. To her, it was normal family life.

To help make ends meet, she went to work for a prestigious hotel where the workplace culture was built around being courteous to every guest, even the ornery ones. She saw how good it made customers feel to be treated royally. Yet what she noticed most was how good it made her feel. She truly enjoyed doing small, unexpected acts of kindness for guests.

One day it dawned on her to try the same approach with her family. She began doing daily little acts of service for her family members, even the grouchy ones. She started using language that was positive, gentle, and kind. If someone forgot to say "thank you" after she had just helped them, she bit her lip and would say, as she did at the hotel, "It's my pleasure!" With time it transformed the culture of her family, and other family members started to return the courtesies.

At one seminar, a man came up to me and said, "Stephen, I like what you're saying about doing little kindnesses, but every situation is different. Look at my marriage. My wife and I no longer have the same feelings for each other that we once had. I guess I just don't love her anymore, and she doesn't love me. What can I do?"

"Love her," I replied.

"I told you," he said, "the feeling of love just isn't there anymore."

"Then love her," I replied with a little more emphasis.

"You don't understand, Stephen. The feeling just isn't there."

"My friend," I said, "love the 'feeling' is a fruit of love the 'verb.' So love her in the verb sense. Listen to her. Appreciate her. Affirm her. Sacrifice for her. Do little kindnesses for her. Are you willing to do that?"

He agreed to give it a try.

You see, love really is a verb. The man and his wife were so focused on love the "feeling" that they forgot how to love each other in the "verb" sense. They had stopped making little deposits. All I was really asking was for him to do small acts of kindness.

As M. Scott Peck said: "Love is an act of will—namely, both an intention and an action. Will also implies choice. We do not have to love. We choose to love."[2]

Little kindnesses are small investments that increase trust in a relationship and return the benefits tenfold. What is a little kindness you can do for a family member today?

Insight from Sandra

A mother was extremely worn out after giving birth. Her body was going through all kinds of adjustments and the smallest of things that went wrong easily upset her.

One evening, she took her emotions out on her husband. She blamed him for things that were not his fault. He exploded in return, all the while wondering what was going on with his "previously sensible" wife. The more they talked, analyzed, and tried to fix things, the more frustrated they became with each other.

At one point, the husband started to walk out on their conversation. "Stop," his wife pleaded. "Don't leave. I've had no sleep. I don't know what's up with my body. I have nothing left to give. Don't speak. Just hold me. Please just hold me!"

When the littlest of things seem to bother a family member, that may be the exact time when the littlest of things will heal them. Don't talk. Don't analyze. Don't leave. Just hold them. Just love them.

GIVING SINCERE APOLOGIES

Saying "I'm sorry" is a small, proactive way to take responsibility for your mistakes and offenses. It is also a grand deposit. In contrast, making lame excuses or blaming others for your mistakes is a trust-busting withdrawal.

Emotional Bank Accounts can take months if not years to build and yet can be destroyed in mere seconds. So when we "blow it" with a family member from time to time—make a withdrawal—it is best to acknowledge our errors quickly and apologize sincerely.

Sincerity is key to an apology. One time I was working at home and writing on the subject of patience. My door was shut but I could hear all kinds of noise in the hallway. There was lots of yelling and banging on doors and walls. I could feel my patience evaporating as I continued to write about patience.

And then I lost it! I opened the door and there stood our son David. He was pounding on the bathroom door. "David, do you have any idea how disturbing this is to me? I'm trying to write!" I really let him hear it. "Now, David, go sit in your room."

As David stomped off, I looked around the corner to see Sean bent over on the ground. The boys had been playing tackle football in a narrow hallway. Sean caught an elbow to the face and was bleeding from his mouth. Our daughter was in the bathroom showering and couldn't hear David knocking on the door in an attempt to get some tissues for Sean. So he started pounding louder to get her attention.

In my short-tempered fit that went against everything I was writing about patience, I could see that I had overreacted and taken out my frustration on David, not knowing he was only trying to help.

I went directly to apologize to David. As I opened his bedroom door, he immediately said, "No, I won't accept your apology, and I won't forgive you."

"Why not, David? Honestly, I didn't realize you were trying to help your brother. Why won't you accept my apology?"

"Because you did the same thing last week," he replied.

In other words, he wasn't accepting my apology as sincere because I was a repeat offender. He was saying, "Dad, your account is overdrawn." He had good reason to be waiting for some new proof that I was sincere in my apology.

Apologies need to be sincere and backed with evidence before people accept them as genuine deposits. Sincere apologies are a source of family healing. But if your self-worth is based on always being right, then to apologize may be more than your ego can handle.

Even if you are much less at fault than the other person, ultimately you are responsible for your portion. So don't focus on trying to correct the other person or manipulate them into admitting their faults. Instead, accept responsibility for your part, apologize sincerely, and move on.

Insight from Sandra

Years ago, our daughter Colleen offered to drive me to an appointment, but then another obligation arose and she said she couldn't do it. When Stephen discovered what the other obligation was, he became upset. "You're being selfish!" he blurted.

Surprised by his abrasive response, Colleen was deeply hurt. She was so used to Stephen being understanding and considerate that it offended her that he would think of her that way. All the way home she harbored negative feelings.

Shortly after she got home her phone started ringing. "It's your dad," her husband said. "I don't want to talk to him," she exclaimed, still feeling hurt. But she answered anyway.

"Darling," Stephen said, "I apologize. There's no excuse that could justify my losing my temper with you." He shared some of the stress he was under and how he felt sorry that she had received the brunt of it. But mostly he continued to repeat, "I'm so sorry. I apologize."

Stephen's apology was a big deposit in Colleen's Emotional Bank Account. So much so that she went out of her way to rearrange her schedule and take me to the appointment. There were no hard feelings remaining. If anything, Colleen and Stephen grew closer.

BEING LOYAL TO THE ABSENT

Loyalty is an important principle of human effectiveness in families. Our children knew the best place to find it in our home was with Sandra. In fact, the following confession from our daughter Jenny reveals how Sandra's loyalty to our children bordered—at times—on going too far.

Once when I was in high school, Mom received a phone call at midnight from the police department: "Mrs. Covey, does your daughter drive a white car?"

"Yes, my daughter Jenny drives a white car," Mom responded. "Is she okay? Did she get in an accident?"

The officer went on to tell Mom that I was fine but that I had been caught with my friend using giant water guns to soak people outside of the movie theater.

Of course, I worried about what Mom was thinking as the officer finished describing what had happened. At first, the phone went silent for a few seconds of pause. And then my mom burst out laughing. "Oh," she said. "That makes me so happy. Jenny needs to relax a little and have more fun. She's always so stressed and serious. This is just great news! Thank you so much for calling and telling me, Officer!"

The officer himself then paused before eventually muttering, "You're welcome," as he hung up.

Lucky for Jenny, Sandra is very loyal to her family in many ways (and the officer was very understanding). However, the specific type of loyalty I am thinking about is a different kind of loyalty. It's being loyal to the absent. It's being true to people by not talking behind their backs or gossiping about them in their absence.

Think about what happens when family members criticize and gossip behind each other's backs. You know, when family members say things like: "Did you hear what my son did the other day? He talked back to his teacher. I was so embarrassed!" Or, "I can't believe my mother-in-law! She tries to control everything we do." Or, "I promised my sister I would not tell anyone, but she got caught cheating on a test. Don't tell her I told you about it."

Such behind-the-back comments are huge withdrawals.

Not only do they break trust with the person being spoken *about*, they break trust with the person being spoken *to*. In other words, if you were to discover that one of your family members was making those comments about you behind your back, you'd feel violated, upset, or betrayed. And if a family member made those comments to you about another family member, even if you felt pleased that the person "confided" in you, wouldn't you begin to wonder if that same person might say something equally negative about you behind your back? Wouldn't you resist confiding in that person in the future?

Bottom line: Always talk about others as if they are present. The way you treat any family relationship will eventually affect every relationship in the family.

> Always talk about others as if they are present.

KEEPING PROMISES

Over the years, people have asked if I had one idea that I felt would most help them make their family life more successful. Almost always, I give the same answer: "Make and keep promises."

If an entire family would cultivate the spirit of making and keeping promises to one another, it would lead to a multitude of good outcomes. Our daughter Cynthia shared this memory:

When I was twelve, Dad promised to take me on a business trip to San Francisco. We were going to be there for two days and one night, and we planned every detail. Dad was going to be busy in meetings the first day, so I would hang around the hotel. After his meetings, we planned to take a cab to Chinatown and have dinner. Then we'd see a movie and take a ride on a trolley car. I was dying with anticipation.

The day finally arrived and the hours dragged by as I waited at the hotel. Finally, Dad arrived with another man—a dear friend and an influential business acquaintance. I remember how my heart sank as this man said, "I'm excited to have you here, Stephen. Tonight, Lois and I would like to take you for a spectacular seafood dinner, and then you must see the view from our house."

When Dad told him I was there, this man said, "Of course, she can come too. We'd love to have her join us." "Oh, great!" I thought. "I hate fish, and I'll be stuck alone in the backseat with Lois while Dad and his friend talk."

I could see all my hopes and plans going down the drain. I wanted to say, "Dad, this is our time together! You promised!" But I was twelve years old, so I only cried inside.

I will never forget the feeling I had when Dad said, "Gosh, Bill, I'd love to see you both, but this is a special time with my girl. We've already got it planned to the minute. You were kind to invite us." I could tell this man was disappointed, but he seemed to understand.

Dad and I did everything we had planned on that trip. We didn't miss a thing. I don't think any young girl ever loved her father as much as I loved mine that night.

Few, if any, deposits have more impact on a family than making and keeping commitments. The most foundational promise we ever make to another human being is the vow of marriage. And equal to it is the promise we implicitly make to our children—particularly when they're little—that we will take care of them and nurture them.

When a person breaks a significant promise, such as a marriage vow, they cannot talk their way into making their spouse or other person trust them again. Saying "I'm sorry" isn't enough. Significant breaks in trust take more than a matter of words to heal. They may take months of the right kind of behavior before the lost trust returns. You cannot talk yourself out of problems you behaved yourself into.

> You cannot talk yourself out of problems you behaved yourself into.

Family members feel trust when they can count on others to follow through on their commitments—to do what they say they will do.

FORGIVING

For many people, the ultimate test of their proactive muscles comes in the form of forgiving a family member who has done them wrong. To genuinely forgive another is a powerful deposit.

Perhaps you or someone close to you can relate to the following woman's experience.

> *I came from a very united family. So when my father followed my mother in death, it saddened us all. Yet when the four of us children met to divide our parents' things among us, what happened was an unforeseen shock from which I worried we might never recover.*

We had always been an emotional family, and at times we had disagreed to the point of some temporary ill will toward one another. But this time we argued beyond anything we had ever known. The fight became so heated that we found ourselves yelling, and we each left feeling bitter and resentful. We even stopped visiting or phoning one another.

This went on for four years. I frequently felt the pain of loneliness and the unforgiving bitterness and accusations that divided us. I kept thinking, "If my siblings really loved me, they would call me. What's wrong with them?"

Then one day I came to realize that not forgiving my brothers and sisters was reactive on my part. I felt I was even hurting myself.

That night, as I was sitting alone in my room, the phone seemed to cry out to be used. I mustered all my courage and called the number of my oldest brother. When I heard his voice say "hello," tears flooded my eyes, and I could scarcely speak.

When he learned who it was, his emotions matched mine. We each raced to be the first to say, "I'm sorry." The conversation turned to expressions of love, forgiveness, and memories.

I then called the others. Each responded just as my oldest brother had. That was the greatest and most significant night of my life. For the first time in four years I felt whole. The pain that had been ever present was gone—replaced by the joy of forgiveness.

Forgiveness opens the channels through which trust and unconditional love can flow. Refusing to forgive is a stubborn roadblock to change, and, in the end, the one you harm the most is yourself. As I suggested in Habit 1, it isn't the snakebite that does the serious damage. It's constantly chasing the snakes of your past that drives the poison to the heart.

DEPOSIT OR WITHDRAWAL?

There are many ways to make a deposit into the Emotional Bank Accounts of family members. I have shared only five examples of what could be many types of deposits.[3]

Indeed, most any family situation is an opportunity to make a deposit. But who ultimately decides whether something is a deposit or a withdrawal? Couldn't one person's deposit be another person's withdrawal?

Sometimes we think we are making a big deposit when, in fact, we are making an enormous withdrawal. A friend of mine was a dean at a prestigious university. He planned and saved for years to provide his son the opportunity to attend that same university. But when the time came for it to happen, the son said he didn't want to go to that university.

My friend couldn't believe it. Graduating from that university would be a great asset to his son. Besides, it was a family tradition. Three previous generations had graduated from that university.

The father pleaded with his son to change his mind. He would say things like, "Son, can't you see what this means for your life? I only want the best for you. Stop being foolish." And his son would reply, "It's my life, Dad. You just want me to turn out the way *you* did. I don't know if I even want to go to a university."

Now let me pause this story and ask: In the view of the son, was the father's offer to pay for his education at the prestigious university a deposit or a withdrawal?

On the surface, the father was making a very generous offer. Beneath the surface, however, the message he was communicating to his son was "I know what gift is best for you. You don't." He was determined to get his way, so much so that he never asked his son what options he might prefer. And the more the father pushed, the more the son resolved to reject the offer.

To his credit, after setting aside his ego, tapping his conscience, and accepting that not everyone likes the same traditions, the father recognized that what he thought was a win-win deposit for his son might in the son's view be a lose-win—a withdrawal. So he chose to back off. He went to his son, apologized, and turned responsibility for the choice over to his son. It was an extremely difficult thing for the father to do because the family's university tradition was so close to his heart.

Interestingly, with the pressure off, the son no longer felt he had to defend his feelings. In fact, the more he researched his options, the more he realized that he really did want to attend that university and that it would be a win-win, after all. So it was his turn to humble himself, to apologize to his father, and to accept the win-win offer.

The key to making deposits is to listen and come to an understanding of what is a win for the other person at any particular moment in time.

It is common to project our paradigms of what a deposit is onto other people, as if everyone sees things the same way we do. We think, "If this is a deposit for me, then it must be a deposit for them." We give gifts that we would like rather than gifts the other person would like. But we never know what constitutes a true deposit for others until we seek to understand what is of importance or enjoyment to them.

Furthermore, what is a deposit for a person may change from one day to the next. So the key to making deposits is to listen and come to an understanding of what is a win for the other person at any particular moment in time.

Insight from Sandra

My friend's husband said to her regularly, "I love you." Occasionally, he also brought her a beautiful rose. Each time, she considered the gestures a delightful deposit.

Years passed and there were times when my friend became frustrated when her husband didn't complete projects that she wanted done around the house, such as painting a room. One night, they were talking and she began to reminisce about how her father had always worked on projects to beautify their house or repair broken items. Instead of buying her mother roses, her father had planted and maintained a bed of rosebushes for her.

The more she thought about it, the more my friend realized that the things her father did for her mother represented a deeper communication of love than merely saying, "I love you," or handing her a rose. So the regular "I love you" and occasional rose began to make less and less of a deposit in her Emotional Bank Account.

By talking about it openly with her husband, my friend's husband came to realize that what once was a deposit was becoming a withdrawal. So he began doing things for her instead of just saying things. He still from time to time brings her a rose and he continues to regularly say, "I love you," but those things now have a refreshed meaning for her.

WIN-WIN AGREEMENTS

Making deposits and building the trust account with family members really is at the core of trying to build any type of win-win relationship. It's better to go for no deal than a bad deal.

Some of the most common contentions—withdrawals—in families occur when expectations are not clearly established or met. So in the remaining portion of this chapter, I will share a tool that will help you and your family set and meet clear expectations. Because the tool focuses on establishing clear wins for all people involved, I call it a "win-win agreement."

To introduce what a win-win agreement is and its potential value, I will share two examples that were shared by two mothers, beginning with this one:

We have a daughter who is very social. When she entered high school, it seemed like a dream to her. There were so many opportunities for fun and socializing, and especially getting to know all the new boys. But it wasn't long before her grades started to drop and our home became more of a place just to sleep. It was as if in her attempt to fit in at school she had lost any connection with good logic.

My husband and I were deeply concerned because we could see a smart girl starting to go down an unhealthy and unproductive path. So one night we sat down with her and shared a little about our concerns, and described what win-win thinking is and how it works.

We asked her to tell us about her needs—her wants. There were many. She wanted more freedom, more involvement in high school activities, later curfews, money to attend the dances, nicer clothes, parents who were more understanding, and so on. As we listened, we could tell that these concerns were very important to her at this stage in her life.

We then asked if we could state our concerns—our wants. We listed things such as her getting acceptable grades, planning for the future, helping out at home, obeying curfews, being nice to her brothers and sisters, and hanging out with friends who had good habits. Naturally, she had objections to some of the things we brought up, but she was impressed that we really wanted to find ways that everyone could be happy.

We were able to capture her wants and our wants on a sheet of paper, and to draw up a win-win agreement very quickly. There were gives and takes on both sides, but basically we agreed that if she met our wants, she could have her wants. She insisted that we each sign it.

Since that evening, she has significantly relaxed. She knows our expectations and has agreed to them as we have agreed to hers. It's as though she doesn't have to prove to anyone anymore that she is getting older and needs new boundaries.

She has referred to the agreement several times since, mostly to point out when we have forgotten something we agreed to.

The second mother shared a similar outcome after developing a win-win agreement with her son who was battling drug issues:

My husband and I divorced when our son was sixteen. Our son experienced great emotional pain, which led him into drugs and other problems. When I had the opportunity to attend a 7 Habits course, I invited him to come with me, and he thankfully did.

At first, he went further downhill. But he eventually used the habits to help pull himself up again. There were definitely up and down times, which caused some mistrust, so we agreed to develop a win-win agreement. Part of the agreement was that I would help him purchase a

*car, which he desperately needed since he was in finan-
cial difficulties and couldn't get a loan. He agreed that if
I helped with the loan, then he would go through drug
therapy. I was very specific about five or six issues that
needed to be taken care of, and he agreed to each of them.
We wrote down our issues and commitments in the form
of a win-win agreement, and we each agreed to do our
part.*

*We have both struggled to keep our side of the commit-
ments at times, but we keep working at it and gradually
my son is becoming more responsible for his past and is
traveling down a better road. In a three-month period, he
has made significant headway.*

In each of these situations, you can see that a win-win
agreement is where two or more people come together to
jointly identify and agree upon the expectations and wins
for all involved in a situation. Courage and consideration are
needed on the part of everyone. If established correctly, all
parties will want to honor their portion of the agreement and
keep their commitments because in the long run it will lead
to wins for everyone.

THE FIVE ELEMENTS OF A WIN-WIN AGREEMENT

Win-win agreements can be formal or informal. The lower
the trust in the relationship, or the more that things can be
misunderstood or forgotten, the more helpful it is to put the

agreement into writing. The higher the trust, the less things need to be spelled out.

Win-win agreements take into consideration five elements:

1. **Desired results:** What are the wins for you and for me?
2. **Guidelines:** Who will do what? Are there specific rules or guidelines that need to be followed?
3. **Resources:** Who can help? What budget or resources are available?
4. **Accountability:** Are there timelines to be met? How will progress be measured?
5. **Consequences:** What will happen if we meet or do not meet the expectations? What are the natural consequences?

Years ago, I had an experience that taught me a lot about creating win-win agreements with children. People call it the "Green and Clean" story. As you read what happened, notice how all five elements of win-win agreements were applied.

During a family time one evening, our eleven-year-old son Stephen volunteered to take care of our lawn. Before he accepted the assignment, I wanted him to have a clear picture in his mind of the desired results, or what a well-maintained lawn looks like. So I took him next door to see our neighbor's yard.

"Look, son," I said, "see how our neighbor's yard is green and clean? That's what we want for our lawn: green and clean. Now look at our lawn. See the yellowing colors? That's not green."

We then set up the guidelines. "Now, how you get the lawn green, son, is up to you. You're free to do it any way you want, except to paint it. But I'll tell you how I'd do it if it were me."

"How would you do it, Dad?" he asked.

"I'd turn on the sprinklers. But you may want to use a bucket or a hose. Or you can spit all day. It makes no difference to me. All I care about is that the color is green. Okay, son?"

"Okay, Dad."

"Now let's talk about 'clean,' son. Clean means no messes—no paper, strings, sticks, or anything that clutters up the lawn. In fact, let's just clean up half of the yard right now and look at the difference."

So we got out two sacks and picked up the trash from one side of the yard.

"Now let's compare the two sides," I said. "See the difference? This side is clean. That side is not."

"Wait!" he called. "I see some paper behind that bush!"

"Good eye, son!" I said. "Now let me tell you a few more things, because when you take on the job, I don't do it anymore. It's your job. I trust you to get it done."

I went on. "Now who's going to be your boss?"

"You, Dad?" he answered.

"No, not me. You're the boss. You boss yourself. How do you like Mom and Dad nagging at you all the time?"

"I don't."

"We don't like doing it either. It causes a bad feeling. So you boss yourself."

Next we made it clear what his resources were.

"Now guess who your helper is, son."

"Who, Dad?"

"I am," I answered. "You boss me."

"I do?" he responded, as if shocked.

"That's right. Sometimes I'm away, but when I am here, you tell me how I can help. I'll do anything you want me to do."

"Okay!"

The setting up of how accountability would be handled came next.

"Guess who judges you," I said.

"Who?" he asked.

"You judge yourself."

"I do?"

"That's right," I said. "Once a week the two of us will walk around the yard, and you can show me how it's coming. And how will you judge your work?"

"Green and clean, Dad."

"Right!"

Now what about the consequences?

At that time, I didn't set up any extrinsic consequence such as an allowance. I focused instead on helping him understand the intrinsic satisfaction and natural consequences of a job well done. I explained how important he was to our family, and how much the neighbors would like it. We were a family working as a team. His siblings would do other jobs. He would be an important contributor.

I worked with him for two weeks before I felt he was ready to take the job. Finally, the big day came and I felt he was ready to go on his own.

"Is it a deal, son?" I asked.

"It's a deal," he committed.

It was a Saturday, and he did nothing that day.

Sunday, nothing.

Monday, nothing.

As I drove off to work Tuesday, I looked at the yellow, cluttered yard and the hot July sun rising. "Surely he'll do it today," I thought. What else did he have to do with his time?

All day I could hardly wait to return home from the office to see what he had done. As I approached our house, I was met with the same scene I had left that morning. He had done nothing. And there he was playing with a friend. This was not acceptable. I was upset. We had a lot of effort and money invested in the yard, and I could see it all going to waste. Besides, my neighbor's yard was beautiful and the situation was beginning to get embarrassing.

I was tempted to break the agreement and go for win-lose. I wanted to say, "Son, you get over here and pick up this garbage right now, or else!" I knew I could get him to do it that way. But what would happen to his internal commitment?

So I faked a smile, held my tongue, and waited until after dinner. Then I said, "Son, let's do as we agreed. Let's walk around the yard together, and you can show me how it's going with your job."

As we started out the door, his chin began to quiver and tears welled up in his eyes. By the time we got out to the lawn he was whimpering, "It's so hard, Dad!"

"What's so hard?" I thought to myself. "You haven't done a single thing!"

But I knew what was hard—self-management, self-supervision. So I asked, "Is there anything I can do to help?"

"Would you, Dad?" he sniffed.

"What was our agreement?"

"You said you'd help me if you had time."

"I have time," I responded.

So he ran into the house and came back with two large sacks and handed me one.

"Will you pick that stuff up?" he asked, as he pointed to some spilled garbage from Saturday night's barbecue. "It's gross. It makes me sick!"

I did exactly what he asked me to do. And that was the moment when he signed the agreement in his heart. It became his yard, his stewardship.

He only asked me for help two or three more times that entire summer. He kept the yard greener and cleaner than it had ever been under my stewardship.

As can be seen, it was initially hard for even me to live by the agreement. I kept reminding myself that I was raising boys, not grass. But I came to appreciate the power of a win-win agreement and all five of the elements.

Without setting clear expectations up front, my son would have eventually said things like: "Oh, was that what I was supposed to do? How was I supposed to know?" Or, "Oh, are we still doing that? I thought that was my job just for last week." Or, "You never said I had to have it done by today."

It may appear as if the five elements of a win-win agreement take a lot of thought and time to set up. But it is far more effective and efficient to invest the time to clarify and agree to expectations early on than it is to deal later with the consequences of not establishing the expectations.

LET THE AGREEMENT GOVERN

The main lesson I took away from this experience with our son Stephen was: You cannot hold people responsible for results if you micromanage either them or their methods. When you are constantly nagging and telling people what to do and how to do it, you remain responsible for the results, not the other person. So what I suggest is that you let the agreement do the governing.

Consider this example of how the following mother established a win-win agreement with her children, and how she restrained herself and let the agreement govern the situation:

> You cannot hold people responsible for results if you micromanage either them or their methods.

When my children were young, I made sure their clothes were clean, neatly folded, and put away. But when they reached their teens, I felt the time had come for them to be responsible for their own clothes.

So at one of our family times just before school started, we talked about what a win-win agreement was and what would be a win for them and a win for me in caring for their clothes. We literally set up a win-win clothing agreement.

I agreed that I would provide them with some money for a "clothing allowance" each week. In turn, they agreed that they would wash, fold, and put away their laundry each week, keep their clothes closets orderly, and not leave clothes lying around. We set out a box for anything I found that was left lying around. Each item put in the box cost them twenty-five cents from their clothing allowance to get it back. We also agreed that every week we would have an accountability session.

The year started out great. They were excited about having money to buy their own clothes. We taught them how to use the laundry machines, and then we went through several wonderful weeks with clean, folded clothes. But as they became more involved in school activities, they began to miss a week here and there. Messes were appearing again all over the house.

It was a big temptation to nag them about it, and sometimes I did. But after a while I began to realize that I had given them a responsibility, and as long as I was reminding them, it was my problem, not theirs.

So I held my silence and let the agreement play itself out. Every week I cheerfully sat down with them and discussed how the week had gone. If they had done their clothes, I gave them their clothing allowance. If not, I didn't. If they had left clothes out that ended up in the box, I deducted twenty-five cents. Week after week they were brought face-to-face with their own performance.

Before long, they began to say, "I really need some new clothes, Mom!"

"Great!" I said. "You have the money from your clothing allowance. When would you like me to take you shopping?"

The reality suddenly seemed to get through. They realized that some of their choices for what they had done with their clothes may not have been the best. But they couldn't complain. They had helped create the agreement in the first place.

It wasn't long before they began to take a much greater interest in getting their laundry clean and put away. The best thing about this whole experience is that the agreement helped me to be more calm and let them learn. I was supportive, but I wasn't being pulled into "Mom, please get me a new shirt!" They knew they couldn't come to me and beg for money for clothes. So the agreement governed the situation, not me.

Did you notice how the mother restrained her impulses to micromanage the situation, and how she let the win-win agreement govern the relationship? Rather than nagging her children, she let the agreement do the governing. It freed her to be kinder and more loving with her children.

CULTIVATING THE SPIRIT OF WIN-WIN

Besides growing trust relationships through building Emotional Bank Accounts and establishing win-win agreements, what else can be done to cultivate a spirit of win-win within a family? Let me share a few insights.

Parents Don't Always Have to Win

In raising our children, Sandra and I decided that we would not fight our children on every minor issue or activity they wanted to do. For example, if our children wanted to build a fort in the middle of the house and leave it up for a few weeks, Sandra and I generally let them do it, even if it looked messy or caused inconveniences. We would let them win those kinds of battles instead of asserting our authority by insisting, "We don't want the mess." It was a win for the children and since it built our relationships it turned out to be a win for us also. It let the children know that Sandra and I were not focused solely on our wins, but that we were happy for their wins. When it came to larger matters, especially matters of principle, the children were far more likely to allow us our wins. So there was give and take on all sides, and that in the long run turned out to be a win for everyone.

Don't Overdo Competition

There are plenty of situations where competition is healthy and fun, and provides great moments to teach children how to work as a team, how to play their best, and how to be a gracious winner—or loser. But some parents (and coaches) take competition to the extreme.

Once, I was at my granddaughter's soccer match. It was the key game between two top teams and parents on both sides got really engaged as the players battled back and forth in a close game. Finally, the game ended in a tie, which to our coach was better than a loss, though not much better.

Players from both teams began the process of shaking hands and saying, "Good game. Good game." But our team was clearly demoralized. The coach tried to comfort the girls but even he couldn't hide that he was deeply disappointed. So they were all walking with their heads pointed downward with somber faces.

As they approached the group of parents where I was standing, I spoke up enthusiastically, "All right, girls! That was a great game! You had five goals: to try your best, to have fun, to work together as a team, to learn, and to win. And you accomplished four and a half of those goals. That's ninety percent! That's tremendous! Congratulations!"

Their eyes brightened up. Smiles appeared. It wasn't long before players and parents were celebrating together. My point that day was that even in a competitive situation, such as in athletics, there are things you can do to create the overall spirit and context for win-win outcomes. Not everything has to be a big competition that ends with a bunch of losers.

Avoid Comparisons

All a parent needs to do to put a dagger in the heart of a family relationship is to constantly compare one sibling to another. Consider this father's experience.

My oldest brother, Bret, is nearly perfect. He is great at everything, including always treating me respectfully. Yet sometimes I leave our conversations upset with myself because I find myself not liking him. Inwardly, I've always sensed that I must be jealous of him, so I kept telling myself, "Grow up and get over it. Be happy for his successes." And so forth.

It took years to realize that my challenge was not with my brother. It was with my mother. She was always telling me about my older brother and how wonderful he was. No matter what I did well, she said things like, "You finally figured out what Bret figured out years ago." Or, "Well, look at how Bret does it with his family."

In short, Mom was always comparing me with Bret and my family with his family, and I and my family always came out the losers. So until then I had developed a resentment toward Bret. Once I realized what was happening, my concerns with Bret went entirely away. Now I am working hard to be more careful in not comparing my own children.

This mother was actively creating and sustaining a sibling rivalry—a win-lose family culture—and my guess is that she didn't even know it. I'm almost certain she never wanted it to be that way. Yet constant sibling comparisons were turning every interaction into a lose-lose outcome in which no one in the family really wins. That's why one of the fastest ways to nurture a win-win culture in a family is to stop the comparisons.

Be Happy for the Successes of Others

A quick way to assess whether you are naturally inclined to think win-win as a family is to examine whether family members are truly happy for the successes of others. If the successes of others make family members feel jealous or like they are somehow less of a person because another family member did something they didn't, then your family will struggle to think win-win as a whole. People with jealousies tend to pull others down, not build them up.

Learning to be happy for others is a good place to start working on creating a win-win culture as a family. The more you personally model how to be happy for the successes of others, the more your family members will be happy for each other's successes.

Insight from Sandra

When our family was spread from teenagers to toddlers, it was difficult to find an activity that everyone could enjoy. Sometimes we would go bowling and everyone could participate at the level they were at, but the overall winners were always the same children—the stronger and more skilled ones.

We tried to figure out a way that it could become a win for everyone and finally found a system that worked. Instead of adding up individual scores and having the person with the most points win, we added up the total of everyone's score. We set an arbitrary goal of how many points we had to reach for us to win as a family. If we met the goal, we would be able to have ice cream sundaes as a reward for meeting our goal. So instead of getting upset when someone else had a strike or did much better, we were cheering for all of us to do our best so our points would add up to our goal.

Instead of having winners and losers, we all hoped each person would do their best, and we cheered for each other's successes. We had a common goal. It became a win-win for the entire family.

THE KEY TO THINKING WIN-WIN

Wise parents put a lot of emphasis on teaching children to become *independent*. But an equal focus needs to be placed on teaching children to become *interdependent*. As Gandhi once said, "Interdependence is and ought to be as much the ideal of man as self-sufficiency."[4]

Family is a "we" experience, not an "all about me" experience. When family members have an abundance mentality instead of a scarcity mentality, great things happen and a spirit of "we" results. This is why the deposits we make into the Emotional Bank Accounts of family members are some of the most worthwhile investments we will ever make.

Habit 4: Think Win-Win is based on the principles of mutual benefit, courage, consideration, and fairness. But as I observed at the beginning of this chapter, many of us have been so scripted to compete, compare, and go for win-lose in our childhood that it carries with us into adulthood and we sometimes forget that going for win-win is the only effective option when it comes to growing a nurturing family culture.

I've had some people say to me, "Well, win-win will never

happen in my family, Stephen, because everyone goes for win-lose. We are so competitive! It will never happen!" To such individuals, I again suggest to work from the inside out. One person who insists on going for win-win can change an entire relationship. Let that person be you. Build trust by being trustworthy. Don't agree to situations where you win and the other person loses. Don't agree to situations where the other person wins and you lose. Choose instead to balance courage with consideration.

As you will soon discover, building trust and balancing courage and consideration are vital parts to improving family communication, which is the focus of Habit 5: Seek First to Understand, Then to Be Understood.

REFLECTIONS AND APPLICATIONS

With Self

Looking back over Habit 4: Think Win-Win, what is the one idea or learning that if you were to apply it better would have the greatest impact on the well-being of your family?

_____

_____

_____

_____

With Adults and Teens

- Discuss the consequences of win-lose, lose-win, or lose-lose thinking. Ask: Can you think of any situation in which any of these alternatives would work better than win-win in a family?

- Discuss how even one person with a win-win attitude can change a situation.
- Talk about the difference between a scarcity and an abundance mentality. Identify a situation in which an abundance mentality would benefit your family.
- Try creating a win-win agreement with a family member. Live with it for a week. Discuss the benefits and challenges.

With Young Children

- Share the opening story about the two young brothers who had such a competitive relationship that they couldn't enjoy being together on vacation. Discuss situations that might create competitive relationships in your family.
- Open a savings account for a child. Explain deposits and withdrawals.
- Draw family members' names from a box. Encourage everyone to do little kindnesses throughout the coming week for the person whose name they drew and to notice how it makes them feel.
- Go to a place such as a park, and talk about how wonderful the sun is and how there is enough for everyone. Point out that it doesn't take anything away from the sun whether one or one million people are enjoying it. There is an abundance of sunshine, just as there is an abundance of love. Loving one person doesn't mean you cannot love other people as well.
- Take the family to a sporting event and explain that the plan

is for everyone to take note of the "best" things they see—best teamwork, best sportsmanship, best coordination—from either team. After the game, compare notes and have them point out the "best" things they observed.

- Select an issue that has been a struggle between you and your children. It might be something such as doing chores without being asked. Discuss what would constitute a win for each person involved in the situation and try to come up with a true win-win solution.

SEEK FIRST TO UNDERSTAND, THEN TO BE UNDERSTOOD

Getting to the Heart of Family Communication

When corporate consultants assess the cultures of organizations, poor communication is nearly always at the top of all complaints they hear. And as any family counselor will tell you, the same is true of family organizations.

Though I have not specifically mentioned family communication to this point, each habit that has been covered thus far has been either directly or indirectly tied to improving family communication. Habit 1 encourages family members to pause and think before saying something regrettable. Habit 2 emphasizes the need to get input from all family members, to tell value-based stories, and to communicate people's worth and potential. Habit 3 talks about establishing systems for mealtimes, weekly family times, one-on-one times, and traditions—all times when family feelings and priorities can be communicated and discussed. Finally, Habit 4 suggests voicing apologies, speaking words of forgiveness, speaking positively about people when they aren't there, having courage to voice what is a win for you, and clarifying expectations through the use of win-win agreements. So you can see how every habit that has been covered to this point contributes either directly or indirectly to effective communication within a family.

Habit 5: Seek First to Understand, Then to Be Understood will now offer a few additional principles and skills that will enable you and your family to improve your communication. There are two parts to the habit: 1) seeking first to understand, then 2) seeking to be understood. There is wisdom and logic to that order.

GETTING TO THE HEART

The primary focus of Habit 5 is on the heart-to-heart communication that happens between two individuals. As the fox in the classic novel *The Little Prince* points out, "It is only with the heart that one can see rightly; what is essential is invisible to the eye."[1]

Seeking to understand a family member's heartfelt feelings is one of the most fundamental deposits we can make into their Emotional Bank Account. Not seeking to understand is one of the greatest withdrawals. Consider the impact that seeking first to understand made in this family:

Around the time our daughter Karen turned sixteen, she began to treat us very disrespectfully. She would make a lot of sarcastic comments and cynical put-downs. I didn't do much about it until it came to a head one night. My wife and I were in our bedroom and Karen came in and made some very inappropriate comments. I'd had enough.

So I said, "Karen, listen. Let me tell you how life works in this household." I then went through a long, authoritative argument to convince her that she should treat her parents with respect. I went on and on about the things we had done for her recently, like the dress we had just bought her. By the time I finished, I was expecting Karen to almost drop on her knees and worship us as her parents. Instead, she somewhat belligerently said, "So what!"

I was furious. I said angrily, "Karen, go to your room." With that, she went storming off and slammed her bedroom door.

I was so angry. And then suddenly it hit me. I had been pretty abrupt and had done nothing to try to understand Karen. I was totally focused on my own feelings and agenda.

When I went to her room a few minutes later, the first thing I did was apologize. I didn't excuse any of her behavior, but I apologized for my own. I then said, "Look, I can tell that something's going on here, and I don't know what it is." I let her know that I really wanted to understand where she was coming from.

Somewhat hesitantly she began to share her feelings about being brand-new in high school and the struggle she was having in trying to keep good grades and make new friends. She had just started a new part-time job and was wondering how her boss felt she was doing. She was also taking piano lessons. Her homework schedule was extremely busy.

Finally, I said, "Karen, you're feeling totally overwhelmed."

That was all she needed. Tears came. But more importantly she felt understood.

Karen had been feeling overwhelmed by all these challenges, and her sarcastic comments and disrespect to her family were basically a cry for attention. She was saying, "Please, somebody, just listen to me! Please understand me."

I got my wife involved and the three of us brainstormed ways that Karen might simplify her life. Ultimately, she decided to stop taking piano lessons—and she felt wonderful about it. In the weeks that followed she eliminated other items. She was a totally changed person.

Karen's disrespectful behavior was camouflaging her real heartfelt concerns. Not until her father stepped out of the role of being a judge and instead became a genuinely concerned listener did Karen feel safe in opening up her heart. Only then did her real concern begin to emerge, and only then did she become open to advice.

> As long as we are in the role of judge, prosecutor, and jury, we rarely have the kind of influence we should have when communicating with a family member.

As long as we are in the role of judge, prosecutor, and jury, we rarely have the kind of influence we should have when communicating with a family member.

LEVELS OF LISTENING

One of the deepest hungers of the human heart is to feel understood.

When you think about it, isn't the reason people shout

and yell at each other because they want to be understood? They're basically yelling, "Understand me! Listen to me! Respect me!" But yelling is so emotionally charged and disrespectful that instead of resolving matters it creates even more defensiveness and anger. It further wounds the relationship. Much time, effort, and distress would have been saved had the individuals practiced Habit 5 in the first place.

Helping someone to feel understood does takes time. Trying to be fast when listening to a person—especially in an emotional moment—is putting efficiency ahead of effectiveness. People don't typically let their feelings out all at once. Like peeling layers from an onion, feelings come out one layer at a time—and that takes time.

So what keeps us from being good listeners, especially in emotional moments? Sometimes the answer is sadly a lack of willingness. We are not interested enough in the other person's feelings or we do not want to be interrupted, so we simply choose to *ignore* them.

But ignoring people is rude and we don't want to appear rude, so on many occasions we instead take our listening up a level and we *pretend to listen*. We repeat back a few words to the person or we nod our heads while keeping our eyes glued to our digital devices. We hope that the person will at least think we are listening.

Or, taking our listening to the next level, we *listen selectively*. We do our best to catch the main points of what the person is saying without giving them our undivided attention. We may even agree with a comment that is made and say something like, "Yeah, I know what you mean."

It is not until we get to the level of *attentive listening* before we show our full willingness to give a person the time they deserve—to hear them out. At this level, we pause whatever we are doing and give the person our undivided attention. We focus our ears and eyes on every word the person says. We pay close attention to their body language to make sure we capture the full content of their message.

Attentive listening is sufficient for most family conversations. For example, when a child is giving directions for where they need to be picked up at a friend's house, attentive listening is all that is necessary. It's just a matter of accurately capturing the content or facts of what is being said.

But certain conversations require an even higher level of listening. The conversations I am referring to are when things get emotional. It's when someone is hurting emotionally or when trust has been broken in a relationship. It's when people are angry or anxious. It's when not just facts but also feelings are being communicated—deep feelings.

This higher level of listening is called "empathic listening," or listening with empathy. Empathy is not to be confused with sympathy. Sympathy is feeling sorry for someone. Empathy is understanding a person from their point of view. Empathic listening requires us to lay aside our viewpoints in an attempt to see the world from the other person's viewpoint. It requires us to pause, set aside any distractions, and use our ears, our eyes, and our heart to listen—with an emphasis on the heart.

Insight from Sandra

I love the quick access to my children and grand-children that cell phones provide. I can call them or they can call me at any time, even if I'm half a world away. I love it.

Yet cell phones can also greatly disrupt family communication. I constantly hear parents complain about how their children spend too much time on their phones or withdraw from family activities to be on their phones. While this may be true of children, what concerns me even more is the number of parents I observe who seem obsessed with their digital devices to the extent that they ignore their children.

Psychology Today recently cited research that identified some of the potential harm that can occur when a parent is distracted or less attentive to their children as a result of being on their phones rather than attending to their children. They include:

- Children feel unimportant because they have to compete for their parent's attention.

- Mothers stuck on cell phones have children who are more negative and less resilient.
- Distracted parental attention harms children's social-emotional development.
- Children feel sad, mad, angry, and lonely when parents overuse cell phones.

Such results ought to be a cause for concern for any parent who cannot put down their phones long enough to listen to a child.[2]

AUTOBIOGRAPHICAL DOOR SLAMMERS

Generally speaking, most people understand the need for good listening skills. Yet when it comes time to listen in empathic situations, they often end up unintentionally slamming doors on communication instead of opening doors. This is because they are prone to listening not from the other person's viewpoints but from their own viewpoints—their own autobiographies. Let me explain.

If I were to write my life story, I would write it from my viewpoint—how I view my experiences and contributions. It would be my autobiography. If Sandra were to write my life story, she would write it from her perspective—how she views my life. It would be a biography. The two versions of my life story would have significant differences because Sandra and I view some things differently. And if you were to read either my version or Sandra's version of my life story, you would evaluate and interpret it from your own unique perspective—how you view things. Why? Because we all experience and view the world differently and view things through our own lenses.

This is one of the main reasons why so many communication problems occur in families. People try to listen to others—not through the other person's eyes—but through their own autobiographies. They aren't willing or patient enough to set aside their own autobiographies and biases long enough to get into another person's world and see things from the other person's viewpoints.

I have identified four autobiographical "door slammers" that people commonly use when listening. They are evaluating, advising, probing, and interpreting. See if you use one or more of them.

Evaluating

When listening to another person, it is tempting to begin evaluating what the person is saying even before they finish their sentence or thought. We may judge what they say to be good or bad, smart or ignorant, clever or dull, and so forth. When we judge in this way, it is typically through the lens of our own autobiography, and it sets us up to prejudge or misjudge what is being said.

When people feel they are constantly being evaluated, they tend to shut down and say less. This is what happened in the case of Essie and her daughter, as described by Essie:

When I was thirteen, my mother started selling me on the street to get money for drugs. I never knew who my father was. For three years, my mom, who should have been protecting me, was actually feeding off my pain. I would come home and she would demand money from me to get back into the apartment. I lived in fear.

I had a baby daughter when I was sixteen, and I didn't know who the father was. This made me useless to my mother so I had to go out on my own. I dropped out of school to get a job. I was alone with my daughter and had nothing. Fortunately, I got some counseling from a neighborhood help center and gradually started to get on my feet.

Today I have a husband. We struggle to live off his wages, but my main concern is my daughter. When she turned eighteen she declared herself free from my guidance. She got into drugs, worked as an exotic dancer, and wanted to be a singer. The last few years, I have worried myself sick over her. For a long time, I was so angry and disappointed that she would choose that kind of life.

Eventually, I reached a point where I finally gave up. Occasionally, she would call me on the phone and rant and rave at me about everything that was wrong in her world. I wanted to say, "I told you so. You should have listened to me," but I had no more energy to fight her. I would just listen with little or no response.

Then a strange thing happened. The more I just listened to her and stopped fighting and judging her, the more she opened up about her life, the horrible things

*she was going through, and the men around her. I hurt
because she hurt, and she could tell that I was hurting with her instead of judging her lifestyle. We cried
together.*

*Today she talks to me every day in ways we never
talked before. Mostly I listen. She knows I listen because
I care. Now she's starting to listen to me too. She's stopped
judging me as well.*

Prior to when Essie "gave up," everything she did with her
daughter involved judging her and evaluating what she was
doing. And how did she judge her? Through her own autobiography. Until Essie quit playing judge, her daughter refused
to open up about her world or build a relationship.

**When you truly
come to understand
another person, you
judge them less.**

Evaluating people, prejudging, or
critiquing people slams the door shut
on communication. When you truly
come to understand another person,
you judge them less.

Advising

Well-intended advice is of little worth and may even be
harmful if it is not dealing with the correct issue. Many people are so eager to give advice that they do not take the time
to diagnose the real problem. They prescribe a remedy from
their own autobiography before they diagnose the underlying
issue. In medicine that is called malpractice. In families it is
called a communication door slammer.

People who are overly eager to advise often listen with the intent to reply, not with the intent to understand. They interrupt before the person is finished speaking because they are so eager to share their advice. In contrast, effective listeners diagnose before they prescribe; they seek first to understand before they attempt to advise.

Probing

Probing is asking a lot of questions. Probing can be very helpful in conversations. But once again, many listeners only ask questions from their own autobiography. They are so eager to be the hero problem solver that they prematurely start digging for hints: "How long ago did it happen?" "Why did you say that?" "What did you do next?"

In my experience, most probing questions are actually "leading" questions. The listener is attempting to lead the person toward a particular solution or trying to get to the root cause before they have identified the real concern. This too slams the door on communication.

Interpreting

Perhaps you know someone who is always trying to "figure you out." They're forever playing psychologist. In their mind they're thinking, "Tell me your story and I'll tell you why you are feeling the way you are feeling." Once again, the problem with this is that people are constantly trying to figure out the "why" without first identifying the "what." They interpret what the other person is saying through their own biases, experiences, or prejudices, not through the perspective of the other person.

So there is a quick overview of the four autobiographical door slammers that inhibit family communication: evaluating, advising, probing, and interpreting. "But Stephen," people will say to me, "aren't evaluating, advising, probing, and interpreting helpful at times?" Yes, they are. But not before the real concern has first been identified. Once people know you truly understand their true feelings and concerns, that is when they become open to evaluation, advice, probing, and interpretation.

STEPS TO EMPATHIC LISTENING

Empathic listening requires people to set aside their views for a moment, and to truly try to see the world through the other person's lenses. So how does a person open the doors to empathic listening? Consider three steps:

Step 1: Be a Faithful Translator of the Content

I was in Indonesia and happened to be teaching about empathic listening when I looked over the audience and saw people wearing headphones. The thought came to me, "If you want a good example of empathic listening, think about what the translators are doing right now."

The translators were listening to the *content* of what I was saying in English and then restating what I had just said into the Indonesian language using their own words. The translators were not evaluating what I was saying, or advising, or probing, or interpreting. They were simply trying to faithfully communicate the content of my message to the listeners.

One of the most effective ways to learn how to listen empathically is to see yourself as a faithful translator.

The experience convinced me that one of the most effective ways to listen empathically is to see yourself as a faithful translator. When you become involved in a conversation or disagreement with a family member and things start to get emotional, pause and think of your main job as being to communicate accurately back to the other person the very same content of the message that they are communicating to you. Do it until they feel fully understood. Don't change the message. Don't insert your interpretation. Don't evaluate. Simply restate the message in your own words, trying to be as faithful as possible to the content the person is speaking.

Step 2: Reflect the Speaker's Feelings

This step involves listening not just with your ears and eyes, but also with your heart. It is listening for *feelings*.

Perhaps there have been times when you have had people misread your emotions. They've asked you something like, "Why are you so angry with me?" And your response has been, "I'm not angry at you, I'm frustrated with myself." Or perhaps you have been told, "You seem to be really excited about giving your speech," and you respond, "I'm not excited.

I'm very nervous and I can't sit still." In each case, people have totally misread your emotions.

When conversations turn emotional, there is a high need to make sure you identify the correct emotions. And that's where the ears, eyes, and heart each play a part. With your ears, you listen for content and for any tones of voice that will give you clues into how the person is feeling. With your eyes, you look for body language, such as facial expressions, that will give you clues as to how the person is really feeling. And with your heart, you also listen for how the person is feeling, their emotions.

In short, step 1 has you reflect back in your own words the *content* of what the person is saying, and step 2 has you reflect back the *feelings* associated with the content. For example, imagine your daughter says to you with a smile on her face, "My boyfriend broke up with me this afternoon." You may not know if her smile indicates she truly is happy that her boyfriend broke up with her, or if the smile is meant to cover up her heartbreak. So to check for understanding, you might respond, "You seem to be happy that your boyfriend broke up with you," and then wait for a confirmation.

In that example, notice how your reflection included both the content: "Your boyfriend broke up with you," and the feeling: "You seem to be happy." The goal is to be correct about both content and feelings. Notice also how you didn't evaluate what was said, saying, "Oh, that stinks," or advising, "Go get a drink and get over it," or probing, "Where were you when it happened?" or interpreting, "I think he was just trying to get a reaction out of you." All you did was repeat the content in your own words and reflect the feelings.

Step 3: Ask Clarifying Questions

Clarifying questions are different from probing questions. Probing questions try to go deeper, take different angles, or explore various options. Clarifying questions simply confirm the accuracy of what you believe was said. If your daughter responds, "Yes, that's right," then move on. If she answers, "No, I didn't say I *broke up* with my boyfriend, I said I *woke up* with my boyfriend," then that's an entirely different conversation.

Until you feel you truly understand and until the other person feels truly understood, feel free to ask clarifying questions. When the speaker and the listener are at one with both the content and feelings of what was said, that is when you have reached empathy.

Do recognize, however, that some people might not feel comfortable sharing contents or feelings. They might give you surface-level answers to see how you react before they are willing to go deeper. Again, it's like peeling away an onion one layer at a time. Be gentle. Be patient. When you walk into people's hearts, you are walking on sacred ground.

When you walk into people's hearts, you are walking on sacred ground.

It's not unusual for people to be unsure about what they are trying to say or how they really feel. When you sense that someone might want you to help them identify or clarify their emotions, you might consider asking such clarifying questions as:

You seem concerned. What is your main concern?
You seem undecided. What is most important to you?

You appear anxious. What are your most pressing needs or
worries?

You seem unsure. What are the possible consequences of
such a plan?

I'm trying to see it from your point of view, and what I sense
is . . .

Clarifying questions demonstrate your sincere desire to
achieve full understanding—full empathy. As long as the person
trusts your intent, they will be patient with your listening skills.

LET'S GIVE IT A TRY TOGETHER

The goal is to be able to restate the other person's content and feelings as well as, if not better than, they can state them.

Again, when you find yourself in an
emotional situation, you are trying
to: 1) restate the other person's content in your own words, 2) reflect
their feelings, and 3) ask clarifying
questions, as needed. The goal is to
be able to restate the other person's
content and feelings as well as, if not
better than, they can state them.

Let's use two short scenarios as examples of how to get to
the heart of your communication with a family member.

Scenario 1

You sense your daughter is unhappy. When you've attempted
to ask her what's wrong in the past, she's replied very abruptly

and in a sharp tone. However, you're alone with her one night and she begins to open up: "Our family rule that I can't date until I'm seventeen is really embarrassing. All my friends are already dating and it's all they talk about. I hate it when John keeps asking me out, and I have to keep telling him I'm not old enough. If I tell him 'no' one more time, he'll for sure give up on me."

Okay. You're the parent. How would you typically respond?

Would you say: "Don't worry about it. If John gives up on you it just means he's no good anyway." Or, "I know just how you feel. I had to deal with the same thing when I was your age." Or, "What you're feeling is insecurity. You need to have more confidence."

Any one of those statements might be a typical parent response, but not an empathic one. They're autobiographic door slammers, not door openers.

So what might an empathic response be? Think of the three steps. First, reflect back the content of what your daughter said. Second, try to capture her feelings. Third, ask clarifying questions until she feels you truly understand.

For example, you might say, "You feel embarrassed about the family dating policy because everyone else can date except you. Is that it?"

Your daughter might respond, "Yes, that's exactly what I'm feeling." And then she might continue, "But what scares me is that I won't know how to act around boys when I do start dating."

Here again, you reflect back both the content and feelings to ensure understanding: "You feel scared that when the time comes to date you won't know what to do. Is that correct?"

She might say "yes" or she might say, "Well, not exactly. What I really meant is that I don't know what to do with John. I'm not interested in dating him, but I don't want to lose his friendship either."

Can you see how each time you reflect both content and feeling you end up getting a little closer to the full picture? Each time you peel away one more layer of the onion you build the trust. You come closer to understanding.

Scenario 2

Daughter, Alejandra, starts this one off.

ALEJANDRA: *Oh, Mom, Meggie got suspended from school today. She was caught in the parking lot with her boyfriend and he was drinking beer. If you get caught drinking at school, you get in big trouble.*
(Evaluate, Advise, Probe, Interpret)
MOTHER: *Meggie should know better. It serves her right for keeping bad friends.* (Evaluating)
ALEJANDRA: *I think it's unfair because Meggie wasn't drinking beer, just her boyfriend.*
MOTHER: *People judge you by your friends. I think you need to start looking for new friends.* (Advising)
ALEJANDRA: *I like Meggie. Why are you always against my friends?*
MOTHER: *Well, why wasn't she in class? Is this the first time she's been suspended?* (Probing)
ALEJANDRA: *Mom, it's okay! Don't get so upset.*

MOTHER: *I think you don't see yourself as highly as I do. If you did, you'd have better friends.* (Interpreting)

ALEJANDRA: *All I wanted to do was tell you something about Meggie, and instead I get a lecture on my bad friends and how you don't trust me.*

So how do you think that conversation went? Did it open up communication or shut it down?

Let's try a second version of this same scenario, and see what happens when Alejandra's mother uses empathic listening and seeks first to understand:

ALEJANDRA: *Oh, Mom, I have some bad news. Meggie got suspended from school today.*

MOTHER: *Honey, you really seem upset that Meggie got suspended.*

ALEJANDRA: *I feel so bad about it, Mom. It wasn't her fault. It was her boyfriend's. He's a jerk.*

MOTHER: *You feel bad because it was her boyfriend's fault. You don't like him?*

ALEJANDRA: *I sure don't, Mom. He's always in trouble and he drags her down. It makes me sad.*

MOTHER: *You feel he's a bad influence on her, and it makes you sad because she's your good friend.*

ALEJANDRA: *I wish she'd drop this guy and go out with someone nice. Bad friends get you in trouble. How do you think I can help her, Mom?*

Did you feel the difference? The first version ended with Alejandra on trial. In the second version, Alejandra's mother didn't evaluate, probe, advise, or interpret. Instead, she responded in a way that led to a better understanding of what Alejandra was saying and with Alejandra asking for advice. Very different outcomes. And did you notice that it took less time than the first version of the conversation? It was more effective and more efficient since neither the mother nor Alejandra needed to deal with all the extra baggage.

NOW YOU GIVE IT A TRY

Now it's your turn. Give it a try on your own.

Select a family member with whom you can practice empathic listening. I recommend that for your first attempt you choose someone you are comfortable with rather than someone with whom you have a difficult relationship. Invite the person to choose a current or past emotional situation that they feel comfortable sharing, one that they can speak about for at least three to five minutes. Once they've identified the situation, go for it. Practice empathic listening using all three steps.

When you are finished, ask the person if they feel understood. Reflect on what you did well and what you might have done better.

One of my colleagues gave this same challenge to the participants of a multiday workshop he was facilitating in Singapore. The next day he asked if anyone had accepted the challenge and had something to report. A man who had not said anything the first two days raised his hand and volunteered:

Last night, I told my teenage son it was time to go to bed, and the same argument that we have almost every night started to erupt.

"Why?" he demanded. "How come you always make me go to bed so early? My friends' parents let them stay up as late as they want."

Instead of listening while he was scolding me, I began preparing my response. It was going to be the hundredth time I gave him the same lecture. I was irritated, tired, and didn't want to deal with it again. And then I remembered your challenge.

I started to listen for content and for feelings and to reflect them. At first, my son looked at me like something was wrong with me. But he kept going. He let me know how unfair and uncaring I am. I then asked some clarifying questions, and one conversation led to another.

We talked until after one in the morning. Mostly I listened. I was so tired when we ended that I was not going to come here this morning. But I needed to come because I wanted to thank you. My son and I became more than father and son. We became friends.

You might be surprised how many times I have heard similar experiences. It starts with pausing long enough to listen, and then reflecting both contents and feelings. It requires you to leave your world—your autobiography—and to get into the other person's world. You don't have to agree with them, just understand them.

Insight from Sandra

A key to listening empathically—to unlock the hearts of family members—is to meet them where they are. I'm not thinking in terms of where they are physically, I'm talking about where they are emotionally.

We have a friend who was a schoolteacher. He always made doing well in math and science a high priority for his children. Yet his son preferred doing things with his hands and muscles. So the father kept on saying, "You need to pay more attention to your math and science homework." He also put down careers that required only physical labor.

As a result, their father-son relationship had nearly come to a halt. Ego battles were their primary form of communication. Fortunately, the father eventually saw what was happening and instead of trying to persuade his son to come to his way of thinking, he decided to switch to a "meet him where he is" approach.

The father got the idea for a project. He and his son would build a scaled replica of the Great Wall of China behind their home. His son loved the idea. It took them weeks to build, but in the process they learned about Chinese history and had a lot of fun talking about other topics. So while the project was to build a wall, the father's real intent was to tear down the wall that had stood between him and his son.

And that's what empathic listening is about. Entering into another person's world, going where they are, and not expecting them to always come to where you are.

You may think your child is so emotionally distanced from you that you need a passport to get to where they are emotionally, but I suggest you give it a try. First go to where they are.

ZIP THE ZIPPER

As important as it is, be careful not to make empathic listening more complex than it needs to be. Sometimes all it requires is to keep the lips closed. A father shared:

Our ten-year-old daughter, Amber, loves horses more than anything. Recently, her grandfather invited her to go on a daylong cattle drive. She was so excited and thrilled that she would get to ride a horse and be with her grandfather.

The night before the cattle drive, I came home to find Amber in bed with the flu. I said, "How are you doing,

Amber?" She looked at me and said, "I'm so sick!" And she started to cry as she said, "I won't be able to go on the cattle drive."

Through my mind went all of the things I thought a dad should say: "Oh, it will be fine." "You can do it some other time." "Don't worry. You'll feel better soon."

But instead I didn't say anything. I just listened and felt her pain.

Well, she was whimpering and shaking all over as I held her for a couple of minutes.

And then it passed. She gave me a hug and said, "Thanks, Dad." And that was it.

She didn't need any advice or pep talks. She just needed someone to listen . . . to make her feel understood.

This father did not give his daughter any miracle cure or advice. He did not probe for root causes. He didn't interpret her situation. All he did was remain quiet—and listen.

Jane Covey is fond of saying, "If there is only one thing to remember about listening, it is this: When you are seeking first to understand, put a zipper on your mouth—an industrial-sized zipper."

And sometimes that's all it takes.

WHEN IS EMPATHIC LISTENING NOT NEEDED?

A common question I get asked about empathic listening is "Stephen, do I really need to listen that way every time I talk with my kids or partner? Do I really need to always reflect content and feelings? That seems exhausting! People will think I'm weird."

If you listen empathically all the time, people would have good reason to think you're a little strange. Because, no, you don't need to always reflect the content and feelings of what a person is saying. In fact, I'm reminded of the teenager who was complaining to his parent about how much he hated school. The conversation went something like this:

TEEN: *I hate school.*
PARENT: *Oh, you don't like school.*
TEEN: *Yeah! And the cafeteria food is so plain!*
PARENT: *You feel the cafeteria food is plain?*
TEEN: *And the students, they're so low-caliber.*
PARENT: *You feel that the students are low-caliber?*
TEEN: *Yeah, and what is wrong with the way I'm saying it?*

As noted earlier, most conversations involve nothing more than passing on information—content. For that, attentive listening is adequate. It's only when things turn emotional—when heartfelt feelings are being shared—that it's time to open up the ears, eyes, and heart to listen for both content and feelings.

If you are sure you understand what the other person is saying, if trust is high, and if the content and feelings are clear, that's your signal that you do not need to listen empathically. Give the conversation the "green light" and continue talking.

If, however, you are not sure you understand, or if the other person feels understood, then give the conversation a "yellow light." Proceed with caution. Do a little empathic listening to see if it is really needed.

But when things truly get emotional, when trust is low, and when understanding is important, then give the conversation the "red light." Stop and listen empathically.

However, don't force it. If the person does not want to open up, respect their will. If the history of your relationship has been one of judging and evaluating, then you may need to first work on rebuilding your Emotional Bank Account with the person. Put trust back into the relationship. This is why Habit 4 comes before Habit 5.

Insight from Sandra

Children do not like parents to play manipulative games when trying to get them to open up and talk about life. Straight talk is better.

Stephen and I had been trying to encourage one of our sons for several weeks to improve his schoolwork. We worried that something unknown to us might be distracting him, and felt it would be good to do some empathic listening. So we asked if he wanted to go out for dinner with us as a kind of special date. He asked who else would join us. We said, "No one. This is just a time to be with you." He immediately said he didn't want to go.

We eventually talked him into it, yet throughout the entire meal there was very little openness on his part, in spite of our best efforts to listen to what was going on in his life. Near the end of the dinner, we began talking about an issue that was only slightly related to schoolwork, and that's when our son blew up: "This is why I didn't want to come to dinner."

He had rightly sensed it would be another "we need to straighten you out" conversation. It took us weeks and a lot of deposits before he became open to talking with us again.

. . . THEN TO BE UNDERSTOOD

It turns out that the first half of Habit 5, Seek First to Understand, is essential to applying the second half of Habit 5, . . . Then to Be Understood. It's why there is wisdom and logic to the order of the two parts of the habit.

Once you truly understand a person, you are in a better position to influence them. Why? Because when you truly understand their points of view, you can then share your feelings within their frame of reference. You can teach them, inspire them, confront them with love, give them feedback, and share your thoughts through the lens of their autobiography, not yours.

One woman shared:

For a long time, my husband and I did not see eye to eye on matters of spending. He would want to buy things that I felt were unnecessary and expensive, and I couldn't seem to explain to him the pain I felt as our debts kept mounting. We spent more and more of our income on interest and credit card bills.

I decided I needed to find a different way to express my point of view. I tried to listen to him more, to understand how he was thinking. I came to realize that he was more of a "big-picture" thinker, and sometimes he just didn't see the connection between his spending decisions and the consequences they brought.

Seeking first to understand his way of thinking allowed me to see how to better explain my feelings. So when he would say, "You know, it would really be nice to have [some item]," instead of arguing with him, I began to say, "You know, it really would be nice to have that. But let's see what will happen if we buy it. Let's look at the big picture." I would then take out the budget and say, "Now, if we spend this here, we won't have money to do that."

I found that when my husband saw the consequences of spending decisions within the big picture, he came to the conclusion himself that we were better off not buying the item.

Through seeking to understand her husband's ways of thinking, this woman was better able to communicate her viewpoints to him. She could express her ideas using his language and in the manner he preferred.

SHARING CONSTRUCTIVE FEEDBACK

Giving feedback is an important and common way that family members communicate their feelings. If feedback is not communicated with respect, it can be the source of much contention and hard feelings.

When trust is low, communicating feedback and feelings can be very risky. When trust is high, giving constructive feedback is much easier and beneficial.

When I was launching my speaking career, I was invited to speak to over a thousand business leaders on the same program as Ken Blanchard, one of the premier leadership experts of all time. When it was over, many people came up to me and told me what a great job I had done. I left the beautiful concert hall feeling confident and pleased.

On our way home, Sandra had not said much about my presentation, so I asked her what she thought. "Well, Stephen," she responded. "I felt it wasn't your best speech. I feel you were too serious and too complicated. I feel like it would help if you told more stories like Ken Blanchard."

At first, her words hit me with a truckload of embarrassment. "Did I really not do all that great? Were all those people who complimented me just being nice?"

The reason Sandra could be so candid with me was because she had such a large trust account built up with me. I knew she had my best interests in mind and that she was balancing courage with consideration in giving the feedback. I also knew she was correct in what she was saying, and that her intent was not to attack me but to encourage me.

Not all family feedback sessions are so trusting or friendly. Some people forget the principle of mutual respect when giving feedback. They don't seek first to understand. That's why a common point of contention in families occurs when feedback is not given or received properly. Words get spoken that never should have been uttered. Negative labels get attached. Personal attacks are made. Such attacks create more problems than they resolve, and some of those problems may take years to resolve. Harmful words are nearly impossible to fully erase. That's because destructive feedback tears down, whereas constructive feedback builds up.

> When you really love someone, you care enough about them to approach them with constructive feedback—and you do it in ways that show respect.

When you really love someone, it means you care enough about them to provide them with constructive feedback. Everyone has "blind spots" that need to be revealed and refined. But those blind spots are best revealed in very tactful ways that maintain people's dignity and respect.

"I" MESSAGES

When you encounter a need to give a family member constructive feedback, consider four best practices:

1. *Seek first to understand.* First seek to know what is important to the other person and how your feedback will connect to their goals, abilities, and interests. There's no sense giving feedback if it is not connected with

something that is important to them. Nor is it helpful if the person cannot realistically do something about the feedback.

2. *Check your ego and motives.* Ask yourself, "Will this feedback truly be helpful to this family member, or does it just fulfill my self-serving need to set this person straight?" Is it genuinely meant to serve the other person or is it more intended to serve your ego or your desire for revenge?

3. *Be sensitive to blind spots.* Feedback often comes as a complete shock to a person. Their "blind spots" may truly surprise or embarrass them if pointed out. Some feedback may even damage their feelings of worth. So tread carefully when dealing with the feelings of others. It may even be that a different person is in a better position to provide the feedback. Most often such feedback is better shared in private.

4. *Use "I" messages.* Attacking a person tends to push them into a defensive mode. It may motivate them to attack back at you. So instead of attacking or describing a person by saying something like, "You are lazy and selfish for not helping me," describe your feelings: "When I don't get help with cleaning the dishes after I have already cooked the entire meal, I feel like I am being treated as an unpaid, non-valued servant." This is referred to as giving "I" messages rather than "you" messages. "I" messages come from your point of view: "This is how I see it." "This is the way I feel." "This is what I have observed." The moment you start sending "you" messages—"You are so self-centered!" "You

are causing so much trouble!"—is the point when you start attacking people, evaluating their intentions, and making yourself the judge of that person. It becomes a huge withdrawal.

Once, Sandra and I were concerned about what we felt was a selfish pattern developing in one of our sons. It had been going on for some time and was becoming offensive to everyone in the family. We could easily have given him quick feedback, reprimanded him, or blown up at him in front of his siblings and hoped the pattern would change. But we've done that before and it has never worked. So I said to myself, "I've really got to pay the price on this one. This is a deeply embedded tendency he's developed, but it's not his nature. It's a blind spot. He needs to know how people feel about his actions."

I waited for a good time and sought out the right occasion. Finally, I said to him, "Son, your mother and I have a concern. Would you mind if I shared it with you?"

He said, "Not at all, Dad."

So I shared with him what we were feeling. He wasn't offended because I was describing our feelings—not attacking his character. I was saying, "This is our concern. This is what we feel. This is our perception." I wasn't saying, "You are so selfish. You are offending the entire family."

I also shared our perception of his true nature and how we knew he too had higher expectations for himself. His immediate response was so positive. He said, "Oh, I can see that being an issue. I guess I've just really been into myself a lot lately, and I can see why others think it's not right."

Things immediately changed for the better, not just for the family but for him. He was no longer unknowingly offending others.

In short, we simply must care enough to confront other family members with constructive feedback when it is needed, timed correctly, and done with a voice of love. When done in the right setting and frame of mind, people ultimately appreciate constructive feedback—straight talk.

Insight from Sandra

Years ago, I covered one wall in our home from floor to ceiling with photos of our family at all stages of their lives. There are baby photos, school photos, and wedding photos. There are photos of our children with pimples and braces. There is a grandchildren's section and a place for grandparents and great-grandparents. I've updated it over the years.

People who visit our home are inevitably drawn to the photo wall. Our children and grandchildren flock to it and say things like: "Oh, I remember that dress. It was my favorite!" "Dad, did you really wear braces too?" Our sons were thrilled when I hung up a poster of them in swimsuits after they had their muscles all pumped up. They point it out proudly to their sons.

There is a purpose to the wall. I want all my family members to see one another as I see them. When I look at photos of our thirty-three-year-old son with four children, in my mind's eye I see him as a four-year-old coming to get comfort for a scraped knee. I see him as a twelve-year-old facing his fears on the first day of middle school. I see him as a seventeen-year-old athlete fighting to be cheerful after a championship defeat. I see him as a nineteen-year-old leaving home to spend two years in a foreign country. I see him as a twenty-three-year-old embracing his new bride, and as a twenty-four-year-old holding his first child. I see him in light of the bigger picture of life.

When I see each child in this way, I feel their ongoing worth and potential. It changes the way I behave toward them, listen to them, and give feedback to them. It reminds me of who they are and how much good they have done over the years. It humbles me to be their mother.

To give constructive feedback with that kind of big-picture vision—instead of the emotion of the moment—makes all the difference in parenting. Perhaps when giving feedback we ought to envision everyone in the family wearing a sign that says, "Be patient; I'm not finished, yet."

TIMING IT RIGHT

You've heard me previously mention the importance of timing. The absolute worst time to give constructive feedback is in the heat of a moment, when people are mad and yelling at each other. "Oh yeah, you think I'm bad. Well, let me say a thing or two about you!" That's destructive feedback, not constructive feedback.

Constructive feedback is at its best when it is timed correctly. I arrived home exhausted one evening after a full day of navigating crowded airports. I was met by my son who had spent much of the day cleaning a work area. The project involved tremendous effort—carrying heavy boxes, cleaning out "yucky" things, and throwing away junk. He was only a little boy but did his best to judge what to keep and what to throw out based on the guidelines I had given to him.

Yet when we entered the room to observe his work, my first observations were very negative: "Why did you do that? Why didn't you do this?" I forget the specifics of what he did or didn't do, but what I do clearly remember—and will never forget—was watching the light go out of his eyes. He had been so thrilled with what he had done, and had waited for hours in anticipation of what he thought would be my great delight. To his surprise and dismay, however, my first reactions were negative. Gentle as my first words may have been, they were to criticize.

When I saw the light go out of his eyes, I knew immediately I had made a mistake. I tried to apologize. I tried to explain myself out of the situation. I tried to make excuses and blame my rudeness on my rough day. I tried to focus on the good things he had done and to express my love and appreciation. But it was to no avail. The light never came back into his eyes that evening.

When people have done their best, then whether their work meets your standards or not is irrelevant. It is the time to express appreciation and praise. Praise the heart that went into the work. Praise the worth of the person. You are not compromising your integrity when you take such an encouraging, appreciating, affirming approach. You are simply focusing on the person, who is more important than the task or project. But in that moment, never give negative feedback—even though it may be deserved. Wait for a better time. Give the constructive feedback at a time when you are more emotionally ready to give it and the person is more ready to receive it. And preferably do it in person rather than on the phone or via text messages where feelings and body language can be easily lost or misunderstood.

Recognize too that there are developmental stages when a child is ready—or not ready—for feedback. Carefully adapt your feedback to match the development phase, maturity, and readiness of the individual.

MAKING DIGITAL DEVICES A FAMILY FRIEND

It's interesting. Parents refer to their cell phone as a "smartphone." Yet when those same parents refer to their child's phone, they say, "I wish they'd get off of that dumb phone!"

So which is it? A smartphone or a dumb phone?

Entire books are written about what digital devices do to family communication. Most emphasize the negative impacts of digital devices, and are loaded with suggestions for how to control a child's usage.

There is good reason for a parent to be concerned with controlling their children's device usage. Many parents see digital devices as warehouses the size of the universe that are filled with nothing more than creepy people, undesirable content, and addictive time wasters. At times, it's hard to disagree. Yet the more a parent tries to control a child's digital device usage, the greater the probability is for tensions and contentions to arise. Parents prefer, for example, to meet their children's friends face-to-face rather than spying on them via social media to figure out who they are. Meanwhile, their children find it disgusting and intrusive to have a parent "friend" them online. Before long, loud arguments break out over the family's digital rules. As parents fight for more control, children fight even harder for more autonomy: "Give me liberty."

Parents further worry about what digital devices might do to a child's physical, emotional, and mental well-being. They sense that the more time spent on digital devices, the less time that is spent exercising, playing outside, building muscles, reading books, doing homework, burning calories, or building relationships. They recognize that late-night digital use can disrupt sleeping patterns and diminish alertness and attentiveness during school hours. Parents who once dreamed of their children learning a musical instrument, developing as an athlete, or growing other talents now find themselves instead having nightmares about why their child prefers to go to their room, turn out the lights, and lock the doors for hours at a time. "Hey, what's going on in there?"

There is no realistic way a parent can monitor everything that gets communicated and consumed on digital screens, even with the best censoring software. It used to be that the big battle was over who would control the one single digital device in the home—the television. Now more than 70 percent of children between the ages of eight and eighteen have a cell phone and they carry it with them wherever they go and at all hours of the day. Posters on bedroom walls have been replaced by wall-mounted televisions, while laptop computers shift from room to room. Again, there's just no realistic way a parent can monitor them all, and that's why many parents give up. The devices are left to reign.

A friend of mine recently attended a pricey concert. A family arrived late and sat down in the row directly in front of him. Almost in unison, every family member instantly pulled out their phones and for the entire concert they scrolled through social media or played video games. When the concert ended, they stood up and hurried off to beat the traffic. My friend wondered if they even knew a concert had happened.

Or perhaps you have experienced what I have seen in some families. They gather each evening to watch a favorite television show. Simultaneously, they are all fully engaged and doing their own thing on their individual devices. I applaud the fact that they are together because in many families the children are in one room while the parents are in another; however, when does family communication happen for these families?

For all the talk about how children overuse their digital devices, of equal concern is the frequent usage of digital devices by the adults in the family. People complain of their spouse's attachment to digital media and how it detaches them from the relationship. Time attending to social media replaces the time that was once meant for nurturing children. Some parents turn babysitting chores over to their child's digital device: "Here's a game for you to play." Indeed, for as hard as adults try to control their children's digital usage, it is surprising how often they cannot control their own. And for the parents who don't know how to use digital technology, this creates a different kind of problem, a generation gap—and a communication gap—between them and their digitally native children.

So yes, there are a lot of negative things to be said about children's and adults' usage of digital devices. And yes, there is a need for parents to take preventative or restorative actions to protect their children. But since this chapter is about improving family communication, I will point out that there is a lot that families can do to make digital devices a family friend.

In addition to the standard benefits of digital devices—being able to contact children for safety purposes, having quick access to valuable information, calendaring, and resourcing online learning tools—digital devices can be a great way to communicate and stay in contact with children and a wide range of family members.

For all the talk about how children overuse their digital devices, of equal concern is the frequent usage of digital devices by the adults in the family.

Whereas some parents become entirely irked when observing their children constantly texting on their phones, one mother decided to join in the fun. Each day, she texts short inspirational messages and expressions of love to her children—small, daily Emotional Bank Account deposits. One of her sons was in the middle of a high school class one day and had forgotten to turn off his cell phone according to class rules. When his phone beeped—a little too loudly— signaling he had just received a text message, the teacher heard it and decided to make a case out of it.

"Oh, is that a text from your girlfriend?" The teacher smiled. "Should I read it aloud to the class?"

"If you really want to," the son responded.

The teacher took the phone and began to read aloud. It was a love note all right. It contained an inspirational quote for the day, followed by the words "I sure love you, Mom."

The girls in the class sighed and the teacher looked at the young man as if to say, "You're very lucky to have a mom like that!"

Mission accomplished, Mom.

I mentioned earlier how my brother, John, and his wife, Jane, spend time each morning texting uplifting messages to their children and grandchildren. They don't consider themselves the world's most technology-savvy grandparents, but the grandchildren think it's cool that Grandma and Grandpa are thinking of them and sending texts.

Some families set up regular virtual group calls to connect with family members who are scattered around the globe. They are getting together and communicating virtually far more often than they ever did in person. Other families set up family blogs. Still others communicate weekly, if not daily, via group chats on their phones. Cousins play virtual games with cousins, even when on the opposite sides of a country. Videos of new grandchildren or family activities are sent out at the click of a button. Funerals of relatives can be viewed online for those otherwise unable to attend.

I honestly believe that if parents spent as much energy using digital devices in proactive ways to communicate with their children as they do in trying to control their children's device usage, they might have more success in helping their children monitor themselves. For the best censors are not the software type but what goes on in a child's mind and the choices they make.

As I mentioned in the beginning of the book, the 7 Habits are at their best when they have a problem to solve. So in the case of too much device usage of a child, ask: How might the 7 Habits help me? Consider Habit 1: How can I be a better model of cell phone usage? How can I share the pros and cons of too much usage with my child, and help them see the natural consequences of their choice to use the phone so much? Habit 2: How can I better establish family values around how we as a family spend our time? How do I better communicate my child's worth and potential, and how too much usage can diminish some of that potential? Habit 3: How can we use family time or one-on-one time to involve children in setting ground rules for phone usage, knowing that when there's no involvement in setting the rules there will be no commitment to keeping those rules? Habit 4: How do I build the Emotional Bank Account with my child so that they will trust me in acknowledging the hazards of improper device usage? Can we set up a win-win agreement around device usage? Habit 5: How do I seek first to understand my child's feelings about cell phone usage without judging, advising, probing, or interpreting their motives? How do I set aside my own cell phone long enough to listen? How do I give them feedback without attacking them with "you" messages?

Again, the 7 Habits may not solve all your digital challenges, but can you see how they get you thinking toward effective solutions?

So yes, there is a lot of worrying that can come with digital devices in a family. I will emphasize that some of those worries can only be alleviated by parents who first build trust with their children so the children will talk to them or ask for help when significant problems with digital devices do arise. I once attended a conference where the governor of the state told of a nine-year-old boy who was acting out of sorts. One day he blurted out, "Dad, I can't stand it anymore!" He told his father how a friend of his was showing him terrifying scenes of violent acts and graphic pornography on his home computer. The images truly disturbed him. While I lamented the fact that the boy was subjected to such scenes, I thought, "Congratulations to that father for having a trusting relationship with his son, so that his son was willing to confide in him about what was going on." I dare say that much of that trust was built by the father applying Habits 1 through 5.

I also say congratulations to parents and families who are finding creative ways to use their digital technologies to keep their family communications open and frequent enough that they are able to continue nurturing their family culture via virtual means. Nothing in my mind quite beats being together in person, but when that is not possible, do all you can to make your digital devices a family friend.

As for the question of whether your phone is a smartphone or a dumb phone, that is not a matter of age or opinion but rather it is a matter of the proactive choices the user makes.

SKILL AND INTENT

As is clear by now, there is far more to Habit 5 than is seen at its surface.

Returning to my research of two hundred years of success literature that led to the discovery of the 7 Habits, as I sifted through the many, many articles and books on how to be successful, I observed a distinct shift that took place during those years. The first 150 years focused on people's *character.* Successful people in those years were described by their inner character traits, such as being honest, hardworking, kind, visionary, disciplined, and so forth. In contrast, the remaining fifty years described successful people more by their outward, visible traits and *personality,* such as being tall, dressed for success, effective listeners, able to give persuasive presentations, and so forth.

I like to illustrate this observation using the image of an iceberg. I label the portion of the iceberg that is above the ocean surface as the "personality ethic," and the portion that is beneath the surface as the "character ethic." The visible personality ethic focuses on people's outward skills and personality, whereas the character ethic focuses on people's inner values, character, and motives. If you are familiar with icebergs, then you know that the mass below the surface contains approximately 90 percent of the iceberg.

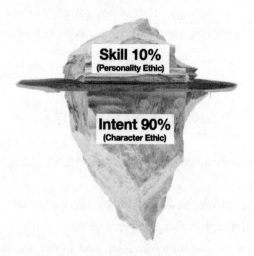

Skill 10%
(Personality Ethic)

Intent 90%
(Character Ethic)

The same is true with Habit 5. While the above-the-surface communication skills are important—including skills for attentive and empathic listening—if people lack the beneath-the-surface character and have less than honorable intentions, people will not trust what they say and will not open their hearts to them. If a family member does not trust your intent, it will not matter how great your skills are for listening empathically or giving "I" feedback. Your attempts will be rejected. If, on the other hand, you are a highly trusted family member—you have strong character and pure intentions—then your skills for listening can be relatively poor and yet there will still be a good chance that the family member will open up to you.

This is why trust is one of the most essential ingredients in effective family communication. In fact, my son Stephen, who you might remember as my "Green and Clean" son, has since matured and moved on from cleaning lawns to writing a bestselling book called *The Speed of Trust*.[3] One of his most central themes is that when trust is high, then things such as family communication go fast. When trust is low, family communication goes agonizingly slow.

> Trust is the most essential ingredient in effective communication.

Good skills and good intent equate to high trust, and that leads to strong family communication. This is one of the main reasons why Habit 4 comes before Habit 5.

Insight from Sandra

A mother came to me for advice on how to deal with teenagers. She was so down on teens and could not wait for her son to get out of that stage.

I looked at her, smiled, and replied, "Ah, teenagers! I love that time of life! I think it's one of the most creative, fun times ever. The main thing is to listen to them, even if you have to stay up with them half the night. Don't tell them what to do with their life but rather say, 'Here are some possible things that might help you.' Because teens are very creative, and they can come up with ideas in half the time that you can."

I honestly believe that if teenagers know you have an interest in them, that you will not judge them no matter what, and that you truly care about them, you will be surprised at how much they want to talk, how much they want to confide in you, and how interesting their conversations can be.

And once you have earned their trust, then get ready to talk with them again and again. Because they'll come back to you again and again.

IN CONCLUSION

A common question people ask me is: "Stephen, of all the 7 Habits, which habit is the hardest for you personally to live?" This is where I don't hesitate in answering, "Habit 5."

At times I can hardly resist my natural tendency to jump in and give advice, or evaluate, or probe, or interpret before I fully diagnose a situation. Yet I know it is the better way. I also know that it involves much more than some surface-level listening techniques. It truly involves stepping out of my shoes—my own autobiography—and into the shoes of the other person for a time. It involves living by principles such as honesty, openness, empathy, and mutual respect. It's not always easy, but it's worth it.

In reading this chapter, I hope you feel my passion for effective family communication. Family life is filled with every emotion imaginable, and given the importance of family, it is vital that those emotions do not get lost or tangled in poor communication habits.

REFLECTIONS AND APPLICATIONS

With Self

Looking back over Habit 5: Seek First to Understand, Then to Be Understood, what is the one idea or learning that if you were to apply it better would have the greatest impact on the well-being of your family?

_____

_____

_____

_____

With Adults and Teens

- Invite one or two family members to share a fun memory or an emotional story. As they are talking, use one or more of the autobiographical door slammers. Afterward, discuss how it feels when people use door slammers.
- Discuss together: Why is it important to truly understand and empathize with each family member? How well do we really know the members of our family? Do we know their

stresses? Their fears? Their views about themselves? Their hopes? How can we get to know them better?

- Ask family members: When have we seen the results of *not* seeking to understand in our family, such as frustration? Share specific examples, if any, and explore how the situation could have been handled more empathically.

- Review the steps of empathic listening on pages 214–218. Then take turns giving the steps a try with someone in your family. Give each other constructive feedback.

- Discuss why seeking first to understand is fundamental to seeking to be understood. How does it help you to better communicate your feelings in the language of the listener?

- Practice with real scenarios or pretend situations giving constructive "I" messages. Discuss why "I" messages are better than "you" messages.

With Young Children

- Encourage children to share experiences of times when they felt misunderstood.

- Gather several pairs of eyeglasses of varying types and strengths. Let each child look at the same object through a different set of glasses. They might say it's blurry, dark, blue-tinted, or clear, depending on what glasses they are wearing. Explain that the differences in what they see represent the different ways people see things in life. Let them trade glasses to get an idea of seeing something the way someone else sees it.

- Prepare a "taste" platter with a number of different items of food on it. Let everyone taste each item. Compare responses and talk about how some people may really love a particular food that others find distasteful. Point out that this is an example of how people experience life differently, and discuss why it is important for family members to really understand how other people experience things differently.

- Play "mood charades." Ask children to demonstrate a mood such as anger, sadness, happiness, or disappointment, and let the rest of the family guess what they're feeling. Point out that you can learn a lot about others by simply watching their faces and body movements. Teach children to listen not just with their ears but also with their eyes and heart.

SYNERGIZE

Uniting the Strengths of Everyone

What I truly love about Sandra is her differences. The differences I'm talking about, of course, are her strengths and her unique perspectives on life.

Sandra has talents that I do not have. She has brought music into our family. She has opinions that contrast mine, and hearing them helps me to be a more understanding person. Sandra works with young people in ways that I can only envy. Sandra understands the developmental phases of children and has the patience to allow them to go through their stages. I could go on about Sandra's strengths.

Fortunately, Sandra appreciates a few of my differences— my strengths—as well. The result is that we are able to solve problems and make decisions that have better outcomes than either of us can come up with on our own. Indeed, in many situations we are more effective and creative working together than we are alone. Now add in the different strengths and perspectives of each of our children and you can see why we are even better together as a family.

All of this is because of our differences, not in spite of our differences. And the result has been synergy in our marriage and in our family culture.

WHAT IS SYNERGY?

The goal of Habit 6: Synergize is to achieve synergy. Synergizing is the process; synergy is the outcome.

Synergy is difficult to describe but you know it when you feel it. The feeling of synergy is different than the feeling you get after you have worked alone.

Synergy is perhaps easiest to explain using a little math. Take any two people and give them a project to complete. What you will get is one of four outcomes:

- Conflict: $1 + 1 = 1/2$ or less
- Compromise: $1 + 1 = 1\ 1/2$
- Teamwork: $1 + 1 = 2$
- Synergy: $1 + 1 = 3$ or more

Conflict happens when two people assigned to a project argue, compete, and battle against each other to the point that the final outcome is worse than what either of the persons would have accomplished alone. Compromise happens when two people can't agree on things so they end up with both sides "giving in" a little. Teamwork happens when two people combine their maximum efforts to get a fully united result. Synergy happens when two people combine their strengths in a way that creates innovative ideas or solutions that are even better than the combined sum of what they would have done individually. This is why some people define synergy as the whole being greater than the sum of its parts.

Synergizing is interdependence at its best. Synergizing occurs in a family when each person brings their best ideas, talents, and efforts together, and then uses them to solve a problem, create something new, or resolve a disagreement. One family member's ideas trigger a new idea in another family member, which then triggers a new idea in another family member. Before anyone realizes it, a better solution has been identified than any family member could have come up with independently.

Synergizing is interdependence at its best.

Synergy does not result from luck, happenchance, or serendipity. It is a form of work. In fact, the process of synergizing is so difficult at times that strong disagreements can be expected to arise from it. When this happens, some people give up and quit. They are not willing to put in the effort and patience that is required, and so they never get to synergy.

Some people never even make an attempt to achieve synergy. They prefer to go it alone. I'm reminded of a college student who described a time when one of her professors assigned a project and let the students choose whether to work alone or in a group. She thought about how difficult and frustrating it might be to try to blend all the differing opinions and schedules, and concluded that it would be easier to do the project on her own.

When the day came to present the projects in front of the class, she was the first to present. She felt very good about her presentation until the group that followed began presenting their project. They were only seconds into their presentation when it became obvious to the young woman that they had much more content than she did (multiple students had gathered content), far better presentation slides than she did (one student was a graphic artist), and much better speaking skills than she did (two students were very articulate). She saw that their presentation was more interesting and better prepared than hers was. She also saw how they had optimized each other's strengths, and were having a lot of fun together.

When the presentations finished, the young woman swore she would never go it alone again if given the option to work in a group. She had witnessed synergy and wished she had chosen to go for synergy.

Insight from Sandra

Isn't it impressive that so many marriages and relationships actually work?

People come from entirely different families and backgrounds, and have such widely varying ways of doing things like communicating, handling finances, eating, raising children, and so forth, and yet they somehow work things out.

When we first married, I loved the arts and theatre and things like that. Stephen liked basketball games, football games, and jumping into lakes at midnight. People must have wondered how we ever came together. In hindsight, we can see that those differences have turned out to be a great benefit to our children because they are more well-rounded and enjoy a greater variety of hobbies—all in thanks to our differing likes and interests.

Every family has differences and every family chooses to do things a little differently. So I have said to our children when they marry, "Take the best traits from our family and the best traits from your spouse's family, and then go and do things the way you want to do them. You don't have to do things the way we did them. Create your own synergy."

SYNERGY—THE FRUIT OF ALL 7 HABITS

The same type of synergizing and synergy that happened in the student presentations can happen in a family. So why is it that when some families work together the outcomes turn out to be pure chaos—not synergy?

The answer is found largely in the previous five habits. Within each of the first five habits are qualities that *drive* a family toward synergy, whereas the opposites of the habits *restrain* a family from getting to synergy.[1] A light review of the first five habits (drivers) and their opposites (restrainers) shows why.

DRIVERS	RESTRAINERS
Habit 1. Family members use their imagination and independent will to pursue creative ideas. They control their anger and emotions.	Family members are reactive. They think their way is the best way, and get angry when they do not get their way.
Habit 2. Family members are united in their purposes and values.	Family members are divided in their purposes and values. Each has selfish motives.
Habit 3. Family members make time to be together and focus on the things that matter most to the family.	Family members are so busy with less important tasks that they seldom come together to share ideas or explore solutions.
Habit 4. Family members have courage to express their ideas while considering others' ideas. Trust is high.	Family members have courage to express their own ideas but lack consideration for others' ideas. Trust is low.
Habit 5. Family members seek first to understand others' ideas without judging, and express their own ideas without attacking others.	Family members listen with the intent to evaluate and criticize others' ideas, while seeking to promote their own ideas.

↓   ↓

Synergy   **Chaos**

In short, the first five habits are instrumental to achieving the outcome of synergy in a family. Living opposite to any one of the habits presents a barrier to synergy, and will likely lead to chaos. Habit 6 will now add principles and skills that can drive a family toward getting to synergy. They include:

- Choosing humility over pride
- Maximizing strengths, minimizing weaknesses
- Discovering unity amidst diversity
- Going for the third alternative
- Letting children lead
- Surrounding your family with greatness

CHOOSE HUMILITY OVER PRIDE

No single factor restrains synergy in families more than pride. For synergy to occur, the principle of humility is needed.

One of the most common forms of pride is the need to be right all the time—to always have things your way. A friend of mine shared an experience he had with his son, and how it required him to overcome his pride in thinking that his way was always the right way.

After one week of practice, my son told me he wanted to quit the high school basketball team. I told him that all our other sons had been basketball players and that the hard work and cooperation involved in being on a team helped them mature. I felt it would help him too.

With some emotion, my son replied, "Dad, I'm not my brothers. I'm not a good player. I have other interests besides basketball."

I listened but was so upset that I eventually walked away.

For the next two days, I felt frustrated each time I thought of this son's decision. Several more times I tried to talk to him, but he simply would not listen.

Finally, I began to wonder what had led him to make the decision to quit. I determined to find out. At first, he didn't want to talk about it, but after some time he began to get teary-eyed, and said, "Dad, I know you think you understand me, but you don't."

He expressed the pain he felt when constantly being compared to his brothers. He said his coach expected him to play ball as well as his brothers. He felt that if he went down a different path and blazed a new trail, then the comparisons might end. He said he felt I favored his brothers because they brought me more glory than he did.

His words humbled me. I knew that what he said about the comparisons with his brothers was true. I apologized. But I also told him that I still thought he would benefit from playing ball, and he still insisted on quitting.

Finally, I asked if he liked basketball. He said he loved basketball but disliked all the pressure associated with playing for the high school team. He said that what he would really like was to play for the city league team. He just wanted to have fun playing without trying to conquer the world. I slowly found myself feeling good about what he was saying.

He started telling me the names of the guys that would be on the city team, and I could sense his excitement at

playing with them. I asked when the city league team
played games so that I could attend. He told me he wasn't
sure, and then added, "But we need to get a coach or they
won't even let us play."

At that point, a new idea came into both of our minds
at the same time. Almost in unison we said, "I/You could
coach the team!" And all of a sudden my heart felt light
as I thought about how much fun it would be to coach the
team and to have my son as one of the players.

The weeks that followed were among the happiest of all
my athletic experiences. They provided some of my most
memorable experiences as a father. And my son—who had
hated to have the high school coach shout at him—would
beam each time I would shout, "Way to go, son! Good shot!
Nice pass!"

That basketball season transformed the relationship
between my son and me.

I admire how this father set aside his pride and humbly accepted that there might be a better way than his. The solution
turned out to be not his way or his son's way but a better way.

Consider another situation. In this case, the pride was
deeply ingrained in a long history of anger and negative
emotions from a broken marriage. It took a lot of humility to
overcome the pride and to be open to exploring synergistic
solutions:

When I first met my wife, June, she had a six-month-old
boy named Jared. She had married her ex-husband, Tom,
when they were very young and neither was ready for

marriage. They divorced when June was five months pregnant, and many bitter feelings remained on both sides.

After June and I married, I took a job that required us to move to another state. Maintaining and arranging monthly visitation rights became very complicated due to the distance, but even more because the feuds between June and Tom never ended.

I did most of the communicating between June and Tom because half of the times that Tom would call, June would get mad and hang up. She would also often leave before Tom showed up for visitations. This went on for five years. June wanted things her way; Tom wanted things his way. Neither was about to budge from their opinions.

I knew there was a lot of good in both June and Tom. I sensed that if they could just be focused on doing the best thing for Jared, they could work some things out. So I encouraged them to have a discussion and talk things out, and with time they agreed to do it.

I called my friend Adam who facilitates the 7 Habits, and he agreed to work with them. Adam taught them about empathic listening. He taught them how to set aside their autobiographies and really listen to the words and feelings that were being expressed. He also taught them about win-win thinking.

Adam then offered June the chance to share some of her deepest feelings. When she finished, he said to Tom, "Now, Tom, what did June just tell you?"

Even though June had not said the exact words, Tom sensed her inner feelings and said, "She's afraid of me. And she's afraid if I one day lose my temper I might hit Jared."

June was wide-eyed. She realized that Tom had been able to hear more than just her words. She said, "That's exactly how I feel deep down in my heart. I'm worried that one day you could easily lose it and hurt Jared—like you did with me."

Next, Tom expressed his feelings. And after Tom expressed himself, Adam asked June, "What did Tom just say?"

June replied, "He said he's afraid of rejection. He's afraid of being alone. He's afraid no one cares at all about him." Even though she'd known him for ten years, June had had no idea that Tom had been abandoned by his father when he was young and that he was determined not to do that to Jared. She didn't realize how alienated he felt from her family after the divorce. For Tom it had been like being abandoned all over again.

June began to realize how lonely Tom had been during the divorce. She began to understand how his declaration of financial bankruptcy a few years earlier had made it impossible for him to get a credit card or rent a car. So when he came to visit Jared he was always alone in a hotel room and with no transportation.

In short, once June and Tom started to truly understand each other, they discovered that there was not a single thing on either of their lists of desires for Jared that the other did not also want. They talked for three hours. Independently, they each told me later, "You know, none of this is about Jared. It's about the lack of trust between the two of us."

From then on, the atmosphere was much more congenial. June said to Tom, "When I come down next month for my visitation, let's make time to talk some more."

I thought, "Is this June talking?"

When we dropped Tom off at his hotel with Jared, June asked, "What time are we picking Jared up tomorrow?"

Tom replied, "Well, my shuttle to the airport leaves at four p.m."

"Let us take you to the airport," she said.

"That would be great, if you want to," he replied with some surprise.

"No problem," she replied.

Again I was thinking, "Wow! This is a major turn-around!"

A few weeks later, June went to California for her visitation. One of her issues of contention was that Tom never acknowledged what he had done to her. But when they had their talk, for the first time Tom humbly apologized to her in great detail. "I'm sorry for pulling your hair. I'm sorry for taking drugs. I'm sorry for walking out on you." And this led to June swallowing her pride and admitting, "Well, I'm sorry for what I did too."

June said to me, "The understanding, the letting go, and the forgiving was so unleashing." She even went so far as to say, "Maybe when Tom comes up here we could let him use one of our cars." And again I thought, "Is this really June?"

They're now at a state in their relationship where they are talking about how to make the visitations easier on each other and more beneficial for Jared. It's a whole new world.

As was evidenced in this story, our temper can keep us from getting to synergy and our pride can keep us there. It took much humility and several habits—particularly

Habit 5—before Tom and June were able to swallow their egos and rise above the hatred that had been festering between them for years. It freed them to be open to each other's ideas and to see a new vision of possibilities for doing what was best for Jared.

Living with family members' differences can be hard. Especially when we think our way is always the right way. Is there a relationship in your family where pride is getting in the way of resolving a conflict or finding a synergistic solution to a challenge?

MAXIMIZE STRENGTHS, MINIMIZE WEAKNESSES

Another key to synergizing in a family is found in this one sentence: Never define a person by their weaknesses; always define them by their strengths.

> Never define a person by their weaknesses; always define them by their strengths.

As I mentioned, Sandra and I are better together than we are alone. We are a complementary team.

To *compliment* someone is different than to *complement* them. "Compliment" means you say something nice about the person. "Complement" means you have a strength that makes up for their weakness. So in our case, Sandra's strengths complement and compensate for my weaknesses, and my strengths complement hers. Complementary families occur when each family member's strengths are maximized and their weaknesses are minimized within the family.

I worked with a man who was full of positive energy, but the executive to whom he reported at the office was full of negative energy. When I asked the man how he dealt with this, he responded, "I see my responsibility as finding out what is lacking in my boss and then I do my best to supply what he lacks. My role is not to criticize him but to complement him." Would your family be any different if all family members took that approach to dealing with each other's weaknesses?

Notice how the wife in the following relationship learned to optimize her husband's strengths and minimize his weaknesses:

My husband and I have very different thinking styles. I am more logical and sequential, more left-brained. He is more right-brained and sees things more creatively, holistically, and compassionately.

When we were first married, these differences created a real problem in our relationship. He was always looking for new creative alternatives and new options, so it was natural for him to change course midstream if he thought he saw a better way of doing things. On the other hand, I tended to be more methodical, diligent, and precise. Once we had a clear plan, I would work out the details and stay the course—no matter what.

This gave rise to a number of challenges when it came to making decisions together. We were both caught up in our own ways of thinking and wanting things our way. The only way we could make decisions was if we would both compromise.

For a time, we tried to divide areas of responsibility and work on things separately, and in this way we were both contributing to the marriage and family in our own areas of strength. But then we discovered how we could use our differences to create synergy, and it brought us to a new level of richness in our relationship.

For example, we discovered that we love to write together. He comes up with the big concepts, and the creative ways of presenting things, while I act as a sounding board, organize the content, and get it all in writing. And we love it!

This has brought us to a whole new level of contribution and togetherness.

This husband and wife team went from tolerating each other's differences to valuing their differences, and even to celebrating their differences. They became a complementary team.

This same synergistic spirit is captured by a father I know. He said he had always hoped his children would marry spouses who would *fit* into the family, but to his delight his children married spouses who *added* to their family. The spouses brought talents, knowledge, hobbies, experiences, humor, games, spirituality, and cleverness that his family did not have prior to their joining the family. This turned the family into even more of a complementary team, and brought greater opportunities for synergy.

To get to synergy you must be able

> To get to synergy you must be able to say sincerely to others, "The fact that you and I see things differently is a strength, not a weakness, in our relationship."

to say sincerely to others, "The fact that you and I see things differently is a strength, not a weakness, in our relationship." It's a strengths-based paradigm, not a weaknesses-based paradigm. It recognizes that without differences there's no basis for synergy, no option to create new solutions or opportunities.

Insight from Sandra

Perhaps you have experienced something similar to what I have experienced.

A family struggles with a particular family member. Their relationship is very toxic. Then a tragedy happens and that family member dies. A memorial service is held and all that is said about the person is how amazing and wonderful they were: "He would do anything for me." "She was the one who helped me through my teen years." And on and on goes the raving praise for the person. Little, if anything, is said about their faults.

My question is: Why do people wait until the funeral to focus on people's strengths and minimize their weaknesses?

DISCOVER UNITY AMIDST DIVERSITY

Getting to synergy requires both unity and diversity. So how does that work?

Some years ago, a neighborhood dinner event was organized for couples. It was mostly intended to be a social gathering for the couples to get to know each other, but a guest speaker was invited to draw extra interest. The speaker on this particular night was a family counselor with expertise in how to resolve conflicts in marriages and families.

At one point during the counselor's presentation, a woman in her early forties stood up and boastfully declared that she and her husband had never had an argument in ten years of marriage. They had never even raised their voices toward one another—never. The other couples mostly stared in silent disbelief as the woman went on and on about her marital bliss.

But then, a long-time married woman had finally heard enough. She called out from the back of the room: "Oh, oh, oh! That's too bad! That's just horrible!" she roared. "I feel so sorry for you! You've missed half the fun of marriage!"

At that, the rest of the group burst into laughter.

It was clear to everyone that the older woman and her husband had experienced many vigorous quarrels during their years together. And my guess is that the younger woman and her husband had also disagreed on occasion but knew how to handle their differences without arguing or shouting. They knew how to "agree to disagree" without getting angry. Yet in both cases, the important point is that the couples did not allow their differences to make permanent cracks in their unity. They didn't allow their differences to tear apart that which mattered most to them—their unified commitment to their relationship and their family. Their unity was stronger than their diversity.

Mahatma Gandhi declared, "Our ability to reach unity in diversity will be the beauty and the test of our civilization."[2] He could just as easily have said, "A family's ability to reach unity in the midst of their individual diversities will be the beauty and the test of their family culture."

When family members are united in pursuing common goals and purposes, diversity is a strength. When family members are divided in their goals, values, and purposes, diversity can completely thwart a family's ability to achieve synergy. In fact, it may add to the chaos that already exists.

I arrived home one night after being away from our young children for three days. I was feeling somewhat guilty about my lack of time and connection with them. When I feel guilty, I tend to become lenient with the children, and may even relax the rules.

> "Our ability to reach unity in diversity will be the beauty and the test of our civilization."
>
> —Mahatma Gandhi

Because I was often away, Sandra sometimes compensated for my leniency by being stricter with the children. Thus the discipline system in our home was sometimes driven more by which parent was at home than by the consistent application of timeless principles. You know, "Who's in charge tonight, Mom or Dad?"

Well, when I came home that particular night, I went to the top of the stairs and yelled, "Boys, are you there?"

One of the younger boys ran down the hall, looked at me, and then shouted back to his brother, "Dad's home. He's in a good mood!"

What I didn't know was that the boys were in bed under the threat of their lives. They had goofed off and quarreled that night to the point that Sandra's patience had departed this universe. She had sent them to bed with a final command: "Now, you boys stay in bed—or else!"

So when the boys heard I was home and happy, they felt a new ray of hope.

We started wrestling around and having all kinds of fun until out came Sandra. With a mixture of frustration and anger in her voice, she shouted, "Are those kids still up?"

I quickly replied, "Hey, I haven't seen much of them lately. I want to play with them for a little while."

Needless to say, Sandra didn't like my response, nor did I like hers. So there were the boys watching their mom and dad argue in front of them.

The problem was that Sandra and I had not previously come to a unified agreement about how to handle such moments. We were divided. I had my objectives, and she had hers. I had my way, and she had her way. We were two good parents going in two different directions. The tension was tangible.

The solution to this problem was not worked out on the spot, but eventually Sandra and I talked. We came to a unified agreement that family was more important than the bedtime rule. If I got home late and hadn't seen the kids for a while, then playing with them was important and okay. But if I ever came home and Sandra was enforcing rules over relationships, then I knew there was a good reason behind her actions and not to oppose her. She had been with them while I was gone, so she knew the story behind the story—I did not.

In short, once we became united in our purposes and had an agreed-upon plan for bedtime, we knew exactly how to handle things and we did it without getting upset at each other. In other words, once we had achieved unity regarding our ends in mind, we could go for synergy on specific rules.

The top reason given for divorce these days is what is referred to as "irreconcilable differences." Yet a divorce lawyer once told me that of the couples who do stay together—who do stick it out—they have on average seven irreconcilable differences between them. But they are able to overlook the irreconcilable differences because they have a higher purpose—a united purpose—and are therefore able to minimize or overlook the weaknesses.

So if you are struggling to get to synergy as a family, a first step might be to go back to Habit 2 and identify what your united ends in mind are in regard to your family. Find higher purposes that unite everyone. Then use your differing strengths to pursue synergistic outcomes.

GO FOR THE THIRD ALTERNATIVE

Synergy occurs when something better is created by two or more people. Through the courageous expression of insights and deep empathic listening by everyone involved, a third alternative is born. It's not "my way" (first alternative); it's not "your way" (second alternative); it's "our way" (third alternative).

I'm going to share a real-life situation and invite you to think about how you would resolve it. Be thinking about what you would do if you were in the following situation, as described by a frugal wife:

My husband didn't earn much money, but we were finally able to buy a small house. We were thrilled to have a home of our own even though it put a crunch on our finances.

After living in the home for a month we became convinced that our family room looked shabby because of the old, worn couch that my husband's mother had given us. We decided that although we couldn't afford it, we needed a new couch. So we drove to a nearby furniture store and looked at the couches for sale.

We saw a beautiful couch that was exactly what we wanted, but we were astonished at the high price. A salesman approached us and asked, "How would that couch look in your home?"

We told him it would look grand. He suggested that it be delivered the following day. When we asked him how we could get it without any money, he assured us that it would be no problem because his company could defer the payments for two months.

My husband said, "Okay. We'll take it."

That's when I interrupted and told the salesman that we needed more time to think.

My husband replied, "What is there to think about? We need it now, and we can pay for it later." But I told the salesman that we would look around and then maybe come back. I could tell my husband was upset as I began to walk away.

We walked to a park and sat on a bench. He was still upset and hadn't said a word since we left the store. I decided to just listen and let him tell me how he felt so that I could understand his feelings and thinking. He told me that he felt embarrassed anytime anyone came to see our new home and saw that old couch. He told me that he worked hard and didn't think it was fair that his brother and others got paid much more than he did. He said that sometimes he felt he was a failure. A new couch would be a sign that he was okay.

His words sank into my heart. He almost convinced me that we should go back and get the couch. But then I asked if he would listen while I told him my feelings. He said that he would.

I told him how proud I was of him and that to me he was the world's greatest success. I told him how I could barely sleep at night sometimes because I was worried that we didn't have enough money to pay the bills. I told him that if we bought that couch, in two months we'd have to pay for it and we wouldn't be able to do it.

He said that he knew that what I was saying was true, but he still felt bad that he could not live as well as others.

This couple was faced with a difficult yet very common family challenge: How do we handle a lack of finances? Before I share the rest of their story, think about how you would suggest they handle the situation. Through conflict? Through compromise? Would you go with "his way" and buy the brand-new couch, or "her way" and not buy the brand-new couch? Or would you try to come up with a new solution, a third alternative? Once you have given this some thought, continue on with the story.

> We got to talking about how we could make our home more attractive without spending a lot of money. I mentioned that the local thrift store might have a couch that we could afford. I reached out and took his hand, and we sat there looking into each other's eyes.
>
> Finally, we decided to go to the thrift store. We found a couch there that was mostly made of wood. The cushions were terribly worn but I didn't think it would be too much trouble to re-cover them in some fabric that would match the colors of the room. We bought the couch for thirteen dollars and headed home.
>
> The next week I enrolled in a free furniture upholstery class. My husband used his woodworking skills to refinish the wooden parts. I found some gold fabric and went to work. Three weeks later we had a lovely couch.
>
> As time went by, we'd sit on those golden cushions and hold hands and smile at our prized possession. Years later it still looked great.

I applaud this couple. Think about the financial stress they avoided. Think about the satisfaction they must have felt in resourcefully using their diverse skills. Could you feel their joy as they combined their skills and created something beautiful together? Could you feel their relief at avoiding more debt? They didn't go for "my way" or "your way," they went for "our way," or a higher way. This is what is meant by going for the third alternative.

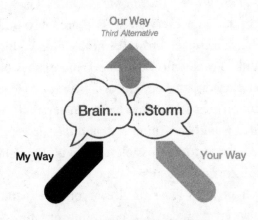

Going for the Third Alternative

In its most basic form, seeking the third alternative involves family members asking each other one question and making one commitment. The one question is: "Would you be willing to search for a solution that is better than what either of us is now proposing?" And the one commitment is: "I will sincerely listen to your ideas until you fully feel your ideas are understood."

To experience how the process of seeking the third alternative can work in your family, try the following activity. Identify an issue that needs to be resolved—an issue where family members have different points of view—then work together to answer the following questions:

1. *What is the problem or issue from everyone's point of view?* Really listen to one another with the intent to understand. Work at it until everyone involved can express

each person's point of view to that person's satisfaction. A problem well-defined is a problem half-solved.

2. *What are the key issues involved?* Once all viewpoints are expressed and everyone feels thoroughly understood, the next step is to break the problem down into logical chunks. People will often agree on more issues, or chunks, than they disagree on. This will help you to identify and focus on the parts, if any, that are in question.

3. *What would constitute a potentially acceptable solution?* Brainstorm possible solutions. Remember that brainstorming means that no one judges or evaluates other people's ideas until everyone feels understood. However, they can ask clarifying questions or offer spin-off ideas. Keep listening and bouncing ideas off of each other. Use your imagination. Stay open to others' ideas. Write down the ideas or solutions that are most feasible so that everyone can remember them and see all of them together.

4. *What option will be the best option?* This is the time when ideas get evaluated. So once you have all the ideas gathered, begin settling on a single solution while ensuring that it is a win for everyone. Remember that synergy takes time and might even involve going through some strong disagreements before you arrive at synergy. Don't give up. Eliminate ideas that are clearly not win-win, then prioritize the remaining ideas until there is a clear winner.

As you go through this process, I believe you will be amazed at the number of new ideas that open up and the shared excitement that develops when people focus on the desired outcomes and real solutions rather than on their egos and their own positions.

LET CHILDREN LEAD

Young children are often the last persons a parent considers involving when searching for how to resolve a family challenge. Yet Sandra and I learned early on that when dealing with matters that impact everyone in the family, leaving children—even young children—out of decisions is a mistake.

Sandra and I raised our children prior to the onslaught of the internet and social media. So in our day, the media battles we faced dealt mostly with watching too much television. Yet the same principles that applied in those days continue to apply to today's forms of too much digital-device screen time.

As parents, we had begun to feel that in many ways our television was like an open sewage pipe spewing into our home. We set up rules and guidelines to limit the amount of TV watching, but it seemed there were always pleas from our children for us to make exceptions. Constantly negotiating about what was and was not okay became a power struggle that caused frequent confrontations between us and the children.

Though Sandra and I agreed there was a problem with the television viewing, we didn't agree on the solution. I wanted to take an authoritarian approach inspired by an article I'd read about a man who threw his family's TV into the garbage can. But Sandra favored a more principle-based approach.

She didn't want the children to resent the decision or to feel it was not a win for them.

As Sandra and I synergized, we realized we were trying to solve this problem for the children when what we really needed to do was to help them solve it for themselves. So at our next family meeting we introduced the topic: "Television. How much is enough?" All the children paid attention so they could defend their opinion.

One son said, "What's so bad about television? There's a lot of good stuff on. I still get my homework done. So what's the problem?"

A daughter added, "If you're afraid we're going to be corrupted by TV, you're wrong. We don't usually watch bad shows. And if one is bad, we turn to a different channel."

Another said, "All the kids at school watch these shows. We talk about them every day. If we don't watch certain shows, we're socially out of it."

Sandra and I didn't argue, we just listened. The children all had something to say and we could see how deeply they were into their feelings.

Once all the children had expressed their opinions, we said, "Now let us see if we really understand what you've just said." We restated what we had heard until they agreed that we fully understood their positions.

Then we said, "Now we would like you to understand where we're coming from."

Before we even got started they said things like: "You just want to tell us all the negative things people are saying about watching TV."

We again held our tongues and listened empathically

while assuring them that that was not our intent. "In fact," we said, "after we've gone over these two newspaper articles together, we're going to leave the room and let you kids decide what you feel we should do about watching TV."

"You're kidding!" they exclaimed. "What if our decision is different from what you want?"

"We'll honor your decision," we said. "All we ask is that each of you be in total agreement about what you recommend we do." They liked the idea.

So together we went over the information in two newspaper articles we had brought to the family meeting that talked about the negative aspects of too much television. We particularly emphasized how it can interfere with family communication and relationships.[3]

After we shared this information, and to our children's continued surprise, we left the room. We asked them to invite us back when they had a solution with which they all agreed. About an hour later, we were invited to return for their verdict.

Our daughter Maria gave us the full report of what happened. She said that her brothers and sisters appointed her as the discussion leader. They knew she was an advocate for watching television, and they anticipated a quick resolution. At first they wanted to get their views known in a hurry so they could get back to their television shows. To satisfy us as parents, someone suggested that they all promise to do their household chores cheerfully and to get their homework done without being reminded before they watched television.

But then our oldest son spoke up about how the two articles had impressed him. He said that at times television had put some ideas into his mind that were not what he wanted. He felt he would be better off if he watched a lot less television. He said he felt the younger children in the family were starting to see things far worse than what he had seen as a young boy.

Then one of the younger children spoke up and told about a show he had seen that made him feel scared when he went to bed. At that point, the spirit of the meeting became very serious. As the children continued to discuss the issue, a new feeling began to emerge. They started to think differently.

One said, "I think we're watching too much television, but I don't want to give it up altogether. There are some shows I feel good about and want to watch."

When the discussion was over, they decided to determine how many hours each week—rather than each day—would be appropriate to watch TV. They all agreed that seven hours a week was about right, and they appointed Maria to monitor that the decision was carried out.

The decision proved to be a turning point in our family life. We began to interact more, to read more, and to play together more. We eventually reached the point where television was not an issue.

By involving our children in the problem, we made them participants with us in finding a solution. And because the solution was their decision, they were invested in its success. As I've said before, no involvement, no commitment.

As a result of our company's Leader in Me work with K–12 schools, two of the main paradigms teachers operate from are: "Everyone has greatness in them" and "Everyone can be a leader."[4] Students as young as five years old are involved in making significant decisions at these schools. They're given many opportunities to lead and to do things that the adults normally do, including interviewing new teachers. Almost always, the young students provide insights and solutions that the adults miss. Adults come to see the value in the students' perspectives.

Sandra and I have experienced these same kinds of results in our family. Our children have occasionally offered suggestions that have astonished us. There are even times when one of the children will need advice but Sandra and I will recognize that the best thing for us to do is to get out of the way and let a sibling provide the advice.

It's been interesting to watch families deal with the generation gaps that arise between parents who don't understand technology and their children who thrive on using modern technologies. I've seen cases in some non-English-speaking countries where parents speak little or no English but their children learn fluent English through school and the internet. Often the children learn technology words that have no translation in their native language. This creates a language barrier. The parents I've seen handle this best are those who essentially dump their pride and say to a child, "I need your help to teach me technology. Let's learn this together." They let their children lead, to be leaders of technology in their family.

So be thinking: What are some ways we can involve our children in important decisions? How can we give them more opportunities to voice their opinions and to lead the family to synergy?

SURROUND YOUR FAMILY WITH GREATNESS

I've had people say, "Stephen, synergy just doesn't happen in our family. We are willing to take the necessary steps but we don't have any creative ideas. We're not talented or smart like some families."

These people bring up an important point. There have been many times when Sandra and I had no idea how to solve a particular challenge we were having with a child or some other family matter. We simply didn't have the necessary expertise or resources. We could have synergized as a family for a month and still not achieved synergy.

> We came to realize that we do not need to be the experts on every topic or to have all the solutions ourselves.

We came to realize that we do not need to be the experts on every topic or to have all the solutions ourselves. There are other people who can help, such as a neighbor, extended family member, work colleague, friend, or professional counselor. There are also various experts whose ideas we have found in books, articles, or podcasts. We've learned to draw upon all these resources for help and advice. In fact, when we shared the two articles on television watching, it was as if we had invited two top consultants into our family meeting. It was free advice.

At times, children go through a stage in which they will listen to anyone on the planet before they will listen to or confide in a parent. They will trust a neighbor or a schoolteacher or a religious mentor or a sports coach or a relative or some other individual before they will go to Mom or Dad. It's just a stage. How grateful we are for those individuals who have offered their strengths and stepped into our children's lives at critical crossroads and helped us in ways we couldn't help ourselves.

We have introduced our children to marvelous individuals with all kinds of backgrounds. Their insights and examples have exposed our children to a wide variety of insights and inspiration for overcoming life challenges. From them, our children have absorbed ideas for how to solve their own challenges, or they have begun thinking about career options.

The point is simple. In addition to the combined greatness that already exists in their family, highly effective families surround themselves with outside greatness. They find ways to meet and learn from all kinds of people.

Insight from Sandra

Some parents think they need to wear capes and be superheroes. They try to be experts at everything and are embarrassed to admit when they are not. That sounds exhausting.

Families that are good at doing a lot of things

are the same families who are not afraid to ask for help. They're courageous and humble in saying, "We don't know how to do this. Can you teach us?"

They say, "We feel we can learn from you since you have already been through some of the same struggles we are facing. Would you be willing to join us for dinner and share with our son how you dealt with your challenge?"

So no, you do not need to have superpowers to be a good parent. But it does help to know a few people who do know how to soar in certain aspects of life.

THE FRUITS OF SYNERGY

So we have just explored some important principles and skills for achieving synergy in your family. I encourage you to review and think about them in terms of how they apply to your family. They are:

- Choosing humility over pride
- Maximizing strengths, minimizing weaknesses
- Discovering unity amidst diversity
- Going for the third alternative
- Letting children lead
- Surrounding your family with greatness

As you can see, synergizing is more than *tolerating* people's differences. Synergizing is more than *respecting* that people have different opinions. Synergizing is more than *valuing* people's diverse talents and backgrounds. Synergizing is more than *utilizing* people's differences. Synergizing at its highest level is about truly *celebrating* people's differences. Synergizing is based on the principles of creativity, cooperation, diversity, and humility, and it is strengthened by each of the preceding five habits.

Now, of course, not all decisions or challenges in a family require synergizing. In fact, some of the worst decisions are made by committee. Yes, sometimes "Mother really does know best" and she doesn't need a crowd of screaming children to tell her what to do. But when challenges grow emotional, when commitment is needed, or when solutions need a lot of creativity, then go for a third alternative. Go for synergy.

Small victories lead to larger victories.

And don't be discouraged if you are not able to solve your deepest challenges overnight. If you get hung up on a tough issue or family members start to quarrel over ideas, put the discussion aside and go back to it later. Break the problem apart and work on the easier portions first. Small victories lead to larger victories. Enjoy the fruits of synergy.

As you and your family establish the pattern of creative cooperation, and as you truly celebrate each other's strengths and make weaknesses irrelevant, synergistic opportunities will arise, outcomes will improve, and your family culture will arrive at a whole new place. Your family will deal with challenges and opportunities at a much higher level.

REFLECTIONS AND APPLICATIONS

With Self

Looking back over Habit 6: Synergize, what is the one idea or learning that if you were to apply it better would have the greatest impact on the well-being of your family?

_____

_____

_____

_____

With Adults and Teens

- Discuss the four potential outcomes that can happen when working together with other people that are found on page 253. Ask: How can 1 + 1 = 3 or more?
- Ask: Does our family celebrate differences? How could we improve?
- Discuss with your partner, if you have one: What differences initially attracted you to each other? Have those differences turned into irritations, or have they become the springboard for synergy? Together, explore: In what ways are we better together than we are alone?
- Discuss: What needs to happen for family members to be able to work together and to identify solutions that are better than any one family member can come up with on their own?

With Children

- Create a list of strengths for each family member, such as the sample chart of strengths below:

Mom	Dad	Maria
Loves crafts	Reads to us	Good with kids
Loves outdoors	Can fix anything	Plays piano
Great cook	Plays games	Likes to bike
Fixes bikes	Musical	Good organizer

Sam	Grandma
Fun	Great storyteller
Good at math	Amateur pilot
Artistic	Bakes pies
Good runner	Was a nurse

- Give family members a small stick. Ask them to break it. They probably will be able to do so. Now give them four or five sticks stacked together and ask them to do the same. They probably won't be able to do it. Use this as an illustration to teach that the family together is stronger than any one person is alone.
- Invite your children to plan and prepare a meal together. Encourage them to come up with dishes such as soup, fruit salad, or a casserole where each of the different ingredients adds unique value. Discuss what unique strengths each of your family members adds to your family's culture.
- Plan a family talent night. Invite all family members to share a talent, such as music, dance, sports technique,

scrapbooking, poetry, drawing, woodworking, or collecting. Point out how wonderful it is that we all have different talents to offer, and that an important part of creating synergy is learning to appreciate others' strengths and talents.

SHARPEN THE SAW

Renewing the Body, Mind, Heart, and Spirit

A common regret I hear from parents is that they have been so busy and so focused on their children or their careers that they have neglected to invest time developing themselves or their marriage.

A former husband shared this experience:

During our first year of marriage, my wife and I spent a lot of time together. We went for walks in the park. We went on bike rides. We had our own special times, just the two of us. It was really great.

The turning point came when we became heavily involved in separate careers. She was working the graveyard shift, and I was working the day shift. Sometimes it would be days before we even saw each other. Slowly, our relationship started disintegrating. She started building her circle of friends, and I started building mine. We gradually drifted apart because we didn't build on the friendship we had with each other. It eventually led to the end of our marriage.

A mother of three shared:

I graduated from the university in computer science and anticipated a promising career. But then I fell in love with a man who had a young child. He was well into getting his career started so we decided that he would continue to work and I would stay home with his daughter until she was old enough to start school. Then I too would enter the workforce.

The next thing I knew, we had three children and I was a very happy stay-at-home mom. I put my heart and every waking hour into our children. Meanwhile, my mother became ill and needed around-the-clock care. I watched her while my dad was at work and my children were in school.

I have no regrets for the time I devoted to my children and mother. But now that I am entering my forties and my mother has passed away, I'm wondering what to do next with my life. My computer skills are outdated and I've invested my entire married life into taking care of my family. I've never invested in me.

Lastly, a vice-president of a multinational corporation shared in a letter:

Summers are very busy for our family. Between my work travel and my children's summer camps and sports competitions, it feels like we never stop. In fact, I'm embarrassed to say that we seem to always get to the end of the summer, school is about ready to start up, and we realize that we did not take a family vacation—again. How do we get off this speeding train we call life so we can take a break and have a little fun?

Stories like these are familiar and common. Perhaps you can relate. We get so busy and so easily distracted that before we know it much of life has passed us by. The irony is that if we would pause long enough to make investments in ourselves and in our relationships, we would be better able to balance the many other things that keep us busy in life.

SHARPENING THE SAW

Sharpen the Saw is an odd name for a habit, so let me explain its origin.

Imagine you are sawing down a large dead tree. You've been sawing for hours and have hardly stopped for a minute to take a break, yet you are not quite halfway through the tree.

You look up and see a man nearby who has also been sawing a tree. You can't believe your eyes! He started the same time you did, his tree is the same size as your tree, and you've noticed that he has stopped every hour to rest. Yet he's nearly finished.

You ask incredulously, "Sir, how have you gotten so far so fast?"

The man smiles and replies, "You watched me stop every

hour to rest, but what you didn't see was that each time I rested I also sharpened my saw!"

When I share this scene with audiences and ask them to identify the moral of the story, many respond with a great big "duh!" In other words, they look at me as if the answer is so commonsensical that it is silly for me to ask.

"It's obvious," they say with a roll of their eyes. "Because the man stopped to sharpen his saw, he was able to cut through the tree faster. He got more done in less time." And they are correct.

That is when I ask my next question. If the answer is so commonsensical, why then, when it comes to real life, do so many people get so busy that they think they have no time to pause to sharpen their saws?

The saws I am referring to, of course, are not real saws, but represent four basic human needs—the physical, social/emotional, mental, and spiritual needs. These needs represent a person's body, heart, mind, and spirit, and I sometimes refer to them as the needs to live, to love, to learn, and to leave a legacy.

The four needs—or saws—can be described independent of each other yet they are highly integrated. When we neglect one saw, we to some extent neglect the others. For example, when a person is ill (physical saw), he will have less energy to socialize (social-emotional saw) or study (mental saw) or pursue meaningful causes (spiritual saw). The opposite is also true. When a person sharpens the physical saw and is healthy, she will be more fit to engage in social, mental, and spiritual activities. This is why I illustrate the four needs as overlapping circles—they influence one another.

In physics, failing to sharpen the saw leads to "entropy."

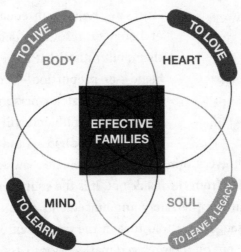

Four Saws for Families to Sharpen

Entropy means that anything left to itself will eventually deteriorate until it reaches its most elemental form. Neglect your body, it will deteriorate. Neglect your mind, it will deteriorate. Neglect your house, it will deteriorate. Neglect the family, it will deteriorate. Anything that is not consciously attended to and renewed will eventually deteriorate.

To avoid family entropy, family members must renew themselves in all four areas of life—as individuals and as a family.

WINNING THE DAILY PRIVATE VICTORY

When individuals neglect one or more of their four saws, the descriptions they often give of their life are: "My life is out of balance," or "I feel stagnant," or "I'm going downhill."

To have more balance in life does not imply that all

To avoid entropy, every individual and family must take time to renew themselves in all four areas of life.

four saws require an equal number of hours or resources dedicated to them, but rather that there is a right blend—or proportion—dedicated to each saw to match a person's specific needs. The right blend will be different for each individual and family.

As with every other habit, Sharpen the Saw works best when started from the inside out. It is the equivalent to what is heard during the safety announcements on an airplane. Adult passengers are told that in the case of an emergency they are to put on their oxygen masks prior to assisting others, including small children. It's not that the airlines don't like children. Rather, if the adult's oxygen needs are not cared for, who then will be able to properly care for the needs of the child?

The same concept applies to sharpening the four saws. If you do not take time to sharpen the four saws yourself, you will be in a lesser position to help other family members sharpen their saws. It's inside out.

Sharpening the saw personally is what I call winning the Daily Private Victory. Personally, I like to sharpen my four saws first thing each day. It's a routine that prioritizes the principle of continuous renewal into my busy schedule. If I wait until later in my day, it greatly increases the likelihood that I will skip it when my afternoon gets busy or I become tired in the evening.

So what might you do to win your Daily Private Victory in all four areas? You will know what works best for you, but a few examples include:

Physical saw: Exercising, eating healthy foods, cleaning the house, or getting more sleep

Social-emotional saw: Building friendships, being empathic, reducing stress, or having fun

Mental saw: Reading, writing, starting a new hobby, developing a talent, or gaining new knowledge

Spiritual saw: Meditating, serving others, reading inspirational literature, or renewing your commitment to principles

Doing something every day—even small things—in all four areas will help you build your individual capacity to help others and strengthen your family culture.

To win the Daily Private Victory may require you to say "no" to requests from others so you can take time for developing yourself. This may be awkward in certain circumstances and in the short run, but will prove tremendously beneficial in the long run.

One approach you can try is to tap your conscience at the start of each week and answer this question for each of the four saws: What is the one thing that, if I were to do it well each day, would have the greatest impact on my effectiveness as an individual and family member? Insert your answers below.

Physical saw: _____

Social-emotional saw: _____

Mental saw: _____

Spiritual saw: _____

Once you've identified your answer for each saw, make a commitment to do just one of those things each day for the next thirty days. Once you succeed at that commitment, pick another one and do it for the following thirty days.

Insight from Sandra

Sometimes what is needed most is time to get away—to enjoy some quiet solitude.

Our daughter Jenny called me after a rough day with her children. She was a tired, discouraged, and ready-to-explode mom. Any parent knows the feeling.

I listened to her. I consoled her. I affirmed her. And, because I had been through so many of those days myself, I was fully ready when she asked for my advice.

"Jenny," I said, "go get a chocolate candy bar and a Diet Coke. Then lock yourself in your bedroom where your husband and children can't get to you. Stay there for an hour. Relax. Do something you want to do for you."

In other words, give yourself the quiet break you need and deserve. Read a book. Exercise. Call a friend and thank them for their influence. Or do nothing.

Every person deserves a personal safe

haven—a quiet place to retreat and find daily
refuge. But be sure not to forget the chocolate.

SHARPENING THE SAW TOGETHER

At this point, some readers may want to shout, "STEPHEN,
you have no clue how busy I am! You've never been in my
shoes. How dare you expect me to find time to invest in myself or win the Daily Private Victory!"

I am sensitive to people's busy schedules and pressing situations. Sandra regularly informs me that I should know better than to tell her or any other busy parent what to do with
their time. Especially not a parent who is in survival mode
and just trying to get from one day to the next.

That said, I will note that for as busy as she is, Sandra
is a master at winning the Daily Private Victory. One way
she does it is by sharpening the saw with one or more of our
children or grandchildren. She finds creative ways to make
sharpening the saw a family activity. And she makes it fun.
In fact, if you ask most children which habit is their favorite,
they will typically say Habit 7. Why? Because they see it as the
habit that includes having fun.

For me, many of my happiest times nowadays are when
I am with our grandchildren. I can be sharpening any one
of the four saws with any one of the grandchildren—or with
Sandra—and I will be happy.

I'm impressed with the extent to which the following busy

father went in order to sharpen the saw together with his family. As a trained engineer from the Caribbean, he emigrated to New York City where he found himself doing his best just to survive, let alone to sharpen the saw. He shared:

I moved with my wife and two young children to the Bronx. I was lucky to get a job as a construction site inspector, which meant I drove around in a truck all day and most evenings to inspect various construction projects. I liked my job, even though I really struggled with speaking English and I never got to see my family. My two kids were always about to go to bed when I arrived home from work. They were growing up without me.

When I heard about Habit 7, I thought, "What can I do? I work sixty hours a week. How can I possibly make renewal time for my family—physically, socially, emotionally, and spiritually?"

Then one evening I needed to visit two construction sites, and I asked my son and daughter if they would like to go with me. They jumped at the chance. In the car we started talking. My daughter said, "Papa, you say you could get a better job if you had better English. We can teach you." It was true. My kids had picked up English much better than I had. So I said, "Okay," and they started teaching me.

That one night turned into many nights. Two or three evenings a week I picked up my wife and children and, as we drove from one construction site to the next, they taught me how to speak better English. The children struggled with math, and I am an engineer and know my math,

*so I tutored them as we drove. They loved to visit the con-
struction sites of buildings in Manhattan. We sometimes
walked from one site to the next. I told them stories about
my childhood in the islands and what my parents taught
me about life.*

Notice how this father involved his wife and children in
sharpening their saws together while driving in a truck. As
they went from one construction site to the next, they taught
each other skills (mental saw), walked to and around sites
together (physical saw), bonded together (social-emotional
saw), and shared stories with family values (spiritual saw). All
of this was done within the very same periods of time that the
father had previously been alone in his truck.

Regular family mealtimes, weekly family time, family traditions, and one-on-one bonding times—all four systems, or
Family Big Rocks—are excellent times to sharpen the saw together on a weekly basis. What follows are a few sample ideas
for how a family might work together to sharpen each of the
four saws. Feel free to use the ideas as springboards to get you
and your family thinking about any other ideas that will best
fit your family's interests, resources, and abilities.

THE PHYSICAL SAW (TO LIVE)

Most any physical renewal activity that is done together as a
family has the potential to not only strengthen muscles and
improve health, but also to nurture the family culture.

Many families find ways to exercise together, whether it

Nature has a way of rewarding even the idle adventurer, providing a source of rest and stress reduction.

be in their apartment, at a park, or in a gym. Getting out into nature is a way some families like to sharpen the physical saw together. Nature has a way of rewarding even the idle adventurer, providing a source of rest and stress reduction. I know several families who like to camp, bike, fish, hike, bird-watch, or play favorite sports together as their way of enjoying the benefits of physical renewal. Other families go on diets together.

Another important way to sharpen the physical saw is to keep the family's physical living space clean and organized on the inside and outside. Our daughter Catherine tells about our family's "ten-minute program":

One tradition we had in our family was the "ten-minute program." Whenever we'd have a big party and there was a total mess left over—or the normal messes we created after school—Dad would stand up and say, "Okay, let's have the ten-minute program before we go to bed." That meant that every person in the family would work really hard for ten minutes to clean up the place. We all knew that if we had all nine children's hands working, it would go a lot faster than Mom or Dad's two sets of hands. We knew it wasn't going to be an hour-long process, and that made it nice.

We also had what we called "work parties." That may seem like a contradiction in terms, but that's what they were. We'd work really hard for three hours to get some-

thing done on a weekend, and we'd eat food and laugh and talk as we worked. We'd also do something fun afterward, and we'd look forward to that.

Working together outdoors can bring multiple benefits, as the following individual remembers:

One of my most vivid memories of growing up is working beside my father in our garden. When he first suggested the idea, my brother and I were excited. We didn't realize that it would translate into spending hours in the hot sun digging, getting blisters, and doing a lot of other things you don't necessarily associate with fun.

The work was hard but Dad worked alongside us. He took the time to teach and educate us so that we could see the vision of what an ideal garden would look like. This provided a great learning experience—from the first time we dug those holes and wondered what in the world we were doing, to a few months later when we were able to find great satisfaction in the fruits of our labors.

When I turned twelve or thirteen, it became a source of great joy to pick bushels of beautiful fruit—peaches and apples and pears—that rivaled the best fruits you've ever tasted, and tomato plants that grew to look like trees because of the care we gave them.

One of the greatest overall learning experiences I had during those years was in seeing what our family could accomplish together. Walking down those garden rows and knowing that we had done this was a source of incredible satisfaction for the whole family.

Working together in the garden not only gave this family time to be together and to get their hands in the soil, it gave them healthy food while acquainting them with how the principles of science and nature work—the laws of the harvest.

Indeed, there are many ways to sharpen the physical saw as a family. What is one way you can sharpen your physical saw with one or more family members?

THE SOCIAL-EMOTIONAL SAW (TO LOVE)

In today's turbulent world, one of the most important needs in a family is to have fun together—to just relax and enjoy each other. This can happen even while doing basic routines.

Our son David talks about some of the ways our family turned basic duties—like taking children to school—into fun and emotionally satisfying times:

I remember when it would be Dad's turn to drive the car pool to school. We'd have this whole car full of kids, and Dad would do the funniest, craziest things. He'd tell jokes. He'd get people to recite a poem or sing a song. He had everyone laughing.

As we got older, we would sometimes feel embarrassed by Dad's behavior. But he'd always say, "Okay. Crazy or boring—take your choice."

"Boring!" we'd say. "Don't embarrass us, Dad." So he would just sit there stiff and silent. But then our friends

would yell, "Crazy! We want crazy!" And off he'd go again being funny. The kids in the car pool just loved it. It was fun.

Holidays and family events are tremendously important times to sharpen the social-emotional saw together. Over the years, we've been accused of celebrating birth *weeks* instead of birth*days*. For an entire week, we focus on letting each child know how special they are to us. We take turns telling them what we love about them.

Thanks to Sandra, we've developed some fairly unique and fun family traditions around sharpening the social-emotional saw. We lived in Ireland for some time and Sandra has since carried on a few traditions related to its culture. As David remembers:

Mom was well known among my friends for her involvement in Saint Patrick's Day each March. She would dress up in her green leprechaun outfit and visit each of her children's classrooms. She would engage the whole class in singing Irish songs and telling stories with an Irish lilt in her voice. Then each child was given a shamrock cookie.

Sharpening the social-emotional saw does not require a lot of time or money. In fact, using kind words and making other small deposits in people's Emotional Bank Accounts are some of the most priceless ways to sharpen the social-emotional saw as a family. There's also not a much better way to sharpen the social-emotional saw with a family member than to offer them the gift of empathic listening—giving them the time to listen to whatever they want to say.

What is one new way you can start sharpening the social-emotional saw with one or more of your family members?

Insight from Sandra

We do some silly things as a family to sharpen the social-emotional saw and have fun. At times, this has come at the expense of Stephen and his bald head.

It started one evening during dinner when Stephen was called away for an important phone call with some key business executives. Our boys were anxious for him to get off the phone, and so they kept motioning for him to hang up. But Stephen just kept putting his finger to his lips in a hushing motion.

Realizing that their dad could not keep up his end of the phone conversation and keep them quiet at the same time, our sons saw his vulnerability. One son got a jar of peanut butter and started spreading it on Stephen's shiny bald head. Another put a layer of raspberry jam on top of the peanut butter, and a third son topped it with a slice of bread. In a matter of seconds, they had built a marvelous peanut butter and jelly sandwich on his head. There was nothing Stephen could do about it.

Every now and then the boys love to find an opportunity to repeat that scene. Fortunately for them and our entire family, Stephen understands the value of fun, and has willingly sacrificed his pride to allow it to happen.

THE MENTAL SAW (TO LEARN)

More important than children memorizing a bunch of random facts is children learning to love learning. Once they find that learning can be exciting and that the adults in their life love to learn, children themselves become enthusiastic learners.

I recently read some research that indicated the top reason why children don't read is that they don't see their fathers read. Years ago, I was shocked when our rather young son Joshua asked me if I ever read. I read a lot. In fact, I cover the equivalent of two or three books every week. Yet Joshua seldom saw me read. I recognized that as one of the mistakes I had made over the years. I wish I'd kept my studies more visible so that my children would have seen me reading more often. I also wish I'd been more conscientious about sharing with the children what I was learning in my reading.

There are many things a family can do to sharpen the

mental saw together. Reading books, watching documentaries, and visiting museums or historical sites are just a few. As Cynthia recalls, Sandra liked to use her captive audience of hungry children at dinnertime as opportunities to sharpen the mental saw together.

Mom was big on educating us during meals. She'd teach us about nutrition, eating customs of different countries, and about table etiquette. Whatever holiday or special thing was coming up, she would share something educational about it, and then we'd have a family discussion, all between bites. Those dinner table conversations got us interested in learning about the world.

We have found much joy over the years and a tremendous feeling of progress as we have identified various ways to discover new knowledge together as a family. Sean remembers:

Our parents took us everywhere. We went with them on trips. Dad took us with him on speaking engagements. We were exposed to a lot of good things. I feel this was a real advantage for me. My comfort zone in situations is really high because I've experienced a lot. I've been in the outdoors. I've been on survival treks. I've tried every sport at least a few times.

Teaching moments are some of the supreme moments of parenting and family life. They are times when you know you've made a significant difference in the life of another family member as a result of teaching them an important concept, value, or principle—such as the joy of learning.

What is one way you can sharpen the mental saw with one or more members of your family?

THE SPIRITUAL SAW (TO LEAVE A LEGACY)

The spiritual saw represents people's need for meaning in their lives—their sense of purpose. People want to feel of worth, to contribute, and to leave a legacy.

The spiritual saw is very personalized to a family and to each individual within the family. It can be of a religious nature or linked to some other form of moral meaning or hope that was spoken of in Habit 2. It involves having an outward focus—doing service for others or being involved in a cause that transcends self and often even family.

Sandra and I made the choice to give our children a religious upbringing. In raising our children, much of what we did to sharpen the spiritual saw as a family was connected to our belief system, which included reading religious materials daily as a family and attending worship services and activities at least weekly. We prayed together as a family daily, and Sandra and I prayed together each morning and night, regardless of whether we were happy or upset with each other. It reconnected us daily with our family values and what matters most to us. I imagine that our family was similar to many other religious families, regardless of which religion they claim. For example, this man's family experience was quite similar to our family's experiences:

> *When I was growing up, it was very important to my parents that we all worship together. At the time I didn't think it was important. I didn't understand why they thought it was important. But they did, so we all went to religious services together and I have to admit as young boys we were often bored.*
>
> *But as I got older, I began to notice that we were more aligned as a family than a lot of my friends were with their families. We had common values and goals. We knew what we all believed.*
>
> *We had lessons at home, where our parents would teach us about what was right and wrong. They would listen as we disagreed, then help us find answers and figure things out on our own. As I got older, I realized how much I learned as I listened to my parents. I learned what was important to them, what they were afraid of or concerned about. I realize that it really drew us all together.*
>
> *I remember when my grandma was in the hospital with cancer. A call went out to our entire family—aunts, uncles, and cousins. We all gathered in family prayer for her. The unity was overwhelming.*

I'm convinced that if you organize your family to spend ten minutes a day reading or listening to something that connects you with timeless principles or some type of moral meaning, you will make better choices during the day in every dimension of life. You will be more principle-centered and connected to what really matters most as a family.

Some families prefer to sharpen their spiritual saw by doing service in their neighborhood, community, or extended family. A wife and mother shared her family's experience with getting outside themselves and serving others:

My husband, Mark, grew up in a Polynesian village where people had to work together to survive. And my mom was always helping people, whether it was in our neighborhood or just someone she heard about that had a need. So Mark and I both grew up with a sense of working and serving together as a family.

When we married and began to have children, we decided that one of the values we wanted to instill in them was a sense of service to others. We've never had much in the way of financial resources, but we realized that there was something we could do: We could make quilts. A quilt is something people can use and appreciate, and tying a quilt is quite simple and something we could do and afford as a family.

So every year we piece together about twelve quilts for different families. We've just started one for a neighbor, who's going through a tough divorce, as a small way of showing our love for her.

The kids have been a big part of identifying people in need, and they really enjoy helping. We sit around the quilting frames and talk about a lot of things that are going on in everyone's lives, so it improves our family communication too. The children love to deliver the finished quilts, whether we do it secretly or not.

The great German philosopher, humanitarian, and Nobel Peace Prize winner Albert Schweitzer said: "I don't know what your destiny will be, but one thing I know: The only ones among you who will be really happy are those who will have sought and found how to serve."[1]

Yet some families make the mistake of thinking that serving others requires donating a lot of money or making some grandiose effort, such as feeding the homeless, rebuilding someone's house, raising money to pay for a medical operation, and so forth. So they give up on finding ways to serve, thinking they don't have the money, time, or resources to do it. But as the previous mother affirmed, many service opportunities can be done at very little to no cost.

> Nothing energizes, unites, and satisfies the family quite like working together to make a meaningful contribution.

Indeed, nothing energizes, unites, and satisfies a family quite like working together to serve others and to make a meaningful contribution to another family. To be a means to a meaningful end, such as rallying around an extended family member who is in need, is truly satisfying.

My own life has been profoundly affected by my sister Marilyn's example of contribution and significance as she lay dying of cancer. Two nights before she passed away she told me, "My only desire during this time has been to teach my children and grandchildren how to die with dignity, and to give them the desire to contribute—to live life nobly based on principles." She was thinking outside herself until the very moment she died. What a legacy she's left to our entire extended family!

Hans Selye, the father of modern stress research, taught that the best way to stay strong, healthy, and alive is to follow the credo "Earn thy neighbor's love."[2] By becoming involved in meaningful service-oriented projects as a family, you and your family members will end up the greatest benefactors.

What is one thing that your family can do together to serve another family or your community?

FAMILY VACATIONS

I feel it is important to make special mention of family vacations as a Sharpen the Saw activity that families can do together. All four saws can be sharpened during one vacation.

I give vacations special attention for two reasons. The first is because vacations make such lasting, bonding memories. In fact, few events are more renewing to a family than a vacation. Planning for a vacation, anticipating it, and thinking about it—as well as looking back at it and laughing about the fun times and the dumb things that happened—is enormously renewing to a family.

Over the years, Sandra and I tried to insert something physical, something emotional, something mental, and something spiritual into all of our family vacations. Yet we are living proof that vacations do not always go as planned. As Jenny reveals:

I remember when Dad decided he would take us camping. Our family has never been big on camping; in fact, we didn't know anything about it. But he was determined to make it a good experience.

*Absolutely everything went wrong. We burned our din-
ner, and it poured rain throughout the night until our tent
collapsed. Our sleeping bags were soaked clear through.
Dad woke us up around 2:00 a.m., and we gathered our
stuff and headed home.*

*The next day we laughed—and we continue to laugh—
about that miserable experience. Despite the disasters, it
created a sense of bonding. Since we had it as a common
experience, we could look back on it and talk and laugh
about it.*

While all of our vacations have not gone as perfectly as we
had hoped, I'm amazed at how often Sandra and I have heard
one of the children say: "Remember the time we were lost on
our vacation? That was hilarious," or "I can't stop laughing
when I think about you falling in the river that one year."
They frequently refer to family vacations that went wrong as
some of the best.

Vacations do not need to be expensive, distant, or lengthy
to be bonding. You can even do a "staycation" where you stay
at home or nearby and do fun things together. Some of our
best family vacations have been visiting a relative and staying
the night with them so that cousins and siblings can bond.

The second reason I make special mention of vacations is
because there is a growing trend for people not to take vacation time off from work. They get so busy on the job that they
fail to make time for a vacation. It's not the hourly, lower-
wage worker that is doing this most. It is the highly paid,
salaried executive who can't seem to make the time for a vacation. That's why many companies are now demanding that

employees take time off for vacation. They know what it can do to renew an individual and prevent burnout.

Finding the right work-life balance in a family may not be easy, but have you ever heard of someone on their deathbed wishing they'd spent more time at the office? Or at the shopping mall?

I find it most helpful to plan months in advance for a vacation. Put it on the calendar as a Big Rock and plan around it rather than wait for the right time to miraculously appear on your schedule—which seldom happens.

Insight from Sandra

Family vacations may be where our family developed our gift of humor.

For one vacation, we had everything planned to the minute. We had visits to historical places and all kinds of learning opportunities planned. We even planned out what we would discuss and do while driving in our car. But then, if something could go wrong, it did. It was miserable. The car kept breaking down. The weather was hot and humid. Our kids kept arguing over who would sit where in the car. We got lost and ended up sleeping in a parking lot one night. We skipped most of our pre-planned car discussions. And on it went.

One of the days was a holiday and, of course, the car's air conditioner quit. The temperature was at one hundred degrees when we limped into a mechanic's shop. He said he didn't fix air conditioners, and that no one else in town was open on that holiday.

We were all dripping in sweat. The mechanic looked at us like we were a bunch of rags. Suddenly, one of the children started to laugh at the bad news about all the shops being closed. Then everyone started to laugh. In fact, we started to laugh so hard that we all couldn't stop laughing.

We asked the mechanic, who undoubtedly thought we were crazy, for directions to the nearest amusement park. We put all the windows down and headed off to have some fun—hysterically laughing at our misery and at ourselves.

It was a trip we will never forget.

EXTENDED FAMILY ACTIVITIES

Another family Sharpen the Saw activity that deserves special attention is getting together with extended family.

I know of families where the siblings grow up best of friends, and then they go off to college, get into their careers, start families of their own, and from then on, the most they do together is to send an annual holiday card or make an occasional phone call. They never see each other. Their children do not get to know their cousins or uncles and aunts. Extended family entropy begins to set in.

Family times when bonds are made with cousins, uncles and aunts, grandparents, great-grandparents, and other extended family members can be precious and more powerful in your family members' minds than you think. I'm thinking of a family who planned for years to go on a special vacation to Disneyland. They were thrifty, saved their money, and blocked out the time to go almost a year in advance. But three weeks before the departure date, the seventeen-year-old son blurted out at dinnertime, "Why do we have to go to Disneyland?"

The son's question took the father by surprise. "What do you mean by that?" the father asked with some frustration. "It seems that nothing we plan as a family is as important to you as being with your friends."

"It isn't that," the son replied. "In fact, it's just the opposite."

His sister then spoke up. "I don't want to go to Disneyland either."

The father sat in stunned silence.

Then his wife put her hand on his arm. "Honey, your brother phoned today and told us his children are really sad that we're going to miss the family reunion campout at Kennally Creek this year. That is what's bothering the children."

Then everyone jumped into the discussion. "We want to see our cousins!" they all cried.

The father responded, "Hey, I want to see the family too. I'd really like to spend time with my brothers and sisters.

But I thought you all wanted to go to Disneyland since we go camping at Kennally Creek every year. I thought this time we'd do what you wanted to do."

The seventeen-year-old spoke up. "We do want to go to Disneyland, but we picked the wrong time. So can we change our plans, Dad?"

They did change plans. And everyone was happy.

The father later shared the background of Kennally Creek.

When I was young, we didn't have much money. We couldn't go on vacation to any place that cost a lot. So every year Mom and Dad would pack all kinds of food, we'd tie the old canvas tent to the top of the car, all the children would pile in like sardines in a can, and off we would go to the mountains of Kennally Creek. We did that every year.

Then one by one, all of us children got married and moved to different locations. The one way we stayed connected was that every summer we would all meet up at Kennally Creek campground.

The year after Dad died, we wondered if we should continue the tradition. Mom said that Dad would want us to do it, so we all went. This continued as the years passed, and each of us had children. We still gathered each year at Kennally Creek. Each night under the moonlight sky, my brother would play his accordion and all the kids would dance.

After Mom died, it seemed in our minds as if she and Dad came back every year and sat by the campfire with all of us at Kennally Creek. We could see them smile as they watched the grandkids dance and eat the watermelon that had been cooled in the stream.

Our family enjoys a similar extended family vacation each year in the mountains of Montana. It is a tradition started by my grandfather some forty-five years ago. On the shores of a lake, the children and grandchildren catch frogs under the dock, build sand castles on the shores, swim in the ice-cold glacier waters, catch fish, spot moose in the meadow, and play volleyball. As our son Stephen recalls:

When I was younger, we used to spend three weeks every summer at Lake Hebgen. It was so enjoyable that I would wish I could be there all summer. It was just so natural to pair up and do things together with our cousins. Everybody loved it.

Joshua adds:

Each year, Mom uses me to help carry out her family schemes and traditions of Lake Hebgen. Among other things, I help out with the traditional Pirate Treasure Hunt. In preparation, we "raid" the dollar stores, buying small dollar items to fill our pirate's chest. We then wrap the chest in huge black garbage bags, and pile into a boat—along with shovels and handwritten clues that are burned at the edges to look old and authentic.

We take the chest to what we call Goat Island, where we search for a place on the beach to bury the treasure. We cover the hiding place with clean sand and throw brush on it so that it looks untouched. Finally, we run all over the island leaving treasure clues in trees and shrubs, and under rocks. We scatter coins for the little kids to find.

Exhausted, we return to the cousins waiting eagerly back by the cabin. As we approach in our boat, Mom waves an old battered pirate flag with its black skull-and-bones logo and screams hysterically that we scared off some pirates who left their buried treasure behind.

Everyone—kids, grownups, and dogs—piles into boats, canoes, rafts, and inner tubes, and invades the island. We run from clue to clue until the treasure is discovered, the loot is distributed, and the tradition is complete.

Many families prefer their extended family activities to be more intimate, and to occur much more often. A couple in their seventies shared:

We have a tradition of having Sunday dinners at which our daughter, her husband, and their children are our guests. Each time, we invite one of the four married grandchildren and their family to join us. In this way we are able to talk peacefully with each family and find out how their lives are changing, what their plans and goals are, and how we might help with those plans.

Our Sunday dinners have been a tradition for thirteen years now. It brings us enjoyment to learn about our grandchildren, to see their growth, and to be part of an extended family.

Being a grandparent myself, I feel that grandparents must never become dulled by the "retirement paradigm" that says there is no longer a vital need for them to be involved in creating a nurturing family culture. You can retire from a job, but you never retire from the family. There is always a need for giving out affirmations, for meeting family members at their important challenging crossroads, for setting a vision of what the extended and intergenerational family is all about, for being a role model, or for providing a listening ear.

No matter who you are, no matter what your talents are, and no matter what your economic or physical status may be, I'm convinced that everyone **You never retire from the family.** can contribute to the extended family if they set their mind to it. The opportunities for intergenerational love and support keep growing as your posterity keeps growing.

I love the attitude of this single woman who is in her thirties and has always lived alone in her adulthood. Over the years she has focused within her Circle of Influence to make her immediate and extended family an ongoing priority:

> I recently bought my own home with the idea of having my entire family come over for holidays. I bought a large table and ten chairs to go around it. Now everyone who comes over says, "You're single. Why do you need this table?" And I tell them, "You don't know what this table represents. It represents our whole family being together. My mom can't cook anymore. My brother is divorced. My sister can't do it at her house. My cousins don't get together much these days. But being together and growing the family ties is important to me. And I want to do it here."

Some families frequently think about reaching out to extended family members but end up not getting around to it. What an omission. Effective families put extended family events on their calendars, sometimes months in advance. They make it a priority—a Big Rock.

Insight from Sandra

Aunts, uncles, grandparents, cousins, and other extended family members have had a tremendous influence on our family. One of Sean's recollections confirms our strong feelings about the power of the extended family. He wrote:

> One of the things I appreciate most about our family is the huge intergenerational support network. My kids are growing up very close to their cousins. A lot of them are the same age, and they're the best of friends. And I think this is going to make a tremendous difference when they are teenagers—and even into adulthood. They'll always have this huge network of support.

SHARPENING THE SAW BRINGS HEALING

Habit 7: Sharpen the Saw is founded on the principles of renewal, continuous improvement, and balance.

Sharpening the saw is one of the highest leveraged activities for individuals and families because it affects everything else we do in life. The four saws are all interconnected and over time they work together to create a robust, happy family culture—even in the turbulent times.

When sharpening the saw together, families further develop their sense of identity, grow in their feelings of connectedness, and come to feel a greater sense of hope. In it they find healing because true healing involves all four dimensions: the physical, the social-emotional, the mental, and the spiritual saws—all four.

> Sharpening the saw is one of the highest leveraged activities for individuals and families because it affects everything else we do in life.

So first find your own ways to win your Daily Private Victory, and then look for proactive, meaningful ways to experience the joy of sharpening the saw together.

REFLECTIONS AND APPLICATIONS

With Self

Looking back over Habit 7: Sharpen the Saw, what is the one idea or learning that if you were to apply it better would have the greatest impact on the well-being of your family?

_____

_____

_____

_____

With Adults and Teens

- Ask family members: What is entropy? Discuss the idea that all things need to be worked at and cared for continuously to stay strong, and how marriages, family relationships, and parenting skills are no exceptions. Discuss: In what ways might entropy become visibly evident in a relationship?

- Ask family members: In what ways are we as a family fulfilling our four basic needs—physical (to live), social-emotional (to love), mental (to learn), and spiritual (to leave a legacy)? In what areas can we improve to strengthen our family?

- Ask family members: What traditions have you enjoyed in our family? What traditions have you noticed in other families that you would like to implement in our family?

- Ask family members what extended and intergenerational family traditions they enjoy or would like to establish.

With Young Children

- Share the story of the person cutting wood on page 291. Ask what family things need to be continuously maintained and renewed in order for the family to grow and remain strong. Describe the four saws and examples of each.
- Ask: What would happen if we ever got too busy to buy gas? To buy groceries? To sleep? What happens when we get too busy to take care of our bodies, have fun, learn new things, or care for others?
- Exercise with your children. Play a sport with them. Go for regular walks together. Sign up for sports lessons or some other type of lessons that will grow children's skills.
- Attend age-appropriate cultural events together, such as plays, dance recitals, concerts, and choir performances. Encourage children to participate in activities that will help them develop new hobbies and talents.
- Involve your children in planning your family vacations. Ask what makes family vacations special for them.
- Become involved with your children in doing family service projects.

GIVING THE 7 HABITS A CHALLENGE TO SOLVE

Several thoughts may be going through your mind.

You may be thinking, "Wow! I want to implement every idea in this book. Where do I begin?"

You might be feeling panic: "Stephen, I already have more to do in life than I can handle. How do I find time to apply even one of the ideas?"

Or maybe you're debating, "I like some of the ideas in this book, but others do not fit my family. Which should I apply?"

What I hope you are not thinking is, "It's too late for my family. We're a mess."

It's never too late to start providing strong leadership in a family. Yet it is also not easy. Trying to nurture the tender feelings and lives of family members can be delicate work.

> It's never too late to start providing strong leadership in a family.

As I have mentioned from the beginning, Sandra and I have built our family culture over several years, not overnight. As you have seen from the stories in this book, our family was not the perfect family, and Sandra and I were not the perfect parents. We've made many mistakes in raising our children. We are still working on our family, and mostly on ourselves.

If there is any one thing we have done really well, it is that we have never given up. The family is too important not to keep trying.

I have shared some of the approaches Sandra and I have applied over the years, including what has and has not worked for our family. I have shared examples of what other families have done. I have not shared them with the intention that they now become a to-do list for you or your family. Rather, the principles and ideas I have shared are meant to be a library of sorts, filled with ideas for you to choose from and adapt to your unique family needs and interests.

But again comes the question of where to begin. In this final chapter I offer four practical approaches for you to consider when deciding how you and your family can best apply the 7 Habits to your specific needs, challenges, and interests. But first, let's review the main insights from each chapter and habit.

LOOKING BACK

From the opening pages, I have acknowledged that all families—even great families—are off course much of the time. Our turbulent world places so many challenges— "grizzly bears"—and distractions in front of us that all families need to course correct at times. And that's okay. The important thing is that we keep trying.

I indicated that I had three main purposes in writing this

book. The first was to emphasize the importance of the family. The second was to highlight your role as a leader in your family. And the third purpose was to demonstrate how the 7 Habits can be of great worth in developing a nurturing family culture and in addressing your family challenges. I further suggested a few ways to create change in a family, including starting with yourself, working from a strengths-based paradigm, living by principles of effectiveness, involving your family members in learning about the habits, and being patient and realistic, as if you were nurturing a tender plant.

Finally, I pointed out that this book is a first-aid resource. If your family has deeper challenges or finds that you cannot resolve your challenges on your own, I encourage you to seek professional guidance from a trusted source.

I then spent the remainder of the book describing the 7 Habits and sharing some family applications. A brief summary of each habit follows:

Habit 1: Be Proactive. Effective individuals and families take the initiative to act on life rather than merely allowing life to act on them. They are influenced by their genetics and environment, but their choices are not entirely determined by them. They use their four unique human gifts—self-awareness, conscience, imagination, and independent will—to grow their freedom to choose and to make wise choices. They work within their Circle of Influence to take an inside-out approach to creating change. They take responsibility for their moods, actions, and thoughts, and use proactive language. They act as transition people to stop negative patterns of past family events and behaviors. Habit 1 is the key that unlocks the power of the remaining six habits.

Habit 2: Begin with the End in Mind. Effective individuals and families create a mental vision for the projects, goals, and activities they pursue. They identify their values, purposes, and destinations, and capture them in personal and family mission statements. They keep their values alive by telling stories that support their family values, and by communicating each other's worth and potential. This helps them to address the lack of identity, connectedness, and hope that is at the root of many family challenges.

Habit 3: Put First Things First. Effective individuals and families organize their time based on their most important priorities—their Big Rocks. They keep their main things the main things by looking at their life through the paradigms of: first relationships, then schedules; first effectiveness, then efficiency; and first importance, then urgency. They set up systems to ensure they keep their focus on what matters most, including: regular family meals, weekly family time, one-on-one bonding times, and family traditions. The key is that they proactively schedule their priorities rather than reactively prioritizing their schedules. They plan weekly and adapt daily, and stay true in their moments of choice by saying no to unimportant activities that try to creep into their weeks and days.

Habit 4: Think Win-Win. Effective individuals and families build trust by making deposits in each other's Emotional Bank Accounts. As examples, they do little kindnesses, express sincere apologies, stay loyal to the absent, honor promises and commitments, and forgive each other. They don't think selfishly (win-lose) or act like a martyr (lose-win) or go for revenge (lose-lose). Instead they balance courage and consideration to foster mutual benefit (win-win). They are happy for the successes of others, and think "we" not "me." They use win-win agreements to establish and meet win-win expectations.

Habit 5: Seek First to Understand, Then to Be Understood. Effective individuals and families listen empathically when emotions are high. They use their ears, eyes, and heart to capture both the content and the feelings of what others say. They diagnose problems before they prescribe solutions. Once they understand and once others feel understood, they then seek to effectively communicate their own thoughts and feelings by giving constructive feedback. They use "I" messages to share their feelings and feedback without attacking people, and improve family communication by making their digital devices a family friend. With the right intent and the right communication skills, they build mutual understanding and lasting relationships.

Habit 6: Synergize. Effective individuals and families maximize each other's strengths and minimize weaknesses. They don't go for conflict (1 + 1 = 1/2 or less), compromise (1 + 1 = 1 1/2), or teamwork (1 + 1 = 2), but rather they go for synergy (1 + 1 = 3 or more). They seek third alternatives when solving problems and generating new ideas. They don't think in terms of "my way" or "your way" but in terms of "our way"—a higher way. They don't just tolerate diversity, they celebrate and optimize it. They utilize and expand their family strengths by letting children lead and by surrounding themselves with greatness.

Habit 7: Sharpen the Saw. Effective individuals and families strive to maintain and continuously improve their effectiveness through winning the Daily Private Victory. They renew themselves regularly by fulfilling four basic human needs: physical, social-emotional, mental, and spiritual. By renewing themselves first, they put themselves in a better position to help others renew. They look for ways to sharpen the saw as a family by doing such things as exercising together; learning together; having fun together; or doing meaningful, inspiring things together.

LIKE A SPIRAL STAIRCASE

The 7 Habits are not a one-time event. They are an ongoing way of living.

If your family is like most families, some days your family culture is in close alignment with the 7 Habits—you are a highly effective family. Other days, you may be far from living the habits and feel like you're a highly defective family. You may even be highly effective one minute and highly defective the next. But the hope is that you will become a little better with each day, week, and year.

You may relate to the parent who wrote to me, "Stephen, our family finds it hard to live by these principles at all times, but we find life much, much harder when we don't!" Yes, living the 7 Habits may not be easy, but living by their opposites makes life even more challenging than it already is.

I view living the 7 Habits as an ongoing process of progress. I compare it to climbing a spiral staircase. Imagine a spiral staircase where each step represents one of the 7 Habits. Step 1 is Habit 1. Step 2 is Habit 2. And so forth. When you get to step 7—or Habit 7—you discover that the next step turns out to be Habit 1 again. Only this time, you are seeing

Habit 1 at a whole new level because living Habits 2 through 7 has taken you to a higher level. At this new and higher level, you are in a position to become even more proactive, and to apply Habit 1 to more areas of your life.

Insight from Sandra

A few years ago, one of my dearest friends, Carol, developed cancer. After months of operations, radiation, and chemotherapy, she accepted what her ultimate fate would be. She never asked, "Why me?" There was no bitterness or feelings of despair.

Carol's whole perspective on life changed. "I don't have any time for things that don't matter," she told me. "I know what's important and where to put my priorities."

Carol's courage touched my heart as I watched her strengthen her relationships with her husband, children, and other loved ones. Her utmost desire was to serve others, contribute, and somehow continue to make a difference to the end. Her death made all of us who loved her want to become stronger people—more willing to love, care, and serve—and more desirous to spend our lives doing only the things that matter most.

I watched Carol apply every one of the 7 Habits in her remaining days. In a real sense, she mentally wrote her mission statement for life on her deathbed, and then carried it out until the day she died. She inspired me to take the way I apply the 7 Habits to a new level.

CHOOSE ONE APPROACH AND ONE CHALLENGE

I truly believe the 7 Habits can help you and your family to build a more nurturing family culture and address your family challenges. But it is far better to make a proactive plan for how to go about it. There are four general approaches to consider:

1. Start with yourself
2. Strengthen a family relationship
3. Work on the 7 Habits as a family
4. Contribute to your community

The four approaches can be thought of as a series of concentric circles rippling from the inside out. By starting with yourself, you will see your influence expand outward to where it touches one of your family relationships. From there it will

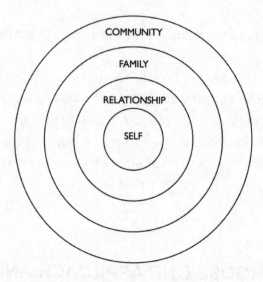

impact your entire family, and from there it will ultimately have the potential to reach your community.

I strongly recommend that you choose only one approach to work on at any given time. Within that one approach, I recommend that you identify only one challenge to work on. Don't try to solve all of life's challenges at once. You can always apply other approaches to other challenges at a later point.

As I said earlier, the 7 Habits are at their best when they have a challenge to solve. In fact, my experience is that the greater the challenge, the more relevant the 7 Habits become. You can take almost any challenge you have and use the habits to create a plan for addressing the challenge. (For examples of common challenges families face and sections in the book that relate to those challenges, see the Challenge and Opportunity Index on page 349.)

Approach 1: Start with Yourself

I always suggest that you consider starting with yourself when attempting to improve a family culture. What families need most is fewer critics and more models.

When we are not at peace with our lives, it is often because we are living in violation of our conscience. We know it and we feel it.

> What families need most is fewer critics and more models.

If we know that we are personally doing things that are disrupting the family culture or disturbing a specific relationship, then why not start by working on ourselves? After all, by improving ourselves we automatically improve our family's culture.

Yet you may be wondering, "How much can I realistically do? I'm only one person in the family. No one even fully respects me. How much impact can I really have?"

Think of yourself as a trim tab for your family. A trim tab is the small rudder that moves the big rudder on a ship or airplane. It's small but its movements ever so gradually change the direction of the entire boat or plane. So while you may feel your influence is insignificant, trust me, you can become a direction-setting trim tab for your family—a leader.

Let's say you have a challenge controlling your anger and you want to overcome it because you feel it is harming your family. In reviewing the pages of this book, you then may choose to focus on Habit 1: Be Proactive, and most particularly the section dealing with Pause, Think, and Choose. Or you may realize that your anger is often the result of your not listening empathically, and so you decide to work on listening empathically more often to avoid misunderstandings that lead you to get angry. Or you may decide that your anger is a function of not getting enough sleep, so you may choose to work on sharpening your physical saw. In this one example, you can see how you can use multiple habits or simply one concept within a habit to address the challenge you select.

If you decide to take approach 1 and start with yourself, I suggest that you begin by tapping your conscience and being 100 percent honest with yourself. Think about what you have read in this book and how it applies to your family, then ask yourself: What is the one thing I will commit to **start** or **stop** doing that will have the greatest impact on my family and its culture? Hint: The first or second thought that comes to your mind will often be the challenge you choose to work on, because you will recognize that it has been working on your mind for some time.

Your Commitment: _____

_____

_____

Once you have identified your one commitment, flip through the pages of this book looking for any ideas or concepts that will help you keep your commitment. Then make a plan for how you will go about keeping your commitment. Keep the plan simple but think in terms of it being a thirty-day plan, which is long enough for it to become a habit but not so long that you lose sight of it. Once you have your plan, I recommend that you share the plan with an accountability partner, someone you trust and who can help you achieve your plan by giving you helpful tips, checking up on you, encouraging you, and celebrating progress with you.

Approach 2: Strengthen a Family Relationship

Dag Hammarskjöld, the former secretary-general of the United Nations, said, "It is more noble to give yourself completely to one individual than to labor diligently for the salvation of the masses."[1] Sandra likes to rehearse that statement to me from time to time as a gentle reminder that in spite of the fact that I am constantly in front of large audiences around the world, my most important audiences—or relationships—will always be within our home.

So a second approach to applying the 7 Habits is to focus on improving a single family relationship. The relationship may involve a spouse, a partner, a sibling, a parent, the child who tests you the most, or an extended family member. Once again, the relationship you choose will often be the first or second relationship that comes to mind because it has been on your mind for some time.

Once you have identified the specific relationship, then go back through the pages of this book looking for suggestions of what you can do to strengthen that one relationship. In many cases, more than one habit or concept will be relevant. For example, suppose you and your partner are experiencing too much contention. You might make a worksheet like the one below and then skim through each chapter and consider how each of the 7 Habits might help you to improve the situation.

The situation: *Too much contention with my spouse/partner.*

HABIT	SAMPLE IDEAS
Habit 1: Be Proactive	*I will work on controlling my own temper. My pause button will be to take a deep breath and say, "I don't want to say any more until I calm down."*
Habit 2: Begin with the End in Mind	*When contention arises between us, I will affirm my husband's worth to me and tell him I don't want to contend with him.*
Habit 3: Put First Things First	*If the contention does not deal with a Big Rock or something important to me, I will not pursue the issue further.*
Habit 4: Think Win-Win	*Instead of insisting I win, I will look for ways we both can win.*
Habit 5: Seek First to Understand, Then to Be Understood	*When an argument starts, I can say, "Let's give each of us a chance to express our feelings. You go first."*
Habit 6: Synergize	*I'll do better at pointing out my husband's strengths, not just focusing on his weaknesses.*
Habit 7: Sharpen the Saw	*I'll watch an internet video or read an article on effective ways to resolve contention.*

Now that you have viewed an example, identify the one family relationship you want to improve, create a simple worksheet like the one above, and then go through the book to identify ways each habit can help you improve the relationship. Again, keep it simple. Choose only one or two ideas from the list of ideas you generate and work on those ideas for thirty days.

Approach 3: Engage the Entire Family

A third approach to applying the 7 Habits is to engage your family in working together on a challenge or series of challenges that will improve the family culture.

One way to do this is to ask family members: What is the one thing out of this entire book that we can **start** or **stop** doing that will help us to be a better family? Based on the answer that family members agree is the one thing to work on, develop a plan for addressing that one thing.

A second way to engage the entire family is to go through the book one habit at a time. As a family, identify for each habit the one most important thing you can do to apply that habit better as a family. Make a plan for doing that one thing for thirty days and commit each other to following the plan.

In the end, you will have identified seven ways to improve your family. Those seven ways make up a sort of Family Flight Plan for creating a nurturing family culture. The following is an example of a Family Flight Plan:

Family Flight Plan for: (Family Name)

HABIT	COMMITMENT
1 **Be Proactive**	*Create a family pause button. Help each other pause and think before or during an argument.*
2 **Begin with the End in Mind**	*Create a family mission statement.*
3 **Put First Things First**	*Make better use of family mealtimes.*
4 **Think Win-Win**	*Be more loyal to the absent.*
5 **Seek First to Understand, Then to Be Understood**	*Don't interrupt each other when talking.*
6 **Synergize**	*Agree on three strengths of each family member.*
7 **Sharpen the Saw**	*Do a physical exercise once a week as a family.*

It is not expected that your family will do all the things on your Family Flight Plan at once. Take them one habit and one commitment at a time. Consider working on one a month. Make them positive experiences and celebrate any milestones—small victories—along the way.

Go through the book at a pace that fits your family. Take turns reading and teaching the concepts. If you have younger members in your family, our son Sean has written versions of the 7 Habits for elementary-aged students (*The 7 Habits of Happy Kids*)[2] and for teens (*The 7 Habits of Highly Effective*

Teens) that can be used as simple resources for introducing the habits to your family.[3]

As you take turns teaching and learning the 7 Habits as a family, you and your family will see many benefits. One of the most significant benefits is that the 7 Habits will provide a common language for your family culture. As one father shared:

> One of the most important things that has come out of being exposed to the 7 Habits as a family is that we now have a common language to talk about things. Our language used to be slamming doors or walking out or yelling something in a rage. But now we can talk calmly and express ourselves when we feel anger or pain. And when we use words like "synergy" or "Emotional Bank Account," our kids understand what we're talking about. And that's really important.

Next from a mother:

> The 7 Habits have made us a lot more teachable and humble. They are a part of everything we do. If I say something unkind to my husband, he'll inform me that it was a withdrawal, not a deposit. Those words are part of our conversation, and so we can acknowledge it. We don't get into a fight about it or suffer in silence with hurt feelings over it. It's a way to say things that aren't hostile or volatile. It's subtle and kind.

The way you teach the 7 Habits and use the language of the habits within your family will be central to your success. Consider the following tips.

1. Model. Model. Model. The best way to teach the 7 Habits is to model them. There is no better way to teach. A child's first and foremost teacher is a parent. Parents who are not cautious with their words and habits often see their weaknesses reappear in the lives of their children—sometimes for generations. As Albert Einstein wrote, "Our death is not an end if we live on in our children and the younger generation. For they are us."[4] It's much harder to teach family members the 7 Habits when you are not living them yourself.

2. Digest the habits in bite sizes. Small bite-sized lessons during meals, family times, or one-on-one conversations are excellent opportunities to teach and discuss short insights. Don't attempt to teach too much about the 7 Habits at any given time.

3. Use the 7 Habits language in positive ways. I've seen parents use the habits as a discipline "stick" to beat down family members: "You're not being proactive!" "Why don't you ever seek first to understand?" Any person—but especially teens—will fall out of love quickly with the 7 Habits if they are used against them in such a way. Parents are better rewarded when they use the 7 Habits language to compliment children: "I loved how you were proactive yesterday when you cleaned your room without being asked." "I always enjoy synergizing with you because you have strengths I don't have."

4. Focus on the principles. Some parents overuse the 7 Habits titles. A child may hear you say, "Be proactive," only a few times before they start to become numb to the words. I can imagine a child saying, "If I hear 'put first things first' one more time, I'm going to scream." It's one reason why I suggest parents refer more often to the concepts associated with each habit, such as Circle of Concern, choose your own weather, or Big Rocks. Or even better, talk about the principles associated with the habits rather than the habit titles themselves. For example, instead of saying, "You were very proactive," say something like, "You are becoming more and more *responsible*," or "You showed a lot of *courage* by standing up for yourself." The principles I've highlighted throughout the book are captured in the following table:

Habit	Examples
Be Proactive	Choice, Responsibility, and Initiative
Begin with the End in Mind	Vision, Purpose, Commitment, and Meaning
Put First Things First	Focus, Prioritization, Discipline, and Integrity
Think Win-Win	Courage, Consideration, and Mutual Benefit
Seek First to Understand...	Mutual Understanding, Empathy, and Trust
Synergize	Creativity, Cooperation, Diversity, and Humility
Sharpen the Saw	Renewal, Continuous Improvement, and Balance

5. Choose a good time to teach. Trying to teach family members the 7 Habits when they are upset with you, emotionally fatigued, under a lot of pressure, or feeling depressed is comparable to trying to teach a drowning man to swim. That's the time when they are looking for a life jacket or a helping hand, not a lecture. Choose wisely the time to teach.

6. Use family stories. Stories are better remembered than facts or lists. Look for and then share examples of how one of the habits has helped you personally, or how a grandparent or other family member applied a certain habit.

7. Empower others to teach the habits. Sometimes adults are so eager to teach that they do it all themselves. Why not invite others to teach, including children? As others study a habit and ponder how to teach it to the family, they will learn the most, and simultaneously examine their own habits and lives more deeply.

8. Use the end-of-chapter activities. Most people prefer to "learn by doing," not by "sitting and getting." Consider using one or more of the family activities suggested at the end of each chapter as part of your teaching.

9. Be patient. Patience is a proactive choice. Don't be shocked if not every family member responds to the 7 Habits with the same level of excitement and enthusiasm that you do. Teach at a pace and level that fits your family.

Those are nine tips for teaching and learning the 7 Habits with your family. And if you want one more tip to make it a Top Ten Tip list, that tip would be to make it fun! This is meant to be enjoyable. Celebrate progress with each habit.

> Patience is a proactive choice.

Approach 4: Contribute to Your Community

A fourth approach to applying the habits in your family is to use the 7 Habits to improve your community. Doing service as a family will unite you in important ways.

In broad terms, your community might include your extended family, a local school, an elderly-care center, a child's sports team, a homeless shelter, a neighbor, or a friend. In other words, community can be any individual or organization outside your immediate family that your family can serve. Perhaps there is a struggling family or individual you know.

Select a service you can do as a family for one individual, family, or organization, then ask such questions as:

- What can we do to help that is within our Circle of Influence (Habit 1)?
- What purposes do we want to achieve (Habit 2)?
- What are the first and highest priorities (Habit 3)?
- What is a win for them? What is a win for our family (Habit 4)?
- What will we do to seek first to understand their needs (Habit 5)?
- How will we communicate our desires to them without offending (Habit 5)?
- How can we combine our strengths with their strengths to create synergy (Habit 6)?
- What four needs—physical, social-emotional, mental, and spiritual—can be addressed (Habit 7)?

Focusing on a challenge that is outside your family will in many cases help to remove challenges that are inside your family. So forget yourselves and serve others for a time.

Insight from Sandra

My advice for addressing a difficult personal or family challenge is to go slow and steady.

I recall when the microwave oven was invented. It was supposed to be the great time-saver. Busy parents were not going to know what to do with all the extra time they would have once they could cook food so much faster. Has that been true for you?

I've seen parents try to resolve a family challenge or a broken relationship with a child using a quick-fix, "microwave" mindset. They want the challenge solved fast so they can save time and do other things. But not taking the time to do things right in the first place ends up taking more time and getting people more upset in the long run.

Just as tough meat requires more time to cook and at lower temperatures, tough family challenges require more time to resolve and at lower tempers.

That's why I approach tender family challenges using a "Crock-Pot" mindset. Because for me, slow and steady still produces the best results.

LET GO AND GET STARTED

So there you have four approaches to consider when looking for ways to apply the 7 Habits and improve your family culture. Again, the invitation is to identify only *one* approach and *one* challenge.

Getting started is the most difficult part. I will never forget the first experience I had rappelling. The cliff was 120 feet high. I watched as several others were trained ahead of me. I even saw them rappel over the edge of the cliff and reach the safety and cheers of the people at the bottom. It all looked so natural and invigorating.

Then came my turn to walk backward off the cliff. All my fantasies of doing it with ease went into my stomach. I experienced sheer terror. I knew there was a rope attached to me in case I should faint, and I had an intellectual understanding of the other safety precautions that were in place. It didn't help that I was one of the speakers at the event and that sixty students were looking on and expecting me to show leadership. I was way outside of my comfort zone.

That first step off the cliff was the moment of truth. Terrifying as it was, I got the courage and did it. When I arrived safely at the bottom, I was totally invigorated by the success of having met the challenge.

That experience may describe how you feel when thinking of applying the ideas in this book. The idea of creating a family mission statement, for example, may be so far out of your comfort zone that you can't imagine how your family can do it, even when it makes intellectual sense. Or maybe you fear doing regular one-on-one bonding experiences with the child who tests you the most. If these are the types of feelings and fear you are experiencing, then all I have to say is "you can do this!"

Again, pick one challenge, choose one approach that fits the challenge best, then take the first step. The more you apply these habits on an ongoing basis, the more you will see how their greatest power is not in the individual habits themselves but in the way they work together as a framework. Wonderful insights and benefits will come.

As Einstein put it, "The significant problems we face cannot be solved at the same level of thinking we were at when we created them." So open your mind to these new ways of thinking—expand your paradigms. Base them on principles of effectiveness. If setbacks occur, that's okay. Keep trying.

Hang on to the rope of courage, let go of your fears, and get started.

ENDING WITH THE BEGINNING IN MIND

Changing the culture of any organization takes time. Creating a nurturing family culture is no exception.

It may take months or years for you to grow your family culture into what you want it to be. And that's okay. But it will not take years or even months before you start to feel a difference. The very moment you commit to work from the inside out and to apply the principles associated with each habit to your challenges, you will start to feel a change in yourself and in your family's culture.

I am convinced that the most important stewardship that you or I will ever have will be that of being a leader within our family. As my grandfather Stephen L. Richards once said, "Of all the vocations that men and women may pursue in this life, no vocation is fraught with as much responsibility and attended with as much boundless opportunity as the great calling of father and mother." His words have impacted me powerfully over the years.

Insight from Sandra

After years of working with my family, I think I'm finally getting the right perspective.

Many times I have blown it, lost my temper, judged before understanding, or not listened at all. But I've also tried to learn from my mistakes. I've apologized, grown to respect children's growth stages, and learned not to overreact. I've learned to laugh at myself, have fewer rules, enjoy life more, and accept the fact that raising children is physically and emotionally hard work.

Yet overall, as in childbirth, you forget about the pain. You remember the joys of being a parent, of sacrificing for that remarkable son or daughter you love with all your soul. You remember the expressions on your children's faces through the years—how they looked in that special dress or that hilarious costume. You remember your pride in their successes, your pain in their struggles. You remember the wonderful times, the fun of it all, the quiet moments of bonding as you gazed into the eyes of the baby you were nursing and how you were filled with the awe and wonder of your stewardship.

> It all comes with the joys and fulfillment of nurturing a family. It makes it all worth it.

Writing this book has been a forceful reminder to me that I need to keep on keeping on, to continue respecting the principles that govern growth, development, and happiness in all aspects of family life. I never feel my work is done. I do my best to live my life in accordance with my motto: "Live life in crescendo." I live each day with the belief that my best contribution is yet ahead.

In fact, I often close a workshop or keynote speech with words from George Bernard Shaw.[5] I've memorized the words because they remind me of how I want to be remembered as a father, husband, grandfather, brother, son, and extended family member. And so I close again with those words and invite you to ponder them as you reflect on the legacy you want to leave your family. Said Shaw:

I want to be thoroughly used up when I die, for the harder I work the more I live. I rejoice in life for its own sake. Life is no "brief candle" for me. It is a sort of splendid torch which I have got hold of for the moment, and I want to make it burn as brightly as possible before handing it on to future generations.

May God bless you in your humble and steady efforts to create a nurturing family culture.

CHALLENGE AND OPPORTUNITY INDEX

This index is designed to help you more easily access content that deals directly with challenges, opportunities, or questions that are specific to the needs of you and your family.

Things have not turned out in my family the way I hoped. How do I bring about change?

How do I engage a child who is struggling or disrespectful?

My family and I feel out of control. How do I get more control over my life?

I'm tired of blowing up at my family. How do I better control my anger?

We have a lot of negative "baggage" from our past. How do we get over it and move on?

How do I help children be more proactive?

My family is content doing little besides social media and television. How can I build more unity and a greater sense of vision?

What do we do when a family member gets emotional?

Every time I give feedback I end up offending the person. What am I doing wrong?

We are all so different from each other. How do we deal with our differences?

NOTES AND REFERENCES

Introduction: Creating a Nurturing Family Culture

1. Stephen R. Covey, *The 7 Habits of Highly Effective People*, Simon & Schuster, New York, 1989. Since its initial release, this book has traveled the world and sold over fifty million copies in more than forty languages, and still continues strong today across the globe.

2. For individuals, I illustrate the 7 Habits according to what I call the 7 Habits Maturity Continuum (pictured on the next page). It illustrates the logical sequence to the 7 Habits and emphasizes how individuals mature from a state of dependence to independence and ultimately to interdependence. The first three habits enable a person to move from dependence to independence, or what I call the "private victory." Habits 4 through 6 enable a person to become interdependent, or win the "public victory." Habit 7 is the habit of renewal and continuous improvement, and it sustains and strengthens all the other habits.

3. Aesop's "The Goose That Laid the Golden Eggs" is found in several collections and with multiple variations. One variation is that it is a hen. To get the hen to lay two eggs a day, its keeper tries to overfeed it. In the end, the outcome and moral is the same.

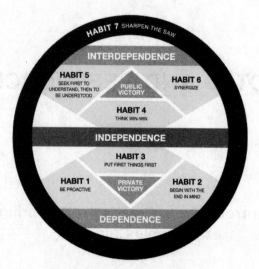

The 7 Habits Maturity Continuum

Habit 1: Be Proactive

1. Viktor Frankl, *Man's Search for Meaning*, Pocket Books, New York, 1959.

2. The Serenity Prayer. Popular opinion attributes the prayer's authorship to St. Francis of Assisi. However, it was penned by Dr. Reinhold Niebuhr, of the Union Theological Seminary, New York City, in about 1932, and has since inspired thousands through the programs of Alcoholics Anonymous.

3. Mahatma Gandhi stated in 1913 that "we but mirror the world." That phrase has come to be translated as "we must become the change we wish to see in the world."

Habit 2: Begin with the End in Mind

1. Henry David Thoreau, in a letter to his friend H. G. O. Blake on November 16, 1857.

2. The Commission on Children at Risk, *Hardwired to Connect: The New Scientific Case for Authoritative Communities*, Broadway Publications, 2003. The principal researcher was Dr. Kathleen Kovner Kline of Dartmouth Medical School.

3. This statement by Jesse Jackson is quoted with variations in several sources, including "Give the people a vision" (*New York Times*, April 18, 1976).

4. Biblical reference from Proverbs 29:18.

5. See Andrew Campbell and Laura Nash, *A Sense of Mission*, Addison Wesley Longman, Reading, Mass., 1994. See also Jim Collins and Jerry I. Porras, *Built to Last: Successful Habits of Visionary Companies*, HarperCollins, New York, 1996.

6. Benjamin Franklin, "Franklin's Formula for Successful Living—Number Three," *The Art of Virtue*, Acorn Publications, Eden Prairie, Minn., 1986, p. 88.

7. Johann von Goethe. The "Treat a man as he is . . ." quote is also attributed to Ralph Waldo Emerson. Since Goethe lived earlier, it can be attributed to him, with a slight variation going to Emerson.

Habit 3: Put First Things First

1. The 7 Habits Benchmark Profile is a 360-degree feedback instrument that has been used to collect leader ratings from peers, bosses, direct reports, and self. From all stakeholders, leaders consistently receive the lowest ratings for Habit 3—by a significant amount.

2. Robert G. Moss, *Learn to Discern*, Zondervan Publishing House, Grand Rapids, Mich., 1992, p. 2.

3. Arlie R. Hochschild, *The Time Bind*, Metropolitan Books, New York, 1997.

4. Charles E. Hummel, *Tyranny of the Urgent*, InterVarsity Press, Downers Grove, Illinois, 1994.

5. Winston Churchill was the former prime minister of the United Kingdom, and one of the most oft-quoted politicians of all time.

6. A quick internet search reveals many benefits to holding regular family mealtimes. Nevertheless, it is estimated that only 30 percent of US families have a regular family mealtime.

7. Kenneth Blanchard and Spencer Johnson, *The One Minute Manager*, Morrow, New York, 2003.

8. As this original book was being launched, I appeared with Oprah on her show. When discussing the idea of a weekly family time, this was Oprah's response.

9. Johann Wolfgang von Goethe started out as a law student and decided he preferred writing books, poetry, and inspirational verses over memorizing judicial rules by heart. It was his way of keeping his focus on "things which matter most."

Habit 4: Think Win-Win

1. Fred Rogers, US Congressional testimony delivered on behalf of CPB appropriations on May 2, 1969.

2. M. Scott Peck quoted in J. S. Kirtley's *Half-Hour Talks on Character Building by Self-Made Men and Women*, A. Hemming, Chicago, 1910, p. 368.

3. See *The 7 Habits of Highly Effective People*, specifically the chapter on "Paradigms of Interdependence," for additional examples of Emotional Bank Account deposits.

4. Quoted in *The Words of Gandhi* by Richard Attenborough, Newmarket Press, New York, 2000, p. 75. It's interesting that Gandhi is celebrated for his quests for independence when his ultimate aim was for interdependence.

Habit 5: Seek First to Understand, Then to Be Understood

1. Frenchman Antoine de Saint-Exupéry's original work *The Little Prince* was released in English in 1943.

2. Dona Matthews, "Why Parents Really Need to Put Down Their Phones," *Psychology Today*, November 23, 2017.

3. Stephen M. R. Covey with Rebecca R. Merrill, *The Speed of Trust*, Free Press, New York, 2008.

Habit 6: Synergize

1. The concept of drivers and restrainers, as well as force-field analysis, was proposed by Kurt Lewin in his book *Field Theory in Social Science*, Harper, New York, 1951, p. 183.

2. Quoted in *Peace: The Words and Inspiration of Mahatma Gandhi*, Mountain Arts, Inc., Boulder, Colorado, 2007, p. 34.

3. See Larry Tucker, "The Relationship of Television Viewing to Physical Fitness and Obesity," *Adolescence*, 1986, vol. 21 (89), pp. 797–806 and his report on "Television and Behavior" by the National Institute of Mental Health, Washington, DC, 1982. See also Susan B. Neuman, "The Home Environment and Fifth-Grade Students' Leisure Reading," *Elementary School Journal*, January 1988, vol. 86 (3), pp. 335–43.

4. Stephen R. Covey, Sean Covey, Muriel Summers, and David K. Hatch, *The Leader in Me*, 2d ed., Simon & Schuster, New York, 2014.

Habit 7: Sharpen the Saw

1. Albert Schweitzer, from a speech to students of Silcoates School on "The Meaning of Ideals in Life," on December 3, 1935. Quoted

in "Visit of Dr. Albert Schweitzer," *The Silcoatian*, New Series, no. 25, December 1935.

2. "Earn thy neighbor's love" became known as Hans Selye's personal motto. It was also the title for his self-published book, *Earn Thy Neighbor's Love: An Essay on Natural Guidelines for Man's Conduct* (1973).

Giving the 7 Habits a Challenge to Solve

1. Dag Hammarskjöld served as secretary-general of the United Nations. Quoted by Beca Lewis in *Living in Grace: The Shift to Spiritual Perception*, 2002, p. 158.

2. Sean Covey, *The 7 Habits of Happy Kids*, Simon & Schuster, New York, 2008.

3. Sean Covey, *The 7 Habits of Highly Effective Teens*, Simon & Schuster, New York, 1998, 2014. See also Sean Covey, *The 6 Most Important Decisions You'll Ever Make*, Touchstone, New York, 2006, 2017.

4. Albert Einstein as quoted in a letter written to the widow of physicist Heike Kamerlingh Onnes, February 25, 1926. See Alice Calaprice, *The Ultimate Quotable Einstein*, "On Death," Princeton University Press, Princeton, NJ, 2010, p. 91.

5. George Bernard Shaw, the Irish playwright and Nobel Laureate in literature, is oft-quoted with this gem. The more complete version of the quote is preceded by:

> This is the true joy in life, the being used for a purpose recognized by yourself as a mighty one; the being thoroughly worn out before you are thrown on the scrap heap; the being a force of Nature instead of a feverish selfish little clod of ailments and grievances complaining that the world will not devote itself to making you happy.
>
> I am of the opinion that my life belongs to the community, and as long as I live, it is my privilege to do for it whatever I can.

ACKNOWLEDGMENTS

This book is the synergistic product of a team of people. Without their wholehearted, unique contributions it never would have come about. I express my deep appreciation to:

- My beloved wife, Sandra, for her many insights and stories in this book, for her constant support and encouragement, for her intuitive wisdom and her education in child development, and above all for her sacrificial dedication over the decades in raising nine marvelous children.

- My dear children, Cynthia, Maria, Stephen, Sean, David, Catherine, Colleen, Jenny, and Joshua, and their spouses and children, for their revealing and often embarrassing stories they contributed to this book, and for the quality of their lives and contributions.

- Boyd Craig, for his superb management of the three-year production process, his unflagging positive energy, and his remarkable judgment and counseling on many key editing issues.

- Rebecca Merrill, for her unusual editorial ability in weaving the ideas, stories, transcripts, and research together in a way that truly sings. Never have I had such a faithful translator.

- My dear brother, John M. R. Covey, for his lifelong loyalty and friendship, his inspiration to me in the development of this book, his gifted ability to model and present these family principles, and his excellent work as a content leader in FranklinCovey Company's home and family area. He is also my personal spokesman for this family material. Also to his wife, Jane, a very gifted person and wonderful mother of a lovely family, whose early work on the book team and contributions of stories and learnings from presenting this material have been invaluable.

- My friend and colleague George Durrant, whose early work on the book team has infused us with an undying spirit of hope; Wally Goddard, for providing the team with decades of the learnings of many scholars in the field of family and human development; and Rick Meeves, for incredible research and documentation contributions.

- Toni Harris and Pia Jensen, for their second-mile administrative support.

- My associates at FranklinCovey Company for their direct and indirect help and support on this project, particularly Greg Link, Stephen M. R. Covey, Roger Merrill, Patti Pallat, Nancy Aldridge, Darla Salin, Kerrie Flygare, Leea Bailey, Christie Brzezinski, Barry Crockett, Julie Shepherd, Gloria Lees, and our outside counsel, Richard Hill.

- Our friends at Golden Books, particularly Bob Asahina, for his splendid professional editing and for always keeping us connected to the pulse of the reader. Also my creative literary agent, Jan Miller.

- The hundreds of families who have so willingly shared their experiences in applying this material in their families.

- The many mentors, teachers, scholars, authors, and leaders who have influenced my thinking over the years.

- My parents, my three sisters, Irene, Helen Jean, and Marilyn, and my brother, John, for contributing to my happy childhood.

And, finally, I express my appreciation for the goodness of an overriding Providence in my life.

FranklinCovey further acknowledges the team that produced this twenty-fifth anniversary edition, including the children of Sandra and Stephen R. Covey, and Dr. John M. R. Covey and his wife, Jane, who contributed several stories, insights, and twenty-five years of experience in teaching this content across the world.

Special thanks to Dr. David K. Hatch who led the project and oversaw synthesizing the refreshed content; Breck England and Annie Oswald for providing editing and publishing expertise; and to Erica Tyson, Robyn Cenizal, Debra Lund, Kalli Sampson, Mary Ann Hatch, Brooke Griffin, and Meg Thompson for subject matter expertise and support. Further thanks are extended to Jody Karr and James Coleman for their artistic genius.

INDEX

ABOUT THE AUTHORS

Stephen R. Covey was an internationally respected leadership authority, family expert, teacher, organizational consultant, and author who dedicated his life to teaching principle-centered living and leadership to build both families and organizations. He earned an MBA from Harvard University and a doctorate from Brigham Young University, where he was a professor of organizational behavior and business management, and also served as director of university relations and assistant to the president.

Dr. Covey was the author of several acclaimed books, including the international bestseller *The 7 Habits of Highly Effective People*, which was named the number one most influential business book of the twentieth century and one of the top ten most influential management books ever. It has sold more than fifty million copies in over forty languages throughout the world.

As father of nine and grandfather of fifty-five, Dr. Covey received the 2003 Fatherhood Award from the National Fatherhood Initiative, which he said was the most meaningful award he ever received. Other awards given to Dr. Covey include the Thomas More College Medallion for continuing service to humanity, Speaker of the Year in 1999, the Sikh's

1998 International Man of Peace Award, the 1994 International Entrepreneur of the Year Award, and the National Entrepreneur of the Year Lifetime Achievement Award for Entrepreneurial Leadership. Dr. Covey was recognized as one of *Time* magazine's 25 Most Influential Americans and received numerous honorary doctorate degrees.

Dr. Covey was the cofounder and vice chairman of FranklinCovey Company, the leading global professional services firm, with offices in more than 150 countries. They share Dr. Covey's vision and passion to enable greatness in people and organizations everywhere.

Sandra Renée Merrill Covey earned a college degree in child development and family relations, attending both the University of Utah and Brigham Young University, where she received the Outstanding Graduate Award. As a mother of nine (five daughters and four sons), Sandra was a memory maker. Each holiday, special family event, and one-on-one conversation was turned into a celebration of life, individual worth, and family.

Sandra devoted herself to many community affairs. She was particularly invested in the fine arts. She worked with the Symphony Guild, was a member of the Provo Arts Council, chaired the Utah Valley Symphony Ball, and served on the Utah Opera Board. She treasured being a soprano soloist for several operettas and musicals. She worked vigorously to help create an arts center in her hometown of Provo, Utah, and felt deeply fulfilled when the Covey Center for the Arts was established in 2007 and named in her honor.

As one who felt the importance of letting one's voice be heard, Sandra chaired multiple political county committees and served as a state delegate. She participated on school PTA boards, joined Stephen on occasion as a public speaker, and held demanding positions in her church, where she was known as a woman who lived her faith.

Though her later years were filled with physical trials and surgeries that left her wheelchair bound, Sandra's social calendar continued to rival any teenager's. Hundreds sought her counsel due to her wise, practical, compassionate, and bold nature.

Sandra and Stephen enjoyed a remarkable fifty-six years of marriage and family nurturing.

ABOUT FRANKLINCOVEY CO.

FranklinCovey is a global public company specializing in organizational performance improvement. We help organizations and individuals achieve results that require a change in human behavior. Our expertise is in seven areas: leadership, execution, productivity, trust, sales performance, customer loyalty, and education. FranklinCovey clients have comprised 90 percent of the Fortune 100, more than 75 percent of the Fortune 500, thousands of small and mid-size businesses, as well as numerous government entities and educational institutions. FranklinCovey has more than one hundred direct and partner offices providing professional services in more than 160 countries and territories. FranklinCovey Education serves millions of students across the world, and features its renowned Leader in Me line of education solutions.